The Interethnic Imagination

Imagining the Americas

Caroline F. Levander and Anthony B. Pinn, Series Editors

Imagining the Americas is a new interdisciplinary series that explores the cross-fertilization among cultures and forms in the American hemisphere. The series targets the intersections between literary, religious and cultural studies that materialize once the idea of nation is understood as fluid and multi-form. Extending from the northernmost regions of Canada to Cape Horn, books in this series will move beyond a simple extension of U.S.-based American studies approaches and engage the American hemisphere directly.

Millennial Literatures of the Americas, 1492–2002
Thomas O. Beebee

The Plantation in the Postslavery Imagination
Elizabeth Christine Russ

The Interethnic Imagination
Caroline Rody

The Interethnic Imagination

Roots and Passages in Contemporary Asian American Fiction

CAROLINE RODY

UNIVERSITY PRESS

2009

Oxford University Press, Inc., publishes works that further
Oxford University's objective of excellence
in research, scholarship, and education.

Oxford New York

Auckland Cape Town Dar es Salaam Hong Kong Karachi
Kuala Lumpur Madrid Melbourne Mexico City Nairobi
New Delhi Shanghai Taipei Toronto

With offices in

Argentina Austria Brazil Chile Czech Republic France Greece
Guatemala Hungary Italy Japan Poland Portugal Singapore
South Korea Switzerland Thailand Turkey Ukraine Vietnam

Published by Oxford University Press, Inc.
198 Madison Avenue, New York, New York 10016

www.oup.com

Library of Congress Cataloging-in-Publication Data

Rody, Caroline, 1960–
The interethnic imagination : roots and passages in contemporary Asian
American fiction / Caroline Rody.
p. cm.—(Imagining the Americas)
Includes bibliographical references and index.
ISBN 978-0-19-537736-1
1. American fiction—Asian American authors—History and criticism.
2. Asian Americans in literature. 3. Ethnic relations in literature.
4. Racially mixed people in literature. 5. Cultural fusion in literature.
I. Title.
PS153.A84R64 2009
813'.609895—dc22 2009006263

9 8 7 6 5 4 3 2 1

Printed in the United States of America
on acid-free paper

With love, for Jahan, Gabi, and Cyrus,
my world-spanning family

PREFACE

> Out of this conflict the ideal American character—a type truly great enough to possess the greatness of the land, a delicately poised unity of divergencies—is slowly being born.
>
> —Ralph Ellison

The final scene of Chang-rae Lee's 1995 novel *Native Speaker* presents a classroom full of children, immigrant New York City children whose families have migrated from many parts of the world, and who have been sent to ESL class to practice their English. But the last lines perform a reversal. As the children stand in quiet attention to be dismissed, their English teacher reads each of their non-English names one by one, "as best she can, taking care of every last pitch and accent"; and the hero, the teacher's Korean American husband, "hear[s] her speaking a dozen lovely and native languages, calling all the difficult names of who we are" (349). Haunting the scene is the memory of the couple's deceased seven-year-old son, a boy of mixed Korean and Scottish descent, whose promise this diverse classroom of children memorializes and re-embodies.

At the close of another contemporary Asian American novel, Karen Tei Yamashita's 1997 novel *Tropic of Orange*, the estranged Mexican American mother and Singapore Chinese American father of a small boy named after the sun finally recover each other and their missing child; and in the middle of the most chaotic, gargantuan possible public spectacle—a wrestling match between a blue-caped superhero of the southern hemisphere's poor and a titanium-clad champion of multinational capitalism—the reunited, transnational holy family ends the book with their intimate "Embrace" (270).

And the final gesture in the comic, prenuptial scene that ends Gish Jen's 1996 novel *Mona in the Promised Land* is given to the two-year-old daughter of the Chinese American-turned-Jewish bride and her Jewish groom, a toddler who loves, of all things, Italian food. Watching the intermarrying heroine's long-deferred reunion with her estranged Chinese mother, in the last line, the young granddaughter, "like a fine little witness, claps" (304).

The proliferation of ethnically mixed children who bless the resolutions of these three 1990s novels by young Asian American writers heralds the birth of a new moment in ethnic American literature.[1] Positioned to leave the stamp of their faces on the books' endings—the liminal moments when fiction sketches futurity—these children are emblems of a new vision, as Lee puts it, "of who we are." Teaching these novels over the past decade and more in increasingly heterogeneous college classrooms, I have come to see these children as inset images of the emerging American readership. And in the era of President Barack Obama, they seem, simply, to image America's undeniably multiracial future.

Mixed children are by no means the only exemplars of the literary historical shift this book raises to view, though genetic mixture is a vivid figure for contemporary literary hybridity. Nor is fictional character the only site, in the contemporary novel, of the interethnic turn, which is also transforming plots, social visions, narrative structures, narrative voices, and currents of intertextual influence. But to illustrate the ways in which the ethnic American novel is becoming what I term the interethnic novel, I begin with characters, astonishing and unfamiliar novelistic characters who embody imaginative engagement with the difference of others. Consider, for example, Chang-rae Lee's "unbeatable" John Kwang, charismatic, populist Korean American city councilman and mayoral candidate in Queens, New York, who seems "effortlessly Korean, effortlessly American," who summons broad, fervent, multiethnic support; who sends his campaign workers out to tell the crowds "in ten different languages . . . *Kwang is like you. You will be an American*"; and who is said to be "unafraid to speak the language" from a public dais "like a Puritan and like a Chinaman and like every boat person in between" (Lee 23, 328, 304). Or consider Gish Jen's Naomi, an African American Harvard-Radcliffe student and "Renaissance woman," who speaks better Chinese than her Chinese American roommate and has mastered *tai qi*, meditation and yoga; but who can also "tease cool jazz from free jazz, bebop from hard bop," loves collard greens and sweet potato pie, "not to say Scrabble, film noir, star gazing, [and] soccer" (Jen 169), and who becomes the novel's image of syncretic American self-realization. Or simply think of the lunch eaten in Los Angeles one day by Yamashita's character Bobby Ngu, a "Chinese from Singapore with a Vietnam name speaking like a Mexican living in Koreatown" (15), who gained entrance into the U.S. by passing as a Vietnamese boat person, and whose polyglot meal of choice includes "Chinese burritos. Fish tacos . . . and Camaron chow mein," washed down with Chinese "*Miraculous Stop Smoking*" herbal tea (101).

All of these characters become, for the reader and for other characters, embodiments and spectacles of charged, riddling, potentially liberating multiethnic fusion. Around these gifted characters (or assemblages of characters) struggle more ordinary and more troubled ethnic seekers—the main fictional protagonists—who propel their novels' plots by experimentation in the ethnic crosscurrents of their cosmopolitan locations. "They all have Ngu names," Yamashita writes about immigrants like Bobby, but her punning meaning ("Ngu" is pronounced "nyu," thus, "new") resonates for many of the characters in this study, whose "difficult names," relatively *new* to the American novel, signal tension with conventional types of the English or American novelistic protagonist. An unexpected turn is achieved, however—a bit of literary alchemy worked—when such names are assigned to fictional personages who creatively, spectacularly master and hybridize multiple cultural codes, and who stand as models for others less divinely visited.

I invoke these special exemplars as figures who embody the spirit of a historic literary shift: in the wake of all that is changing in local and global cultures, in patterns of migration, settlement, labor, communications, and interaction among peoples from all parts of the world, this study claims that what we have long thought of as ethnic literature is becoming interethnic literature. That is, since the last quarter of the twentieth century, the focus of ethnic texts has begun to drift toward the borders of ethnic experience, away from being-ethnic as a problematic in itself, to the condition of being-ethnic amidst a hybrid collective, as part of a "difficult" but undeniable "we." Of course, ethnic American literatures are still rooted in narratives of tradition and memory, and yet, I would argue, they share a growing impulse to engage the heterogeneity of American culture. Certainly they are concerned, as ever, with particular peoples' histories, lives, and cultural traditions, yet ethnic literatures have also begun to elaborate identities that are at home in multiplicity, and to construct textualities that negotiate fruitfully with the multiculture.

In this "ngu" moment, not only are fictional characters, plots, and literary influences increasingly hybrid, but also the English language itself in contemporary fiction is dramatically swelling, crossbred with myriad immigrant tongues that daily enrich it. Of course, all languages are not equal "in the new world-system," Fredric Jameson reminds us, English crowding out many others as "the lingua franca of money and power" (59). But the monolithic character suggested by this account of English is undermined in contemporary fiction; for example, in Jiro Adachi's *The Island of Bicycle Dancers* (2004), a young Korean Japanese immigrant in lower Manhattan attempts to pick up the local talk:

> In New York, there were too many different kinds of English. Sometimes her head was full of her aunt and uncle's Korean English, sometimes Suzie's American English going on about the Indian women who came into the nail salon dripping with yellow gold and the black women who spent all their money on nails that ended up looking like cheap jewelry. Her ear caught snippets of Chinese English from the high school kids on the 7 train, Spanish English everywhere, Russian English and Polish English near Lucky Market; black English all over, even from white people and some Asians—everyone trying to act black. (2)

A dynamic medium of cultural interchange, hegemonic English is heard here in a state of transformation, being reworked on the tongues of multitudes of its new possessors. The sounds of the remaking of the language also move the hero of Lee's *Native Speaker*, who sits in an open window at night to "listen to the earnest attempts of [immigrants'] talk, the bits of their stilted English," no longer, as in youth, "ashamed and angry at those funny tones of [his] father and his workers, all that Konglish, Spanglish, Jive"; now he would "give most anything to hear [his] father's talk again, the crash and bang and stop of his language" (337). And listening to a

Dominican immigrant woman mourning her son, the hero muses, "Half the people in Queens talk like her. . . . I think she's saying it perfectly, just like she should. When you're too careful you can't say anything . . . [and your words] sound like they belong to somebody else" (257).

English sounds better, and sounds more authentic, in both of these recent American novels, when it sounds "ngu," when reinflected by multiple newcomers' differently articulating tongues. Linguistic multiplicity and difference are understood as in themselves good; uniform speech is the enemy of vitality, of beauty, of hope. Invocations of an interethnic, interlinguistic sublime—recalling Bakhtinian dialogism—are the more remarkable in contemporary American fiction because until recently they have been uncommon, for ethnic American fiction has usually been more occupied with representing the distinctive texture, substance, and power of one or another given people's speech. But the fictions of the contemporary interethnic turn render a multicultural English, an English with its ears open to the talking world.

In foregrounding the "multicultural" as the dominant current that contemporary fiction engages, I may raise skepticism from several sides. Let me state clearly that I do not mean to celebrate a triumphant cultural formation that in any way resolves the social and economic inequalities that continue to plague the American present—in historian Manning Marable's words, a "new color line of spiraling class inequality and extreme income stratifications" at work alongside the old color line "more closely coded by physical appearance, legal and racial classification, and language" (B4). Nor do I mean to diminish the reality of the enormous differences of opportunity and mobility among different racial or ethnic groups, nor the class and other divisions within these groups (see Marable). I mean to argue, indeed, that the urge toward cross-cultural literary engagement persists despite profound awareness that the new appreciation of cultural difference has failed to make real progress toward eradicating systemic injustice and exploitation, and despite daily evidence of intergroup conflict.[2] It seems important to add, as well, that interethnic literary involvement has only increased, not the least abated, in the face of rampant xenophobia in the years since the September 11, 2001, attacks.

To be sure, the mass commodification and exploitation of ethnic and racial heterogeneity in commerce and popular culture has made us justly suspicious of any easy celebration of the multicultural and of the globalization of culture. Who would want ethnic texts to go interethnic if the result were a recolonization of ethnic difference, or a flat and homogenized cultural vision? Moreover, between the "twin and not altogether commensurable faces" of globalization, in Jameson's terms, we may well fear that the cultural face, which tends to generate a "joyous" "postmodern celebration of difference and diversity," of increasing tolerance, pluralism, and democratization, may serve to disguise or inevitably be occluded by the "far more baleful" economic face, characterized by mass-scale standardization and the disappearance of local markets and subsistence because of "forced integration . . . into a world system" (56–57).

I discuss (and defend) the politics of interethnicity (and hybridity) in contemporary Asian American fiction in part II of chapter one, but for now I will simply assert that the texts I examine here support Jameson's view that the two faces of globalization are not "logically incompatible" (57). Though it has been argued that globalism as a worldview has Western "free trade imperialism [as] . . . its institutional correlate" (Krishnan 33), and though some have doubted that the conglomerate-dominated publishing industry can do much besides sell us more multinational capitalism,[3] this study argues that literature still works as a space for the exploration of possibilities amidst and beyond those of the market. Moreover, I would claim that contemporary interethnic texts speak out in opposition to the forces of standardization and univocality, speak up for the vital energies of difference and multiplicity, for what Michael Hardt and Antonio Negri have called "the multitude's . . . globalization, or . . . making common, of the desire for human community" (362). Multiculturalism, as a zeitgeist surely contaminated and even promoted by corporate profit but also expressing genuinely liberatory and egalitarian popular impulses, has made something new happen in American and world literature. Here, as in the social world, it breaks down barriers and allows, even amidst mass fear and its manifestations, unexpected new fruition. In the face of both commodification and extremist identitarianism, the contemporary literary imagination seems all the more attracted to the possibilities of shifting, multitudinous identities. I want to bring to light, then, in the texts considered in this study, a strong strain of the visionary, a creative reimagining of the potential of intergroup contact and engagement for our language and literature as well as for our lives.

I came to this conception of the changing terrain of ethnic American fiction in the process of writing my first book. In *The Daughter's Return: African-American and Caribbean Women's Fictions of History* (2001), I set out to examine a "vertical" axis—that is, the axis of specific ethnic history and tradition, in two distinct but related bodies of literature. But (as I noted in that book's introduction), I was surprised to keep bumping up against a "horizontal" impulse, in which African American and Caribbean women's "histories" generated plots of a heroine's encounter, in the imaginative space of "history," with women of other groups. Considering moments like the childbirth scene in Toni Morrison's monumental novel *Beloved,* in which the escaping slave Sethe, in solitary labor in a Kentucky wood, finds a midwife in the vagrant "whitegirl" Amy Denver, I mused upon the eruption of interethnic history in the very womb of ethnic history, the last place one would expect to find it. As such significant encounters multiplied, *The Daughter's Return* grew a counterplot of hybridity to complement its preoccupation with ancestry, and I found my next subject in the interethnic imagination of contemporary literature.

When I first began to collect interethnic literary visions and relations in the early 1990s, it seemed to me that the project of accounting for them would require a broad interethnic design: I envisioned my next book as a big one, with chapters on interethnic developments in all the ethnic literatures in which I had some competence—contemporary Asian American, African American, Jewish American, and Native American fiction—plus short "interchapters" on hybrid topics in excess of these rubrics, such as the inscription of a Native American presence in African American fiction, fictional encounters between Black maids and Jewish housewives, and so on. The vast reach of the thing, as I first conceived it, was meant to be by no means encyclopedic, but still a fairly extensive map of culture-spanning patterns of exchange and interaction in fiction.

I invoke this long-dormant plan to suggest the way that the contemporary interethnic imagination tends to conjure, not only in fiction but also in its readers, visions that stretch possibility, a sense of the momentous. But as the project changed along with my life and family over that decade and a half, and I came to see the desirability of writing an actually completable book, I tossed the grand plan and eventually settled on contemporary Asian American literature as the best illustration, to me, of the broader phenomenon. This was the literature that most compelled me through the 1990s and beyond; I decided that using Asian American fiction as a case study would allow for greater depth and coherence in my readings, while still enabling me to point my argument toward comparable instances across the spectrum of ethnic American literatures. This choice is undergirded by two key factors that will play a part in all the arguments that follow: first, the "in-between" position of Asian Americans in the historically racialized culture of the United States, and second—a factor to some degree stemming from the first—the place of Asian American fiction in the vanguard of the interethnic experimentation this book discusses. A body of literature that has boomed in recent decades, with publications and public notice soaring and notable new authors appearing every year, Asian American fiction is also an enormously inventive literature, one that seems sometimes to have set out to confound those who might seek to confine its sphere. My focus on contemporary Asian American fiction, detailed in part II of chapter 1, rests on the conviction that this literature is the avatar of a historic turn to the interethnic axis across the spectrum of American ethnic literatures.

This study, then, addresses the wide field of multiethnic American literature even though (and partly because) few books do so, even at a moment when ethnic literary critique still largely proceeds in distinct ethnic/racial areas, and when such a project might seem less urgent than studies of transnational literary developments. My strategy is to maintain a multiethnic American field focus in the spirit of comparative, coalitional scholarship that has been foundational to the discipline of U.S. ethnic studies,[4] even while engaging with transnational, hemispheric, and postcolonial critical paradigms, especially as they illuminate the imbrication of localities in global change. It is precisely at this juncture of the ethnically specific and the interethnically mixed, the family and the crowd, the home and the world, that this study locates itself, to consider a contemporary literature characterized at once by deep roots and by unanticipated passages.

Since I first began to track the phenomenon that is this book's subject a decade and a half ago, the hybridity of culture has become a more and more popular critical theme. But while cross-cultural and comparative studies have multiplied, the core of what I have wanted to say, it seems to me, still has yet to be said. It is now broadly agreed that writers, the ethnic and racial groups and cultures from which they stem, and the cultural forms they produce, have always been intertwined. What this book announces is the emergence, in the last quarter of the twentieth century, of a literature that presumes, that is immersed in ethnic interconnection: an interethnic literature, which prophesies our greater and more profound enmeshment as ever more intricately world-crossing neighbors.

Chapter 1, composed of three parts, theorizes interethnicity in contemporary fiction, discusses its preeminence in Asian American fiction, and offers an overview of trends in interethnic Asian American fictional texts. Following the first chapter, three more chapters each focus on a novel that constitutes a particularly compelling example of the complexity of the interethnic imaginative project, and two shorter "interchapters" plus an epilogue take up special "in-between" topics in contemporary cross-ethnic literary encounter.

The literary critical chapters seek to come to terms in the largest sense with the distinctiveness of a novelist's interethnic vision. Though committed to a comparative and a historically grounded ethnic literary scholarship, as a literary reader, I privilege the unique engagement with the world, with history, with human discourse that is any writer's work. Mine might be called a "political formalist" method, in Rita Felski's coinage ("Modernist" 510), a term used to describe close reading practices that "[insist] on the primacy and preeminence of aesthetic form" while performing ideological critique, that draw out social and ideological suggestions through the careful examination of formal elements like language use, tropes, characterization, emplotment, and narrative structure. While each chapter is framed by a critical problematic an author allows me to address, my practice is to give novels sustained and close attention, to see how the author transforms the critical terms or questions at hand, in the subtler, richer orchestration of his or her art.[5] The life of this study, then, is in the readings of some remarkable works of contemporary fiction, books I have found to grow only larger and more capacious in the conversation of classrooms that mirror their visions of our emerging future.

ACKNOWLEDGMENTS

I have been fortunate over the years of the writing of this book to receive the support of many generous people. It is a pleasure to try, at least, to list them here. Most recently, I am indebted to my colleague and longtime mentor Susan Fraiman for a heroic late-hour reading of the whole manuscript, and also to Dean Franco for a most incisive, detailed reading of chapter 3 and the interchapter "Cross-ethnic Jewishness." I continue to appreciate the stalwart support for my work offered by Michael Levenson, Margaret Homans, Silvio Torres-Saillant, and Ann Jones. The editorial suggestions of Eleanor Ty and Donald Goellnicht were invaluable as my essay on Karen Tei Yamashita progressed from their MLA panel to the edited collection that grew from it, as were those of the anonymous readers for Indiana University Press. The manuscript became a far better book because of the wise critiquc and suggestions of anonymous readers for Oxford University Press. I thank my Oxford editor Shannon McLachlin and her assistants Chrissy Gibson and Brendan O'Neill for their labors to bring this study to publication.

At the University of Virginia, this project was aided by several summer grants and a sesquicentennial associateship, and by generous support from Gordon Braden and Dean Karen Ryan. The lively collegiality and ready help of the staff and fellows of the Rothermere American Institute at Oxford University, where I was a Senior Fellow in the spring of 2007, contributed to a lovely and productive residence.

I am indebted to my colleagues in the Department of English for sustaining an atmosphere of remarkably positive, creative dialogue and in particular to Debbie McDowell and Rita Felski, for insightful feedback and support in the first stages of this project. My thanks, too, to the organizers of the 2004 English Department graduate student conference, "Found in Translation," and for the energetic conversation of illustrious former UVA graduate students James Kim, Brenna Munro, Heather Love, Swan Kim, Erika Meitner, and Jolie Sheffer. I appreciate the fine research assistance of Robin Field and Emily Heilman and the indispensable technical assistance of Cheryll Lewis, June Webb, and Gail Moore. And I am happy to have this chance to thank my many wonderful students in undergraduate and graduate courses on Asian American, Jewish American, Ethnic American, and interethnic literature at the University of Virginia, who have been my collaborators in developing this project when they least suspected it.

A true pleasure during these years has been my participation in the intellectual communities of both UVA's Asian Pacific American Studies Minor, in which connection I salute the leadership of Sylvia Chong and Pensri Ho, and also UVA's Jewish Studies Program, sponsor of a colloquium in which I received warm responses to a paper on Gish Jen. I am especially grateful for the collegial friendship and support of Jewish Studies colleagues Vanessa Ochs, Gabriel Finder, Asher Biemann, and Alon Confino. For the joy of conversing with them during their visits to Virginia, I offer enthusiastic thanks to Lisa Lowe and to the writers Karen Tei Yamashita, Chang-rae Lee, and Don Lee.

For their stimulating conversation and their generosity to my project, I thank Thomas Ferraro, Priscilla Wald, and the Duke University Americanist Group, who invited me to give a paper in 2005; Mark Wollaeger; Min Song, chair of an MLA Asian Americanist panel on which I spoke from this project that same year; and my colleagues on a 2008 American Jewish Studies Association conference panel. My thanks to Jelena Šesnić for the pleasure of her ongoing intellectual camaraderie, and to her and her welcoming colleagues in the Department of American Studies at the University of Zagreb, Croatia, for a most memorable visit and lectureship there in March of 2007. And for her zestful friendship, which helped make Oxford a new home, my gratitude to local historian extraordinaire Liz Woolley.

To my mother- and father-in-law, Nesta and Ruhi Ramazani, I offer warmest thanks for their years of loving support. My work would never have been done, of course, without the irreplaceable childcare over the years of Kathy Smith, Holly Jones, Robin Field, Rebecca Sayre, Miriam Todras, and Shannon Bayliss. As ever, I am deeply glad to have the sustaining counsel and hilarity of my siblings Liz Rody-Koenig, Annie Rody-Wright, and David Rody, and of their dear spouses and darlingly irrepressible progeny. To my mother, Emily Miller Rody, I am grateful and then some for her tireless listening, advice, and good cheer, and this time around for going far beyond the call to serve as associate fiction reader and researcher. It is a great piece of luck to have been so lovingly mothered by such an avid and discerning reader. To my father, Robert S. Rody, a lifetime of thanks for his gentlemanly kindness and for his ever-ready wit, still vital and still blessing us all.

Finally and most dearly, I thank Jahan Ramazani—the one and only, in more senses than one only—whose many clarifying readings, and whose formidable patience, generosity, and love have been utterly essential. And how can I thank Gabi and Cy, the wonder brothers, my more than me? I can only hope that their tolerance for my endless work amidst their bouncy lives, their openhearted rooting for its completion, will someday serve their own big ideas.

An earlier version of chapter 4 appeared as "The Transnational Imagination: Karen Tei Yamashita's Tropic of Orange" in *Asian North American Identities:*

Beyond the Hyphen, edited by Eleanor Ty and Donald C. Goellnicht, published in 2004 by Indiana University Press.

I also reprint here several lines from my essay "Impossible Voices: Ethnic Postmodern Narration in Morrison's Jazz and Yamashita's Through the Arc of the Rain Forest" in *Contemporary Literature* 41.4 (2000), copyright University of Wisconsin Press.

CONTENTS

The Interethnic Imagination

1

The Interethnic Paradigm and the Case of Asian American Fiction

We are in the epoch of simultaneity: we are in the epoch of juxtaposition, the epoch of the near and far, of the side-by-side, of the dispersed.

—Michel Foucault

Where the transmission of "national" traditions was once the major theme of world literature, perhaps we can now suggest that transnational histories of migrants, the colonized, or political refugees—these border and frontier conditions—may be the terrains of world literature.

Homi Bhabha

All across the country, people of different races, ethnicities, and nationalities are being thrown together—and torn apart—by the churning forces of first the postindustrial and now the information economy. In search of new economic and social addresses, many African-American families have abandoned the inner city for the suburbs, and some have gone back to the South. Middle-class whites have moved into formerly working-class "minority" districts. . . . Albania and Ireland and Nigeria and China and El Salvador and Korea and Pakistan arrive on both coasts and stream across the heartland, filling in the space between America's traditional black and white poles. In the midst of all this movement, peoples have been running into one another, sometimes violently, sometimes sublimely. It is a terrifying experience, this coming together, one for which we have as yet only the most awkward vocabulary. One for which new languages are being written.

—Rubén Martínez

Part I: Roots and Passages

Contemporary Interethnic Fiction

Interethnicity cannot be called a new phenomenon in the literature of the United States. A venerable roster of American literary texts, especially those dating from periods of robust immigration, has evoked a rich ethnic heterogeneity as the heart of Americanness itself. The claim of this book is that as the unprecedented globalizing, multidiasporic dynamics of our moment have transformed the texture of our lives, the long-present interethnic strand emerges as the dominant weave, and what we have long thought of as "ethnic literature" is becoming "interethnic literature." The phenomena Foucault called human "simultaneity" and "juxtaposition" (229)—mass movements of families and communities under the pressure of want or violence, new possibilities in global communication, proliferating interconnection through trade, media, and travel—all have had the effect of creating, not by intent, but by inevitable byproduct, a multiplication of human encounters, across ethnic differences and antagonisms, and across deepening divisions of class. Amidst this prodigious enmeshment of peoples, U.S. literary sensibilities have turned to an expressive interethnicity.

Ethnicities have always existed in relation to one another, of course, and not simply in the sense that one can be ethnic, by definition, only in relation to an Other. Contemporary theorists tell us that ethnicities are always historical negotiations between tradition and hybridity (Bhabha 2), cultural identities "always multiple, contested, discontinuous, and changing" (Lenz 475). The history of the world is the history of human meeting and separation, the formation and reformation of peoples by means of encounters with others. In the United States, ethnic communities have long been busy "rubbing elbows" with one another, in Gish Jen's phrase ("So"), have developed, historically, in tandem, been "mutually constitutive of one another, not just competitive or cooperative" (Lipsitz 210–11).

But the mass influx into the United States over the decades following the 1965 easing of immigration barriers has deepened and intensified the interethnic character of American life. Waves of newcomers—uprooted by ethnic conflict, economic devastation, or the still-potent promise of an exceptional American form of becoming—have brought accelerated change. We all now live and work more intimately with more different kinds of people, amidst the traces and consequences of more varied histories. These facts are vivid, unavoidable, even determinative in the lives of recent American immigrants and their descendants, who—granted the time it takes any immigrant group to develop the wherewithal, the comfort with the language, the aspiration, to start producing a body of literature—are now generating fictional texts that rework narrative conventions to accommodate their intense imbrication in the lives and stories of disparate other arrivants. What emerges in this body of work—as early as the late 1970s, gathering strength in the '90s and after—beyond the mere economic and civic necessity of adapting to racial, ethnic, cultural and linguistic heterogeneity, and to the staggering economic inequalities that frame and plague this diversity, is an urge to admit those differences into the center of one's imaginative life, even into one's self-conception. The compelling event of our era, interethnic American fiction now reports, is the imaginative encounter with "others."[1]

In a suggestive paradigm, Susan Stanford Friedman discusses a "narrative poetics of intercultural encounter," in which narratives are driven not simply by desire in time, as psychoanalytically informed theories would have it, but also by encounters with otherness across space. Friedman argues that such spatial encounters are often "what generates, motivates, and fuels narrative," and she speaks of "scenes of intercultural encounter" as "motive for some narratives, removing us as readers from the oedipal and post-oedipal scenes of the dwelling (the localized family plot), and directing us to the intersubjective spaces of self-other interaction" (*Mappings* 141, 134). The plot moves the questing subject away from family and ethnos toward resolution, specifically through engagement with others marked by ethnic difference.

The terms Friedman uses evoke, for me, no narrative more strongly than Henry Roth's classic immigration novel *Call It Sleep* (1934), especially the climactic scene in which the young Russian Jewish immigrant boy David bolts from the terrible oedipal dynamics of his family apartment and down many flights of stairs to the teeming street, where he seeks and finds a spiritual apotheosis through an electric shock from a train-rail, in the hallucinatory aftermath of which his consciousness is blended in a sublime Joycean-modernist sound-collage with the mixed voices and idioms of his heterogeneous, immigrant New York neighborhood. This scene, iconic of an earlier boom-period in U.S. ethnic literature, may be seen as a key precursor to the contemporary interethnic visions this study discusses.

For the drive toward encounter across multiple differences describes the animating energy of contemporary interethnic American fiction, in which the accelerated, global flows of our moment have given new primacy to the spatialized literary plot. It is not simply that, in recent fiction, "we see more engagement with the realities of... multiracial, globalized, and many-voiced America" (Suh and Ku 316), but that the new interethnic attention has profoundly changed the nature of ethnic narrative itself, significantly molding the contemporary ethnic novel's deepest psychic structures, its ambitions, its sense of its place in the larger culture, as well as many aspects of its aesthetic form, including its narrative structures, plot types, uses of language(s), characterizations, and, not least, its patterns of literary borrowing and influence. The interethnic imagination of this body of work is by no means the facile celebration of hybridity to which we have become accustomed in mass consumer discourse and imagery—though indeed it often absorbs, parodies, or critiques such commodification. Rather, this literature registers an ironic consciousness of arising from a culture that is profoundly hybridized, yet still urgently in need of reparative cross-ethnic dialogue.

While such claims could be made in relation to many contemporary literary genres, this book, based on my own close observation and teaching of ethnic American fiction, focuses on developments in the novel (and to a lesser extent in the short story). My contention is that what drives ethnic fiction today is not only the "vertical" axis of memory and return, traditionally dominant in ethnic literatures, but increasingly, the spatial, "horizontal" axis of encounter. The texts I will examine displace the primacy of the single-ethnic or familial story—the story of inheritance (Werner Sollors's "descent")—to engage interethnic encounter or dialogue ("consent") as their central narrative donné; as a corollary, they overtly engage the influence of precursor fictions by writers of other ethnic minority groups. Taking the novel beyond its traditional interest in and association with a single people or nation,[2] and including not just ethnic or racial binaries but multiple differences of ethnicity, language, national origin, class, and citizenship status, these texts make the novel instead about the meeting of multiple peoples, a momentous meeting in which the singular protagonist—often read as a representative national or ethnic subject—becomes the living nexus of an expanding interethnicity. Revising and complicating the generative plot of conflict between immigrant parents and American-born children, the new interethnic fictions send young protagonists into complex, unanticipated matrices of multiethnic encounter.

Exemplifying the trajectory from "the localized family plot" to "intersubjective spaces," novelist Chang-rae Lee has explained that in writing his first novel, *Native Speaker*, he wanted to depart from the "very circumscribed family stories, within-the-house kind of stories," "expected of Asian-American writers," and "widen the stage in which my character was going to act," forcing him to "get out in the world and see others," including "different immigrant populations" and "different languages and different forms and stages of English"; "I wanted to put him in harm's way, or at some kind of risk, so that he would have to put himself on the line and speak . . ." ("An Interview" 6). The fictions considered in this study send subjects out of the house and into "the 'unhomeliness' inherent in . . . [the] rite of extra-territorial and cross-cultural initiation" (Bhabha 9). In the process, they transform affective elements common to ethnic narratives—the outsider's yearning, fury, or lament—in the encounter with the challenge and the spectacle of heterogeneity, of participation in the multicultural crowd. The result is a narrative texture crossed by competing strains of desire and fear, imitation and competition, affiliation and appropriation, in tones ranging from ambivalent to enthralled, from historically wary to hopeful. While this interethnic attention sometimes evinces sheer curiosity, a pleasurable fascination born of unlikely proximity, or a competitive urge to master inequality or priority, in the main these fictions evince what Michael M. J. Fischer has called the "ethical and future-oriented" cultural politics common to ethnic narratives (196). That is, they present themselves, in Stephen Knadler's terms, as "reparative and affiliative interventions" in the U.S. social imaginary, evidence of a "coalitional or cosmopolitan consciousness inspired by a desire for justice" (3, 2), by a desire to unsettle the hierarchical, divisive structures of racism. Whether set in city or suburb, then, East or West Coast, the new interethnic fictions are located most saliently in the arena of the contemporary American multiculture, foregrounded as the site of potential threat and of possible dialogue. As Friedman puts it, "the intercultural space in between difference . . . [is] a dynamic terrain that makes things happen" (*Mappings* 149).

The contemporary United States is one such dynamic terrain, a site of the "dwelling-in-travel" that James Clifford argues should replace traditional anthropological notions of static cultures,[3] a "human location" "constituted by displacement as much as stasis" (2). The circuits of migration to and intercultural contact within the United States have given all sorts of localities—urban, suburban, and even rural—a texture of overlaid travels, displacements, regroupings, and connections to points of origin that upset traditional models of ethnic orientation. Arjun

Appadurai has coined the term "ethnoscapes" to indicate "the landscape of persons who constitute the shifting world in which we live: tourists, immigrants, refugees, exiles, guest workers, and other moving groups and individuals constitute an essential feature of the world and appear to affect the politics of (and between) nations to a hitherto unprecedented degree" (*Modernity* 33). In the changing American ethnoscape, Appadurai writes, "The United States, always in its self-perception a land of immigrants, finds itself awash in . . . global diasporas, no longer a closed space for the melting pot to work its magic but yet another diasporic switching point to which people come to seek their fortunes though no longer content to leave their homelands behind" ("Heart of Whiteness" 803).

That the two anthropologists cited above describe an intensity of human flux prevalent not only in the decolonizing zones of empire, but also across the United States helps show the concerns of ethnic American literary study overlapping studies of the postcolonial, the borderlands, the diasporic, the hemispheric, and the transnational, all of which examine cultural changes precipitated by the dramatically expanded scale of contemporary human deterritorialization (Appadurai, *Modernity* 49), and the changing forms of global human migration. Because many authors (and their characters) are postcolonial migrants before they land on these shores as ethnics, and because ethnic or immigrant American literary texts tend to engage both national and transnational (or diasporic) trends, a key aim of this book is to bring the insights of postcolonial theory to bear on the "dynamic terrain" that now produces ethnic American literature; especially germane are theories of linguistic and cultural creolization and other forms of hybridity born of the historical, conflictual yoking of disparate, dislocated peoples. This study aligns itself, too, with recent "post-exceptionalist" Americanist scholarship that conceives the United States as "one node in a vast interlocking network of commercial, political, and cultural forces" (Pease, "American" 123, 125).[4] The far-reaching, global changes of our era have inspired new transnational and anti-identitarian scholarly paradigms,[5] which in turn help make visible interethnic phenomena of the sort that this study examines. As we read the shifting ethnoscape of U.S. ethnic fiction, such paradigms can help us see the need, in Bhabha's words, "to think beyond narratives of originary and initial subjectivities" (1), the need to look, in the words of U.S.-Mexico border critic José David Saldívar, beyond "linear narratives of immigration, assimilation, and nationhood," "to imagine new cultural affiliations and negotiations . . . more dialogically, in terms of multi-faceted migrations across borders" (*Border* 1). We need, that is, to conceive of a dialogic American literature.[6]

Bakhtinian dialogics provide another touchstone for my analyses here. For Bakhtin's sociolinguistic theories can help us see how the novel—for him always characterized by a heteroglossic, dialogic texture—is being shaped in the hands of contemporary ethnic American writers to display a multiplication and heightening of ethnic interactions, to record the ring and clash of multitudes meeting, and in doing so, to redraw social, geographic, and literary boundaries. Indeed, a close analogue to the interethnic texture I want to highlight can be found in Bakhtin's account of the way that in novels, every "word is shaped in dialogic interaction" (279); each novelistic utterance,

> directed toward its object, enters a dialogically agitated and tension-filled environment of alien words, value judgments and accents, weaves in and out of complex interrelationships, merges with some, recoils from others, intersects with yet a third group: and all this may crucially shape discourse, may leave a trace in all its semantic layers....(276)

This description of the linguistic composition of novels might well depict the interplay of ethnic cultures and subjectivities in contemporary American fiction. Historically the most socially capacious and the most adaptable of literary genres, the novel now rises to meet the representational and structural demands of a transformed cultural consciousness in "the epoch... of the side-by-side," rendering a vibrant intercultural, interlingual dynamism. The result, as Salman Rushdie has observed, is that "a new novel is emerging, a post-colonial novel, a de-centered, transnational, inter-lingual, cross-cultural novel" (57).

Another key feature of novelistic dialogism for Bakhtin is its "liberation... from the hegemony of a single and unitary language.... an absolute form of thought" (367); he reads the novel, in Josephine Donovan's account, "as a somewhat anarchical, insubordinate genre that reflects a kind of popular resistance to centralizing official establishments and unifying disciplines" (86). Such resistance is dramatically rendered in the multilingual texture of contemporary interethnic fictions, and again in their scenarios and paradigms—sometimes conflictual, sometimes carnivalesque—of multiplicity overwhelming the singular and the univocal, particularly the monotone voice of racism. We might claim, indeed, that in these fictions, interethnic dialogue is granted the level of importance that ethnic texts traditionally give to inheritance, so that the two are held in balance. To recur to Sollors's generative terms, in these texts "descent" and "consent" (inheritance and alliance) meet and mingle—miscegenate, let us say, producing a hybrid social imaginary (*Beyond* 5–6). Responding to the complexity of life amidst the disparate populations and cultural forms "thrown together" in the United States around the turn of the millennium, as described by Martínez in an epigraph to this chapter, contemporary fiction generates imaginative energies that defy containment by conventional ethnic literary categorization, that produce shifting and surprising new compositions of the "we."

Studying Ethnics/Others

Key to the history of the imaginative shift now become dramatically visible in ethnic American fiction is the fact that this literature's current flowering emerged from two near-simultaneous cultural transformations: the rise of the African American civil rights movement and the subsequent upsurge in cultural expression across the U.S. ethnic spectrum; and the post-1965 immigration wave to the U.S. from Asia, Latin America, Africa, and elsewhere. Flourishing in the wake of these changes, post-1960s U.S. ethnic literatures' commitment to the expression of distinct peoples' experiences from the beginning evinced a self-conscious connection to a larger, worldwide emergence of previously untold stories. In the late century, this ethos of connection intensified and grew complex dimensions, amidst transforming currents of economic and mass cultural globalization.

While a new assertion of public identity has emerged among people of mixed races and ethnicities,[7] people from many backgrounds have become aware of participating in an increasingly hybrid collective cultural life, of daily practices and self-understandings transformed by their interaction with those of other ethnic and national origins. As we live, so also do we read and watch and listen: as audiences of literary, mass media, and other cultural texts, we attend and encounter and identify, increasingly, in interethnic patterns. One now often finds passages like the following in essays on the American present:

> Newcomers . . . are doing things to earn their livelihoods that they could not have imagined when they were in their homelands: Cambodians are making doughnuts, Koreans are making burritos, South Asians are operating motels, Filipinos are driving airport shuttle buses. . . . the Minnesota social worker who clings to the idea of Hmongs as limited-English-speaking refugees from a pre-literate society may be surprised to encounter a Hmong teenager who composes rap music, plays hockey, and dates Chicano boys or girls. (E. Kim, "Preface" xi)

> It is an America where even as we witness the destruction of local cultures by global capital we can find a moment to ask what it means when a Chinese American student in Durham, North Carolina, who speaks only English, has her sartorial, musical, and aesthetic sensibilities shaped by hip-hop videos produced in Seoul by bilingual Korean youth who lived in Los Angeles and moved back; an America where the son of a restaurant worker from Dhaka living in New York City's Lower East Side has mostly Latino friends, goes to the mosque each week with his father, and while everyone else sleeps tonight will be writing Bangla poetry into Asian American literature. . . . (Suh and Ku 326)

In a world transformed by myriad adoptions and reformulations of the unfamiliar, it is not surprising that our literatures now diagram new imaginative journeys. As traffic on the interethnic imaginative axis has accelerated, new fictions exemplify the paradox of the Greek terms *ethnos* and *ethnikos*, which refer at once to a given people and to others (in the sense of heathen or *goyim*) (Sollors, *Beyond* 25). That is, today's ethnic American literatures are increasingly inclined to locate stories by and about ethnic and racial others inside stories of the self, stories of the family, stories of the subject's struggle or reconciliation with the nation. The classic Americanization novel has become a novel of initiation into interethnicity.

For scholars of ethnic American literature, the interethnic turn in recent fiction suggests the need for an interethnic turn of our own. "[E]thnic literary criticism ought to be comparative," Dean J. Franco rightly argues in 2006 (6), and the rise of a comparative practice is a healthy corrective to the tendency to over-isolate subfields in ethnic American literary studies. But I would suggest that our critical practice go beyond comparison to catch up with the dynamic interethnicity already shaping the literature we read. Such a shift would place us definitively beyond the limiting, binary opposition that formerly reigned in debates about U.S. literary ethnicity—an opposition recently complicated and resituated by transnational paradigms, but one that still, it seems to me, needs upending in ethnic American literary studies.

The first of these poles is the ethnic critical paradigm itself, which over several decades has produced lively bodies of criticism about Asian, African, Latino, Jewish, Native, and other American literatures, organizing literary study around ethnicity as a vital category of human history. The second paradigm, enabled by post-structuralist critique and most vividly operative from the mid-1980s to the mid-1990s, introduced a healthy skepticism toward essentialist adherence to "ethnicity" in criticism and canon formation. But those who argued most forcefully for an anti-essentialist view of American literature have taken extreme positions. Werner Sollors, who has produced volumes in the vital project of interrogating prevalent conceptions of ethnicity in literature (eg., *Beyond Ethnicity*, *The Invention of Ethnicity*), and who is at the forefront of what has come to be called, perhaps perversely, the "ethnicity school," has tended to treat ethnicity as a mere structure of differences, of boundary-marking without real content, and, much to the consternation of Asian Americanists and other ethnic specialists, to suggest that those who practice single-ethnicity criticism are guilty of essentialism and, even worse, of "further isolation of the marginalized group, [and] fragmentation of American studies as a discipline" (Sau-ling C. Wong, *Reading* 4). In a related line of argument, Walter Benn Michaels, examining American literature and culture "from the standpoint of anti-essentialism," has claimed that notions of cultural identity, because they rely on the concept of racial identity, amount simply to more racism and that ethnic attachments of identity to particular languages, cultures, and histories make no logical sense (*Our America* 134, 181–82; "You who never was there").[8]

From an interethnic critical perspective, such an ideological dispute is now beside the point. While I, too, want to shake up ethnic criticism's earlier tendency to project static, tradition-bound identities, it seems to me absurd to try to deconstruct "ethnicity" entirely away, or to dismiss all usages of the category of "race" as racist. I think it should be possible to discuss ethnic literatures, authors, texts, without falling into one or another absolutist trap, to speak of ethnicity as constructed and performed and borrowed while also noting how it produces meaning and shapes lives, subjectivities, and texts. As Kathleen Brogan has usefully put it, explicitly revising Sollors:

> One can resist ethnic essentialism and yet remain uneasy about the implication that ethnic culture is essentially contentless. The face-off between form and content (boundary-marking versus "cultural stuff" or differentiation versus essential difference) presents at bottom a false opposition: both are central aspects of ethnic identity. Differences in cultural content exist, and they matter. These differences cannot be separated from the particular histories from which they arise and to which they continue to make reference.... (14–15)

So, in a both/and spirit, I sympathize with those critics, prominent among them some African Americanists and Asian Americanists, who have mistrusted the move away from the specificity of ethnic traditions and toward either hybridity, borders, or cross-cultural synchronicity. I have no interest in unseating the critical model of literary ethnicity—the "vertical" conception that traces one historical tradition, and that has been a crucial, powerful generator of stories to live by, as well as an essential, strategic identity marker for marginalized peoples. Rather, I supplement it by offering the interethnic, a "horizontal" model that attends to the dialogism that postcolonial theorists and anthropologists variously attribute to hybridization, sites of cultural encounter, the contact zone where cultures meet. Like cultural critics ranging from Ralph Ellison and Toni Morrison, to Eric Lott and Michael Rogin, to Ella Shohat and Robert Stam, to historians David Hollinger and Vijay Prashad, I suggest that we regard multiethnic American literature as a space of experiment with cross-ethnic influence, affiliation, imitation, projection, and rivalry. But while Sollors urges us to "develop a terminology that goes beyond the organicist imagery of roots and can come to terms with the pervasiveness and inventiveness of syncretism," I prefer to preserve "roots" even while tracing extra-ethnic "passages,"[9] as they become what both Clifford and Paul Gilroy have called "routes,"[10] the paths that rooted people nevertheless follow into a syncretic culture. I propose the interethnic paradigm of "roots and passages" to account for a remarkable revision of the notion of an ethnic text by writers who must be said to retain profound ethnic investments.

Ellison noted before most others the "metamorphoses and blending of identities, values, and life-styles" set in motion by the dynamics of multiethnic American history. As he saw it, "whatever else the true American is, he is also somehow black" ("What America" 108, 111). But despite his deep sense of American hybridity, writes Henry B. Wonham, "Ellison understood that racial essentialism constituted a necessary critical illusion for members of his generation.... A space of "difference"... was essential to the emergence of black voices in artistic, educational, and political life. That space of difference is real, and its constant articulation remains a necessity" (4). Beyond the necessary revisions of the "ethnicity school," then, and even while engaging paradigms in cultural scholarship named for migrations, national border-crossings, the hemisphere, the globe, or even (as in Spivak) the planet, I would insist on the need for the different space of intra-ethnic literary and cultural study, for reasons aesthetic as well as historical and strategic.

At the same time, I would like to extend across the spectrum of ethnic American literatures the valuable interethnic work that, following in the line of Ellison, has been done since the early 1990s in studies in America's interrelated black and white literatures. Toni Morrison's *Playing in the Dark* played a key role in the trend, reading repressed blackness in canonical works of white American literature. Scholars including Eric Sundquist, Eric Lott, and Shelley Fisher Fishkin have worked "to trace the expressive heritage of a biracial culture" (Sundquist 9). Extending this work "beyond black and white," critics including Ella Shohat and Robert Stam have energetically traced circuits of cross-ethnic borrowing. More recently, scholars including Vijay Prashad, George Lipsitz, Daniel Y. Kim, James Kim, Jelena Šesnić, Yung-Hsing Wu, and the contributors to Heike Raphael-Hernandez and Shannon Steen's 2006 collection *AfroAsian Encounters* have plotted black-Asian literary and cultural intersections in particular. In the spirit of this growing body of work, and of related scholarly projects that cross national and regional borders, I mean in this book to carve out a space of possibility between the two poles of "ethnic criticism" and "the ethnicity school," foregrounding the interethnic dynamism underway in ethnic texts themselves.

It is essential to this project that while speaking of extra-ethnic affiliations, borrowings, projections, power contests, and so on, I also attend to the differences among differences, to the differently determinative power or social weight that ethnicities have carried, the varying access to the ethnic "choice" for different groups, and so on. Multiculturalism is sometimes accused of leveling important inequities, but it seems to me possible to do cross-ethnic thinking while remembering the histories of the differences among the people around us, in the working multiculture in which we live; in Marable's words, "ethnic studies must both have a broad perspective—and at the same time be careful to make distinctions" (B4). In examining the boundary-crossing visions of ethnic fictions in the chapters and interchapters that follow, I find it crucial to observe not only distinctions that arise in the wide range of national and ethnic origins and histories that the texts in this study comprise, but also those that arise by virtue of class and citizenship statuses. As King-kok Cheung has written:

> Bilingual and biliterate writers and academics may thrive on hybridity, whereas those who are less fluent and less privileged may find their biculturalism to be a handicap that marginalizes them in both dominant and ethnic cultures. Similarly, diasporic experience may be enabling for metropolitan intellectuals who can afford to travel back and forth across the Pacific but debilitating for migrant workers and those who suffer drastic occupational "demotion" in the transition from Asia to America. ("Re-Viewing" 14)

In honoring the reality of lived difference, it may be important, too, to acknowledge the inadequacy of the terms with which I work, "race" and "ethnicity"—imprecise and loaded terms with which many scholars have had to make a certain strategic peace, hoping to avoid both the biologism of "race" and the homogenization of disparate histories that sometimes attends blanket usages of "ethnicity." I generally follow Sollors's sensible practice: to prefer "ethnicity" over the "heavily charged term" "race" in describing any given group, thus treating race "as one aspect of ethnicity" (*Beyond* 39). At the same time, I use the term "racialization" to describe the oppression that has attended phenotype- and skin color-based social categorization of some groups, so as to foreground the differently determinative nature of the ethnicity of more oppressively "raced" subjects, African Americans above all, and Asian Americans as well.[11] Next is "multiculturalism," the more race-conscious, less conformist successor to American cultural pluralism, an "understanding of the world as a cacophonous multiplicity of voices and experiences," all equally entitled (Greenberg 57, 55). While multiculturalism has come to be regarded in some quarters as a bland, hegemonic, politically retrograde ideology that aestheticizes cultural differences and quashes real, lived experiences of class and racial disadvantage and suffering, for cultural conservatives it continues to name a radical menace to traditional institutions of culture such as the university and the public schools. I treat it as the prevailing zeitgeist, an imperfect but hopeful cultural formation born of massive global and national change, which, despite its many lamentable co-optations, suffuses contemporary ethnic literatures with a distinctive vigor, a drive toward encounters with others, and an elusive, utopian ideal.[12]

Interethnic Literary History

While the particularly energetic quality of the contemporary interethnic turn feels—to borrow from Yamashita once more—"ngu," interethnicity, as I have argued, has long been an essential dynamic of imaginative literature. In the literature of the New World, indeed, we might have to call it the bottom line. The founding fact of departure from traditional societies, entrance into the unfamiliar, and contact with other peoples gave rise to a literature fundamentally about engagement with otherness, perhaps even—particularly for those with the freedom to desire it—fundamentally inspired by what Chang-rae Lee has called "that initial American desire and yearning, which is the possibility of becoming someone else" ("An Interview" 6).

Native American written literature cannot be imagined without the shaping reality of European conquest and domination, which set in motion the hybridization of cultural forms, the "process of mediation and translation," the "intercultural practice," that "bring[s] differing cultural codes into confluence" in Native American writing today (Murray 69, Krupat 21, Ruppert 209). Moreover, as A. Robert Lee has observed, "Native America, increasingly, has come to be construed... through mixedblood or crossblood populations," and its literature is correspondingly "multivocal, sited in the city as well as the land, open to American mass culture as well as to traditional tribal influence" (9). Cross-race entanglement is of course foundational to the literature of the African American experience, from earliest narratives by ex-slaves who "attempt[ed]...to *write themselves into being*" through the white man's English and generic traditions (Davis and Gates xxiii), and who incorporated white people in their tales as both antagonists and imagined readers, through nearly two centuries of fiction that ranges from the intrigue of race mixture and racial passing to the ordinary encounters, both violent and banal, of intertwined peoples. Sollors's *Anthology of Interracial Literature* (2004) offers dozens of examples of "black-white contacts" produced in American literature by white and black writers both, ranging from Longfellow to Kate Chopin, Charles Chesnutt to Eugene O'Neill, Countee Cullen to Gwendolyn Brooks.[13] All of African American literature, Toni Morrison and, before her, Ralph Ellison have argued, has developed in intimate struggle with the tight grasp of whiteness, just as all white American literature has been structured upon its Africanist other. Ellison wrote in 1946, "[O]n the moral level I propose that we view the whole of American life as a drama acted upon the body of a Negro giant, who, lying trussed up like Gulliver, forms the stage and the scene upon which and within which the action unfolds" ("Twentieth-Century" 28). His vision, as we shall see, holds true even for recent interethnic American texts, in which dramas involving diverse types of lately arriving immigrants continue to circle around that "Negro giant." United States Latino/a literature, in all its variations of region, ethnicity, and national origin, bears witness to a deep historical memory of *mestizaje*, of racial and cultural mixture, a legacy of colonization recently reclaimed by Latino/a writers and cultural critics, to whose work this study is indebted.[14] For Gloria Anzaldúa in the influential *Borderlands/La Frontera: The New Mestiza* (1987), the mixture born of conquest can be realized as a creative, future-oriented ethos for a people's survival.

The shock of encounter with the human multiplicity of America is a drama reenacted over and over in the texts of the ethnic immigrant literature that burgeoned in the decades following the late nineteenth-century migration waves from Europe and Asia. Among the immigration fictions of the early twentieth century, while Roth's *Call It Sleep* most literally renders this shock, a text set at roughly the same period—Filipino American writer Carlos Bulosan's novelistic memoir *America Is in the Heart* (1946)—presents a panoramic view of immigrant encounters on the opposite coast, portraying Depression-era American migrant multitudes struggling in the wake of a harsh arrival. Along with scenes of destitute Filipinos riding boxcars north and south through the California farmlands in search of work and refuge from racist attack, Bulosan also presents stark vignettes of mixed Asian-emigrant crowds clashing violently in crammed urban ghettoes, and the memorable scenario of a global diaspora of tuberculosis sufferers awaiting recovery together, on the tree-shaded porch of a California state sanitarium. Such varying visions of chaotic or comradely American heterogeneity are scattered throughout the texts of mid-twentieth-century ethnic American literature.

But even as this study traces a vital interethnic strand to the earliest moments of American literature, it also argues for the distinctiveness of the wave of "fusion texts"[15] arising around 1980 amidst the heightened consciousness and imperative, in our era, of cross-cultural interrelations. In the contemporary interethnic novel of foregrounded multiethnic dialogue and unabashed cross-ethnic literary affiliation, while sources of deep meaning are still found in the ethnos and its history, transforming moments arise from significant exchange with others.

A few examples from contemporary ethnic American fiction will illustrate. One of the earliest American novels to foreground and thematize the values of intercultural syncretism is Leslie Marmon Silko's *Ceremony* (1977), in which the Navajo medicine man Betonie sets the hero, a half-breed Laguna World War II veteran, on his path to healing through a hybridized practice of Indian medicine. Betonie teaches the hero to regard his mixed blood as an asset, not as a deficiency, and in his healing practice, he mixes traditional elements: "reddish willow twigs tied in neat bundles," "painted gourd rattles and deer-hoof clackers," and a traditional ritual involving chanting, drums, reenactment of myths and a symbolic scalping, with the found detritus of Euro-American culture: "bundles of newspapers . . . barricading piles of telephone books with the years scattered among cities—St. Louis, Seattle, New York, Oakland," and "layers of old calendars, the sequences of years confused and lost" (119–20). "And what do I make from all this?" Betonie asks the startled young hero; "In the old days it was simple. A medicine person could get by without all these things. But nowadays . . . " (121):

> [A]fter the white people came, elements in this world began to shift; and it became necessary to create new ceremonies. I have made changes in the rituals. The people mistrust this greatly, but only this growth keeps the ceremonies strong.
>
> [My grandmother] taught me this above all else: things which don't shift and grow are dead things. (126)

Betonie is the pivotal figure who makes the novel's ethos of hybridity work, a figure for the contemporary artist as *bricoleur*, for the Native American writer preserving tradition while embracing diverse materials, affirming the hope of survival through syncretism that is echoed in a number of Native American fictional texts.[16]

The corpus of the African American historical novel of slavery includes many texts with substantial white characters, including Margaret Walker's pioneering *Jubilee* (1966) and Alex Haley's well-known *Roots* (1976), but nothing to prepare one for the deeply braided lives, the fully developed relationships of black and white across the slavery line in Sherley Anne Williams's *Dessa Rose* (1986) or Charles Johnson's *Oxherding Tale* (1982). Johnson's hero, Andrew, a mulatto slave-cum-philosopher born of the (parodic) coupling of a white slave mistress and a black slave butler, is part of a significant trend in texts about mixed-race but non-"tragic" characters.[17] His fearsome antagonist, the allegorical "Soulcatcher" Horace Bannon, is "a racial mongrel, like most Americans," but with a phantasmagorical difference. Not only does he display his "genetic mix" in a "collage of features" identifiably black and white (67–68), but also when he uncovers his chest at the novel's climax, this murderer reveals the very body—at once marvelous and demonic—of America's interracial history: "An impossible flesh tapestry of a thousand individualities... forms sardined into his contour, creatures Bannon had killed since childhood." In Johnson's sublime revision of the ontology of American slavery, anchored in binary racial division but transcending it, all creatures, ranging from "spineless insects" to human beings, black and white, are united in "the commonwealth of the dead," "their metamorphosis having no purpose beyond the delight the universe took in diversity for its own sake, the proliferation of beauty ... the profound mystery of the One and the Many" (175–76).[18]

While Jewish American literature derives from a diasporic culture that has always thrived in hybridity, in the United States its most visible public face has been that of Americanization, a blander if still complex intercultural process. Still, a distinct interethnic strain can be traced through Jewish American literary history—from immigrant negotiations of the multiethnic streets, to the anxieties of assimilation and intermarriage, to a particularly charged encounter with African Americans[19]—a strain that develops, in a contemporary cultural moment combining intense roots revivalism and self-conscious, postmodern hybridization,[20] into a central, animating preoccupation. A certain culmination is found in Philip Roth's 2000 novel, *The Human Stain*, a variation on the African American passing novel in which a black man passes not simply for white but for Jewish. The problem, for the Jewish narrator compelled by somebody else's American story—the passing hero's assimilative quest—is not the relationship between the two minority groups, but the philosophical and social difficulty of truly knowing others, given the unreliability and even falseness of all public identities, across a variegated American spectrum of gender, race, and class. Contemporary Jewish writers frequently join Roth in privileging the encounter with ethnic others, embedding such interactions in a wide social spectrum and an intense dialogism, as in the diverse ESL class of immigrants that shares a moral dilemma in Lore Segal's "The Reverse Bug" (1989), or in affirmations of interethnic romance such as the Jewish-Indian American love in Lynne Sharon Schwartz's "The Melting Pot" (1987), and in the riotous synagogue outing of a Jewish-Catholic marriage in the family in Galina Vromen's "Secret Diary of a Bat Mitzvah Girl" (2002).[21] Even the legacy of the Holocaust gets an unprecedented dialogic structure in Jonathan Safran Foer's wildly imaginative *Everything Is Illuminated* (2002), which unfolds in an epistolary and novelistic exchange between a young Jewish American man seeking his family's pre-war home and an ebullient Ukrainian teenage tour guide whom one would not have expected to be heir to the same story.

After the success of *Everything Is Illuminated*, the arrival of the young Foer's second novel, about the aftermath of September 11, 2001, in the life of a New York City boy of German descent, drew such high notice in literary circles that the back cover of *Extremely Loud and Incredibly Close* bears an endorsement from that celebrant of the transnational novel, Salman Rushdie. I cite this fact to suggest the global and broadly interethnic readership that major press book distribution now models and enables. Just as a cross-ethnic readership is a constitutive feature of literary publishing today, we need to understand ethnic writers, too, as global readers, crossing ethnic, national, and linguistic lines to read and be influenced by diverse, heterogeneous precursors and contemporaries.[22] Ellison, once again ahead of his time and my authority for the "rooted cosmopolitan" view I claim as the current norm,[23] declared an artist's freedom to "choose one's 'ancestors,'" naming the European and white American authors who influenced him even more than did the African American canon ("The World and the Jug" 140).[24] The conspicuous display of this hybrid process of influence is one of the key features of contemporary interethnic literature. We might say that contemporary literary influence, too, has seen a miscegenation of "descent" and "consent": one can now descend, literarily, from any "ancestors" one chooses, so to speak.

Writers influenced by diverse others may be simply opening their ears to a more and more polyphonic reality. Or they may be purposefully drawing lines of alliance to or working to distinguish themselves from other minority groups, or perhaps asserting an active claim to a shared and hybrid literary inheritance. The wide-ranging, inclusive literary imaginations of the Asian American novelists discussed in this study deliver the sense that not only the contemporary American street, but also the public library, is a vital source of the hybrid vision. The new interethnic fictions, mirroring the heterogeneous range and openness of contemporary reading practices, are written by and for people who, in their lives as readers, dwell in "a third space of fragmented and shifting cosmopolitan affiliations" (Knadler 15); or, if we are not quite denizens of such a promising space when we pick these books up, we are surely encouraged to become such, once in their pages. That is to say, I take myself and all other readers to be summoned, by this literature, to the experience of cross-ethnic encounter, invited to find ourselves unsettled and newly placed within it. And similarly, I regard the interethnic literary turn as a claim to broad freedoms for the ethnic writerly imagination. In my critical practice, I honor the implications of their wide-ranging ventures, their destabilizing of conventional ethnic literary spheres, their suggestion that we, too, think beyond familiar definitions and categories. I derive from these novels our license to become interethnic readers.

Part II: Interethnicity and Asian American Literary Studies

Engaging Asian Americanist Critique

While ethnic Americanist, postcolonial, and transnational theoretical paradigms are all important to this book's investigation of the interethnic imagination of contemporary Asian American fiction, the most crucial body of scholarly work that I engage is Asian Americanist critique. The lively field of Asian American literature has been well served in the past three decades by a thriving, sophisticated, and politically astute body of theory and criticism on Asian American culture. In the swift rise and development of this field, occurring in the short time since the entry of significant numbers of Asian Americans into the academy, one sees a striking historical self-consciousness. The theoretically ambitious work of the late 1990s and early twenty-first century repeatedly invokes its debt to the originary, cultural nationalist projects to assert and define a viable field of literature and of scholarship. Moreover, those earlier critical ventures—to recover and dignify marginalized texts, to illuminate their context by rewriting inadequately told histories of Asian American people, to elaborate the features of a distinctive tradition—still retain real currency, even while their interrogation and revision are energetically underway. This makes Asian American literary critique a remarkably vibrant, contested field, a few years beyond the controversies around issues such as canonization, authenticity, critical authority, and assimilation, but in many ways still engaged in debating the very definition of the field, even the very term that names the field. Many critics have problematized the term "Asian American," but most argue for retaining it as a matter of Spivakian "strategic essentialism" (Lowe, *Immigrant* 82).[25]

Though the name remains the same, this field has expanded dramatically from its initial focus on just a few East Asian immigrant groups, "to include writings by Americans of Bangladeshi, Burmese, Cambodian, Chinese, Filipino, Japanese, Korean, Indian, Indonesian, Laotian, Nepali, Pakistan, Sri Lankan, Thai, and Vietnamese descent," among others (Cheung, "Re-Viewing" 3). Moreover, since the early 1990s, a major "paradigm shift" has led critics to de-emphasize an American national frame (Sau-ling C. Wong, "Denationalization" 2), shifting from "identity politics—with its stress on cultural nationalism and American nativity"—to a reading of Asian American experience within a transnational, diasporic historical matrix (Cheung, "Re-Viewing" 1),[26] which avoids American exceptionalism and attends to global dynamics. While the tension between "nationalist" and "transnationalist" paradigms continues, some of the most interesting work in the field has depended upon this dialectic, placing Asian American subjectivity "simultaneously within both U.S. national and global frameworks" (Lowe, *Immigrant* 34) and, as in the title of Lisa Lowe's influential essay "Heterogeneity, Hybridity, Multiplicity: Asian American Differences" (*Immigrant* 60–83), complicating the U.S. national model by attention to "the multiple axes of ethnicity, gender, class, and sexuality"; to the "panethnic" or "interethnic" field that constitutes Asian American culture (see titles by Espiritu; Cheung)[27]; and to Asian America's historical relations with other ethnic American groups (Cheung, "Re-Viewing" 1; Sau-ling C. Wong, "Denationalization"

18). Thus, Sau-ling Cynthia Wong, considering the shift in a key 1995 essay, suggests, "It would be far more useful to conceive of *modes* rather than *phases* of Asian American subjectivity: an indigenizing mode can coexist and alternate with a diasporic or a transnational mode, but the latter is not to be lauded as a culmination of the former, a stage more advanced or more capacious" ("Denationalization" 17). And writing in 1998, David Leiwei Li appreciates "the multivalenced formations both 'difference' and 'diaspora' can helpfully generate" but urges that we maintain "the notion of Asian America as a compelled solidarity" so that we lose neither " 'race' as a central category of address and analysis" nor " 'nation' as a viable ground for critical alliance" (202). The vigorous reexamination of the Asian American critical paradigm has also involved creative engagement, in various moments, with Marxist, feminist, critical race, postcolonial, psychoanalytic, queer, diasporic, globalization, and other theories. This ongoing intellectual ferment has generated, in Rachel C. Lee's term, a " 'postconsensus' condition" (*Americas* 155, note 19), and in Li's words, "an era of energetic heteroglossia" that can "entertain as never before divergent ideological viewpoints and aesthetic expressions" (189–90).

It is in the spirit of this moment of openness and controversy that I propose a focus on the interethnic imagination of the Asian American novel, aware that this proposal may seem an "extravagant" contribution to the field. I borrow the term "extravagance" from Sau-ling Cynthia Wong's landmark 1993 study *Reading Asian American Literature: From Necessity to Extravagance*, in which the poles of "necessity" and "extravagance" define the spectrum of choices in life and art for Asian American people over a couple of centuries of struggle. This study's approach to contemporary Asian American texts is "extravagant" both in that its moment logically arrives after the crucially "necessary" work of claiming and defining an ethnic literary tradition and also in that it is concerned literally with wanderings beyond bounds, in the obsolete meaning that derives from the Latin (*extravagari*).

The interethnic paradigm, highlighting Asian American fiction's simultaneous engagements with specific immigrant histories and with multicultural American localities intimately tied to global-scale change, can enliven the U.S. national model in ways that are broadly consonant with post-national American cultural and literary studies, and that are also closely attuned to the particularities of cross-ethnic interrelations. At the same time, this approach can be seen as a logical extension of Asian Americanists' recent privileging of "difference" over essentialist identity politics, as when Lowe writes, "To the extent that Asian American culture dynamically expands to include both internal critical dialogues about difference and the interrogation of dominant interpellations... Asian American culture can likewise be a site in which the 'horizontal' affiliations with other groups can be imagined and realized" (*Immigrant* 71).

Others whose work honors the importance of such "horizontal" connections are Wong, who cites the history of and continued need for "coalitions of Asian American and other racial/ethnic minorities within the U.S." as one of the key reasons to continue to privilege the U.S. national over the diasporic framework ("Denationalization" 18); James Kim, who suggests that Asian American studies begin to "adopt a... focus on Asian American relationality, an emphasis on sites where the concerns of Asian American studies intersect with the concerns of other ethnic studies" (153), and who urges scholars to "work toward radical interracial coalitions" (173); and Daniel Y. Kim, whose work "seeks to address... [the] forces—psychic and ideological," "that draw members of different racial minority groups together and also pull them apart" (*Writing* xvii).

With such attention to cross-ethnic relations in mind, I read the interethnic turn in contemporary Asian American novels as transforming the historically resonant claim to Americanness that has been a key topos in Asian American literature.[28] This charged and central claim, which for Wanni Anderson and Robert G. Lee "ought not to be dismissed as merely assimilationist, but may be understood as a radical assertion of subjectivity and transformative of the nation itself" (8), undergoes in the context of cross-ethnic imaginative relationality an enriching expansion, becoming an insistence on a wide range of possibilities for self-invention and identification, and for dialogic contestation across the historic geography and among the intermingled peoples of America. The America that Asian American literature now ventures to claim is no longer the symbolic possession of select, remote Others; rather, this literature now claims the power of free entry into a multiply articulated and contested collective space.

I also see these fictions claiming a place for themselves amidst both transnational and subnational currents. The multiethnic urban, suburban, or regional settings of the novels given chapter-length treatment here tend to downplay the importance of the United States as an ideologically privileged space and to erode the importance of national boundaries, accentuating instead the local manifestations of global-scale movements of people. "Cities," writes James Holston with Appadurai, are "especially salient sites for analyzing the current renegotiations of citizenship, democracy, and national belonging," for they "make manifest... national and transnational realignments... in the spaces and relations of urban daily life" (vii). The novels in this study pay exquisite attention to the imbrication of Asian American lives at once within diasporic networks and within the heterogeneity of local U.S. settings. They collectively ask, with Appadurai, "what is the nature of locality as a lived experience in a globalized, deterritorialized world?" (*Modernity* 52), and with Saldìvar, "How do we tell other spatial stories? How do we tell other histories that are placed in local frames of awareness, on the one hand, and situated globally, geopolitically on the other?" (*Border* 12). Recent Asian American fictions attempt to do just this, I would claim, vividly locating themselves amidst global crosscurrents in New York City, its suburbs, Los Angeles, and many other heterogeneous and changing U.S. ethnoscapes and at the same time firmly within the influence of Asian American literary tradition.

Asian American Fiction and the Interethnic

This brings me to Asian-American fiction, one of the most energetic and interesting fields of American literature today, and a body of work in the vanguard of the interethnic. Why should the interethnic impulse be particularly lively in contemporary Asian American literature? One way of accounting for it is to date the current publishing boom. The rise of Asian American literature today has been fueled by decades of mass immigration, beginning when the 1965 Hart-Celler Act ended longtime U.S. discrimination against potential immigrants from Asia and elsewhere outside Western Europe.[29] For a huge and heterogeneous segment of this new American population, notions of ethnic identity have developed in an era already "multicultural" and increasingly "global," marked by the massive dislocations, the globalized consciousness, and the newly fluid patterns of settlement and interaction in our time. For many from these largely nonwhite immigrant populations, familiarity with histories of "colonialism and neocolonialism (sometimes indeed at the hands of Americans)" in their home countries means that a "critical knowledge of race prejudice is almost second nature" (Mendoza and Shankar xxii), as is a "tendency . . . to critique American culture and find it wanting" (Katherine Payant, qtd. in Mendoza and Shankar xxii). At the same time, the powerful changes in culture and consciousness that were set in motion by the African American civil rights movement across the spectrum of American ethnic groups, as well as the global media literacy that the new immigrants bring with them to this country, tend to engender a multiculturalist consciousness that affirms cultural and racial differences, and "a deep and thoroughgoing rejection of the option of assimilating to America" in the conventional sense (Mendoza and Shankar xxii). Though recent Asian American writers have by no means forgotten the histories of exclusion and alienation, of anguished desire for American acceptance, rendered in the literature of their precursors, the new work often conveys a sense of entitlement to Americanness guaranteed them by the very heterogeneity of the crowds that greeted them at the U.S. airport terminal. Americanness in the new immigrant writing, that is to say, is inseparable from an interethnic ethos. Such narratives have been said collectively to evince "more fluidity of identity, more heterogeneity, more resistance to assimilation, [and] more bilingualism and hybridity" (Friedman, "Migrations" 265). For Asian American writers in particular, both the relatively recent notion of a collective Asian American identity (explicitly since its inception a political construct, a self-positioning),[30] as well as the "in-between black and white" position conventionally granted to Asians in the hierarchy of American race, may tend to foster an interethnic consciousness.

Like the texts of the literature that preceded them, contemporary Asian American fictions remain grounded in histories of immigration, family, labor, and the transmission and transformation of traditional cultures. And like earlier texts, they continue traditional Asian American literary preoccupations: as Rachel C. Lee lists them, "biculturalism, racial conflict, generational conflict, and resistance to U.S. hegemony" (*Americas* 107), and as Patricia P. Chu puts it, "the historical contradiction between a democratic rhetoric of inclusion and the realities of exclusion, discrimination, internment, and cultural marginalization" (4). But at the same time, recent texts make it clear that Asian American literature has come to an ethnic crossroads. In the works this study examines, the historical problematics of Asian American subject formation are embedded within visions of rich human and cultural multiplicity, scenarios notably distinct from the stark, binary face-off between immigrant subjectivity and a generalized Americanness that long marked this literature, from early texts such as the Angel Island poems, written on the walls by imprisoned nineteenth-century Chinese immigrants, up through the best-known works of the canon, such as the wrenching plea for American belonging in Bulosan's 1946 immigrant narrative *America Is in the Heart*; John Okada's portrait of a World

War II Japanese American army resister fighting for recognition as an American in the 1957 novel *No-No Boy*; or Maxine Hong Kingston's catalogue of the American types she was taught to see as ghosts in her breakthrough 1976 autobiographical fiction, *The Woman Warrior*. In contrast to these earlier works, recent Asian American fictions portray less the struggle for a place in the American mainstream than the negotiation of shifting roles in an intercultural arena. Rather than contest the monolith America (as in the Bulosan and Okada texts noted above, in which the word "America" repeats obsessively, like an anguished mantra), recent texts tend to foreground regional U.S. settings, to some degree displacing the national episteme in favor of specific local forces and urgencies. Seeking to make themselves at home in the complex, multiethnic plots of this body of fiction, contemporary protagonists puzzle out an Asian Americanness uneasy with binary notions of "us" and "them."

The Politics of Horizontality

What, we may ask, are the politics of this Asian American shift toward intercultural engagement? As Clifford writes, "there is no reason to assume that crossover practices are always liberatory or that articulating an autonomous identity or a national culture is always reactionary" (10). Cross-ethnic confluences or affiliations do seem at first glance a good thing, familiarly encapsulated in a progressive vision like that of Li, who advocates a "fuller appreciation of [the] plural memberships" of Asian American people in the larger world (193), or of Lowe, whose essay on Asian American heterogeneity ends: "In the 1990s, we can diversify our practices to include a more heterogeneous group and to enable crucial alliances—with other groups of color, class-based struggles, feminist coalitions, and sexuality-based efforts—in the ongoing work of transforming hegemony" (*Immigrant* 83).

But surely fictional texts that affirm plural memberships and alliances would fail to contribute to such a transformation if they simply advocated the sort of thin multiculturalism that, in Lowe's terms, emphasizes cultural diversity but "suppresses tension and contradiction, and overemphasizes resolution and integration," especially in that it fails to consider the differing material burdens borne by various groups ("Multiculturalism" 590). Such concerns about multiculturalism are closely related to the debates on hybridity, a highly contested notion among theorists of postcolonial cultures. Here again, the question is whether the term reveals or conceals the histories and power relations behind the commingling of peoples and cultures, as Shohat and Stam suggest:

> A celebration of syncretism and hybridity *per se*, if not articulated with questions of historical hegemonies, risks sanctifying the *fait accompli* of colonial violence. For oppressed people, even artistic syncretism is not a game but a sublimated form of historical pain. . . . As a descriptive, catch-all term, "hybridity" fails to discriminate between the diverse modalities of hybridity: colonial imposition, obligatory assimilation, political cooptation, cultural mimicry, and so forth. Elites have always made cooptive top-down raids on subaltern cultures, while the dominated have always "signified" and parodied as well as emulated elite practice. Hybridity, in other words, is power-laden and asymmetrical. (43)

Jahan Ramazani has argued that our use of the "hybridity paradigm" "can keep this potential problem in check by continually referring back to the colonial and postcolonial matrices of violence, inequality, and oppression, even as it reveals the cultural interchange across the colonial divide" (271–73; see also 9–10). Similarly, Rita Felski, asserting hybridity's usefulness for the conception of "multiple, interconnecting axes of affiliation and differentiation" ("Doxa" 12), argues that

> To acknowledge the cultural leakages and interconnections between cultures is not necessarily to deny their asymmetrical placement. Neither is it to affirm uncritically a condition of cultural fragmentation and geographical displacement that's often experienced as painful rather than liberating, as has occurred in contemporary celebrations of the nomadic subject. The point is not to idealize and essentialize hybridity as a new source of political value, as a code word for the radically authentic or subversive. It is simply to acknowledge cultural impurity as the inescapable historical backdrop of all contemporary struggles... in a global culture marked by pervasive and ongoing processes of both voluntary and involuntary cultural interchange. (14–15)

Writing on hybridity in the context of Asian American cultural production, Lowe offers a definition of the term that preserves matrices of violence, yet allows for heroic agency:

> Hybridization is not the "free" oscillation between or among chosen identities. It is the uneven process through which immigrant communities encounter the violences of the U.S. state, and the capital imperatives served by the United States and by the Asian states from which they come, and the process through which they survive these violences by living, inventing, and reproducing different cultural alternatives. (82)

All of these critics remind us that the creative potential of ethnically mixed situations and identities arises within difficult, overdetermined historical contexts. This is a reality kept alive in all of the fictions I discuss in this study, which retain the memory of long years of striving for safety, dignity, and prosperity in America even as they engage in newly possible interethnic experiments. Texts that situate Asian American experience amidst what Felski calls the "inescapable historical backdrop" of "cultural interchange" place subjects within a complex field of power relations that generates a form of hybridity not well described by either of the binary terms "metropolitan" or "postcolonial," offered by R. Radhakrishnan: "The crucial difference that one discerns between metropolitan versions of hybridity and 'postcolonial' versions is that, whereas the former are characterized by an intransitive and immanent sense of jouissance, the latter are expressions of extreme pain and agonizing dislocations" (753). The fictions considered here, I would argue, merge painful, postcolonial dislocation and jouissant metropolitan communion. By taking the plots of struggling, postcolonial immigrants into surprising metropolitan encounters, or working them into the complex weave of multiethnic fictional structures or scenarios, these novels generate transforming modes and moments of creative hybridization. These fictions tend, moreover, to grant a healthy density and particularity to other (non-Asian) ethnic presences and experiences, so that interethnic plots are played out within a rich social texture, in which Asian American characters participate with results varying in emotional affect from hope and delight, to profound ambivalence, to bewildering grief.

Certainly we might read in this turn to ethnic interrelatedness more appropriative desires, a will to power that inevitably accompanies intergroup cultural relations, whether "cooptive top-down raids on subaltern cultures," in Shohat and Stam's terms, or parody and imitation by the oppressed. Eric Lott's *Love and Theft*, illuminating the history of blackface minstrelsy in nineteenth-century America, makes abundantly clear the way (white) admiration and imitation of (black) cultural forms and practices can coexist with self-aggrandizing, racist, and rapacious appropriation. If an ethnic fiction's vision of interrelationship indeed advances the protagonist's interests over against those of his or her group or coalition partners, if it should be infected with what David Palumbo-Liu has called "model minority discourse," "a blueprint for the deliverance of minority subjects from collective history to a reified individualism" (415), then its interethnic textuality would be an appropriative sham.

But the texts I will examine, though certainly as rife as any other human document with selfish desires, suggest another valence to the shift away from the more binary social vision of Asian American fiction's bold, embattled early texts. While legal exclusion has ended and the most severe ostracism has largely abated, racialization endures long, as do its social and psychological effects. As Palumbo-Liu has put it, "Their American status continually deferred, Asian Americans have been racially separated from "'Americans,' a distinction buttressed by a belief system deeply ingrained in the American imaginary which insists on the essential difference of racialized peoples" (1, 3). Recent Asian Americanist scholarship has produced several potent theories of and terms for the enduring abjection of Asian American subjects in life and literature; my readings of Asian American literature draw upon the valuable work of Anne Anlin Cheng on racial melancholia, David Eng on racial castration, and Kandice Chuh on Asian American subjectlessness. At the same time, I want to suggest that the interethnic turn in Asian American literature offers a direction beyond such impasses.

Just as interethnicity as a critical paradigm can offer scholars an alternative to rigid or limiting formulations of literary fields, interethnic fictions themselves break out of binaries and offer their protagonists a route out of despair, into new possibilities. In the chapters that follow, I argue that protagonists who, as minoritized subjects living under a racializing regime, might be accurately described in the bleak terms offered by the scholars listed above, are yet given in their authors' interethnic visions another chance; what I term "the horizontal plot" opens for them an axis of interethnic desire through which intersubjective play, borrowing, imitation, comparison, challenge, dialogue, or mirroring can be liberatory, even redemptive. The horizontal plot provides somewhere else to go on the way back to the self, a way out of pain or impasse through cross-ethnic identification.

Chapters and Interchapters

The final part, part III, of this opening chapter offers an overview of interethnic experimentation across a wide range of contemporary Asian American fictional texts, including, among others, works by Bharati Mukherjee, Jiro Adachi, Jessica Hagedorn, Lois Ann Yamanaka, Gus Lee, Don Lee, Patricia Chao, Rishi Reddi, Jhumpa Lahiri, and Chang-rae Lee.[31]

Three novels have been singled out for extended consideration, in chapters 2, 3, and 4 of this study. In these works, the traditional quest of the novelistic protagonist is reshaped by intersection with the mobile and globalizing world, and by potent, perhaps unexpected cross-ethnic literary influences. Their scenarios of danger and of carnivalesque, transforming possibility turn upon cross-group romantic pairings, which result in the distinctive novelistic outcome—uncommon before this era in Asian American fiction—of mixed children. And each of the three novels offers entrance into a different, compelling area of interethnic experiment.

The first of these is the complex problematics of Asian American literary relations with African American literature and culture. The ambivalence of this connection, evincing at once empathic identification, resentment, and reluctance to contribute to a history of racist demonization, is beautifully exemplified, chapter 2 argues, in Chang-rae Lee's 1995 novel *Native Speaker*, an ambitious first novel in which a Korean American New Yorker inhabits his marginalized identity and lives out his life's lingering tragedies as a spy, among a bureau of urban ethnic chameleons trained to spy on their own. The plot of this Asian American hero's self-alienation—his distancing from family, language, and culture, his daily ethnic treason and performance of false identities—opens out into an ambitious interethnic vision, which places Henry Park amidst the conflicting imperatives and attractions of whiteness, Koreanness, and the multicultural crowd. Park is forced to choose his truest public face when assigned to sabotage a Korean American politician, John Kwang, who dreams of uniting all the great city's peoples in the multicultural "family" of his candidacy.

An ambivalent poetics of the crowd is central to the life of this novel, emerging in scenes of the protagonist's wonder before heterogeneous, multicolored assemblages of New Yorkers, and also in moments when amassed others become a source of fear and horror. The novel's attention to multiethnic New York is most vexed in its engagement with African Americans. Lee's title, *Native Speaker*, directly invokes the smoldering irony of Richard Wright's *Native Son*, while his lyrical narration of a secret life on the margins strongly echoes Ralph Ellison's *Invisible Man*. Yet intriguing contradictions mark the novel's relationship to African Americans, suggesting the difficulties of a novelistic vision that aspires to encompass the Korean American and the "multicultural." Though few black characters appear in the novel, urban black-Korean conflict looms as a threat in the mayoral campaign plot. But the conflict fades; Lee ultimately steps back from black-Korean strife, seeming instead to offer, in muted tribute to an African American literary and cultural inheritance that overrides contemporary conflicts, an honoring Korean silence.

When the teenaged Chinese American heroine of Gish Jen's 1997 novel *Mona in the Promised Land* departs from all literary convention by converting to the Judaism of her suburban New York neighbors, she brings the Chinese American novel into a hilarious hybrid with the tales of Jewish Americanization, straining the limits of ethnic literary classification. In a book that bears blurbs from both Amy Tan and Cynthia Ozick, and a narration that slips alternately into the syntaxes of Shanghainese and Yiddish, Jen conducts a spirited investigation of the American freedom of self-transformation—under the conditions of suburban prosperity, 1970s youth culture, and parental absence. "The more Jewish you become," the hip, young rabbi advises Mona, "the more Chinese you'll be."

This buoyant narrative of hybrid development allows me to discuss two contemporary literary projects: the redesign of the Asian American novel as a home for multiethnic experiment, and the contemporary cross-ethnic literary project of writing Jewishness, a surprisingly popular international mode. Chapter 3 begins by investigating the uses of Jewishness for Mona's plot of Americanization and for the book's comic tone and structure, so strikingly different from those of most Asian American novels. It then goes on, beyond the giddy plot of hybrid development, to share in Mona's large questions about responsibility and relations outside the family and the ethnic group. In the spirit of the 1970s, in which the novel is set, Mona and friends take over a lavish, parent-free mansion for a few months one summer, and launch a grandly doomed experiment in American interethnic communalism—Chinese, Jewish, white, and black. In "Camp Gugelstein" this novel imagines a house of American multiethnic coexistence, even if one haunted by violent histories and far too grand in ambition, as it turns out, for anyone to own for long. Jen's book boldly remakes the Asian American novel, too, as a house of encounter, a place where all kinds of voices can enter and, for a short space of time, join in conversation, exchanging beliefs, histories, and uses of the common language.

The debate over national versus diasporic paradigms in Asian American studies provides the context for my argument that both models are indispensable and even inextricable. My exemplary text in chapter 4 is Karen Tei Yamashita's *Tropic of Orange* (1997), a novel that cultivates an interethnic sublime, assembling a cast of thousands in a postmodern, electronically wired, transnational Los Angeles. In Yamashita's tragicomic plot, indebted at once to the magic realism of Latin America and the tradition of Los Angeles disaster film and fiction, a violent freeway crisis is precipitated by the magical northward creep of the Tropic of Cancer across the U.S.-Mexico border all the way to L.A., dragging with it the illegal migration of the entire culture and history of the Southern Hemisphere. Yamashita's transnational imagination remakes the landscape of a multiethnic American novel, connecting a diverse cast of L.A. characters to worldwide human movements across borders. A character who observes it all is Manzanar Murakami, a homeless Japanese American sansei and former surgeon, who spends his days high atop an L.A. freeway overpass, conducting the music of the traffic below. "[S]tanding there," Yamashita writes, "he bore and raised each note, joined them, united families, created a community . . . an entire civilization of sound" (35). Manzanar's name records the World War II internment camp where he was born, and where his painfully acute attunement to the sounds of our civilization must be rooted. Through his character, Yamashita incorporates traces of Asian American history, but extends them into a design for a new sort of Asian American novel, one that embraces a vast, multiethnic, and transnational vision, while being especially tuned in to change, to the reverberations of the world now in the making.

When the novel magically literalizes the impact of Latino migration to the U.S. by sending the whole South physically North, the changes so shake up terrain and identity that the streets of L.A. begin to stretch and curve, all its radio stations start speaking in one another's languages, and one figure, a sarcastic, wildly anti-conventional Japanese American female yuppie, who is bleeding to death under an LAPD helicopter gunship attack intended for the homeless, echoes the resonant question of Rodney King, "Can we all get along?"

How do we understand the cultural and literary politics of such fictions—surprising, contradictory, sometimes raising dread and alienation, sometimes arriving at the comic, or even the sublime? What do they bring to the conversation about the boundaries of Asian American and other ethnic American literatures? How do they engage the transformations of a globalizing culture?

In advancing these sorts of questions, I am wary of the possibility of seeming to celebrate the interethnic literary impulse as a mode preferable to or more developed or mature than the rooted ethnic (see Sau-ling C.Wong, "Denationalization" 12, 17), even of seeming to discard the ethnic model against the interests of Asian American literature itself, only recently establishing its authority and integrity as a field of study. Moreover, an interethnic focus might be particularly unwelcome from a critic who is not an Asian Americanist per se, but a scholar of ethnic American and New World literatures, as well as an ethnic outsider, especially given the justified wariness among Asian American cultural critics about the material side of this literature's rise. Issues of publication, marketing (and the variously exoticizing or homogenizing pressures of the market), and critical authority raise the question of who is authorized to define this field. Asian American literature, writes Leslie Bow, is "hot property" (36), the darling of an Orientalism in the literary marketplace, which ultimately promotes a bland assimilation of ethnics, flattening differences even while rewarding non-Asian readers' exoticizing projections. In these circumstances, my work might risk seeming to celebrate as hybridity what others see as selling out, accommodation of the non-Asian reader, or worse, adherence to what Wong has called "the trajectory of 'growth' prescribed for people of color in this country: that minorities need to liberate themselves from their outmoded, inward-looking preoccupations and participate in the more generous-spirited intellectual inquiries that 'everybody else' is engaged in" ("Denationalization" 13).

My intent, far from disdaining, defining, or suppressing Asian American difference is rather to follow Asian American literary texts as they, themselves, negotiate multiple differences, as they take on the risky subject matter of interethnic experience, placing heterogeneous differences at the heart of Asian American cultural practice. I see in these fictions a strong impulse to try things out, to play them out transgressively, to surprise people, to test the limits of the acceptable and the possible. This phenomenon is in itself a departure from historically stereotyped Asian American cultural behaviors—in Wong's words, "industrious, focused, dependable, accommodating, serious-minded," "prudent," "*subdued*" (*Reading* 210)—and is thus a form of "extravagance" that makes texts less categorizable, containable, or dismissible. We might then read in these texts resistance and struggle against monolithic typing of Asians, and at the same time call the actively interethnic impulse a form of the "play" Wong recognizes as a vital if minor strain in "necessitous" Asian American literary tradition, one that "subverts white society's expectations on the Asian American's proper place and stimulates the creation of a heteroglossic Asian American culture" (210). But if we read these contemporary fictions as risk-taking and playfully transgressive, it must be said that, even as they celebrate the free step out of the ethnic enclave and into the multicultural arena, they evince a distinct multicultural ambivalence. They worry the fate of the simplest, the home-born virtues—loyalty, love, respect, memory—amidst the life of the heterogeneous crowd, and they worry, too, the reductive objectification of Asian American bodies and personhood in the global marketplace of cultural ideas, images, and commodities. Reading recent Asian American texts, we must come to terms with this ambivalence, I believe, with its politics and with contemporary novelists' rich aesthetic elaboration of it in form and theme.

This study's "interchapters" are short essays that extend the thematics of boundary crossing and creative in-betweenness across the structure of the book by examining special topics just beyond the range of the single-author chapters themselves. The first interchapter, "Asian/African: Black Presences in Asian American Fiction," located after this chapter and before chapter 2 (on interethnicity and blackness in Chang-rae Lee), contributes to the growing body of "AfroAsian" scholarship an overview of the history of Asian American fiction's engagement with African American culture and literature. Drawing examples from the work of selected authors including Frank Chin, Peter Bacho, Gus Lee, and Gish Jen, this interchapter investigates the strong strain of sympathetic attachment to black Americans that persists in this tradition alongside considerable cross-race tension and conflict. After chapter 3 (on Jewishness in Gish Jen), the reader will find the interchapter "Cross-ethnic Jewishness in Asian American and Other Contemporary Fiction," which carries the discussion of the meanings of Jewishness in *Mona* to the implications of its cross-ethnic adoption in other contemporary literary and cultural texts in English, focusing on David Wong Louie's *The Barbarians Are Coming* (2000) and Jamaican British novelist Zadie Smith's second novel, *The Autograph Man* (2002). I argue that as an element of global, postmodern cultural pastiche, Jewishness has become a trope for the adoption of identities from other peoples' texts, that is, for the way we read now. And after chapter 4 (on the transnational in Karen Tei Yamashita), this study closes with an epilogue on contemporary Asian American writing titled "Mixed Races, Mixed Children, Mixed Outcomes," which briefly traces a history of the treatment of mixed-race characters in Asian American literature, in texts by authors including Don Lee, Jiro Adachi, Heinz Insu Fenkl, Jessica Hagedorn, and Patricia Chao, so as to consider the special significance of the topos of the hero or heroine's mixed-race child, which appears in all three of the novels examined centrally in this study's chapters.

Interethnic Inheritance, In-Between Status

A final area of crucial yet ambivalent interethnic experiment in the texts studied here, and of dramatic departure from Asian American literary norms, is that of literary influence. More overtly than most any Asian American texts before them, I would argue, these late twentieth-, early twenty-first-century fictions affiliate themselves to extra-ethnic literary precursors; that is, they choose ancestors, in Ellison's phrase, among writers outside the Asian American—and, importantly, the Anglo American—canon. A complicated linkage to African American literary tradition undergirds Lee's *Native Speaker*, for example; Jen's *Mona in the Promised Land* and Louie's *The Barbarians Are Coming* bear a similar relationship to literary Jewishness; and Yamashita's *Tropic of Orange* to the literatures of Latin America. My readings will search out the implications of these texts' extra-ethnic attachments and appropriations for matters ranging from cultural and interethnic politics, to style and narrative mode, to representations of racialized and gendered identities.

In a striking commonality, regardless of primary attachment, each of these novels displays an affiliation with African American culture. For at the heart of Asian American literature's interethnic sensibility, I believe, has been the problem of negotiating a partly imposed, partly owned sense of *thirdness* in the American racial and cultural psyche, an arrival on a scene already structured by the presiding racial poles of blackness and whiteness. Daniel Y. Kim has recently called this condition for Asian American writers a "sense of racial 'belatedness'" (*Writing* 126). While a great deal of scholarly and critical writing has addressed Asian American cultural negotiations with dominant white cultural traditions, the matter of Asian-African American cultural relations has only lately come to the forefront of scholarly attention. This crucial, vexed alignment as a topos in Asian American fiction is the subject of the interchapter that follows this chapter.

For Wong, Asian Americans have long been treated "as a peculiar kind of Other (among other Others)"; their American status continually deferred, they have been seen as "'unassimilable alien[s]'" or "permanent houseguests in the house of America," who inhabit the space "between black and white" (*Reading* 5–6).[32] In contemporary Asian American fiction, diverse experiments in proximity to the poles of blackness, of whiteness, and of both, or in the direction of myriad other ethnic differences, help to complicate the hierarchical structure of American race, and to stake out for Asian American people a third territory other than that historically assigned to them: a space in which binary oppositions are cleared away, and American *bricoleurs* construct their homes by laying claim to whatever materials come to hand.

Setting out to trace the interethnic axis of contemporary Asian American fiction, this book pursues the enigma of evolving American ethnicity, which continues to make us vital and rich, to make us creative inheritors and preservers, but which now seems to realize itself most fully in the force field of the multiculture, a place of hazard and transformation where our particularities, our very histories of difference, give us our clamorous and hopeful membership.

Part III. Reading New Interethnic Asian American Fictions

Tracing the interethnic impulse that has traveled through Asian American fiction since the 1980s, one finds several striking, recurrent tendencies in this group of texts: the cultivation of a sublimity of interethnic flux and enmeshment, prose composed in multilingual counterpoint, an abundance of cross-ethnic romance plots, and the imagining of ethnically other protagonists, along "lateral" or "vertical" lines.

The Interethnic Sublime

Perhaps the clearest case in which multiethnic encounter becomes in itself the occasion for fiction is Bharati Mukherjee's collection *The Middleman and Other Stories* (1988), a pioneering venture into the multicultural American sublime. In this shrewd and comic group of eleven stories, the contemporary United States becomes the stage for the collision of the most unlikely pairings of third-world migrants. Mukherjee's cross-ethnic narration seems the work of a master ventriloquist, one who can do anybody's voice, and anybody's voice in dialogue with anybody else. It is a performance designed to dazzle and, by dazzling, to jar readers into a sense of the momentousness of the societal shifts wrought by global migration.

The sheer heterogeneity of Mukherjee's multiethnic characterization depicts a new American population of astonishing diversity, while the story collection framework presents them as being all, as it were, in the same boat. Each of Mukherjee's immigrants struggles for a foothold in America, and each is on the make, in pursuit of money, adventure, love, or a connection with possibilities. Many characters hail from the Indian subcontinent, but whether or not they share Mukherjee's background, the energies of interethnicity drive their plots. Unlikely romantic pairings predominate, including, among others, a married Indian woman doctoral student in New York City dating a refugee from Budapest; a New Jersey Italian American woman who brings her Afghani political refugee boyfriend to Thanksgiving dinner; and an Iraqi-born American Jew from Queens on the lam in Central America, involved with a woman who is the mistress of a guerilla leader, and formerly, of a president. Mukherjee's subject is mobility: physical, cultural, imaginative, amorous, and her characters seem to have left their distant homes as much to reinvent themselves through unprecedented encounters as to seek a higher standard of living.

In a 1988 *New York Times Book Review* essay published alongside the review of *The Middleman*, Mukherjee decries "the great temptation . . . of the ex-colonial, once-third-world author": to reject the category of "immigration" in favor of "expatriation," which gives arrivants a "cloak of mystery and world-weariness" and conveys "the purity of their pain and their moral superiority." By contrast, "[i]n literary terms, being an immigrant is very déclassé. There's a low-grade ashcan realism implied in the very material" ("Immigrant" 1). Yet it is this low-class immigrant condition that Mukherjee urges writers to embrace, for it offers "some of the richest material ever conferred on a writer": the "time travel" of characters who have "lived through centuries of history in a single lifetime," "shed past lives and languages, and . . . traveled half the world . . . to come here and begin again . . . bursting with stories" (28). She exhorts immigrant writers: "Turn your attention to this scene. . . . See your models in . . . this tradition, in the minority voices, the immigrant voices, the second-generation Jews and Italians and Irish and French-Canadians. We are in their tradition" (29). Rejecting either an Asian or a diasporic model of cultural inheritance, Mukherjee wholeheartedly advocates, and in *The Middleman* exuberantly demonstrates, an interethnic, immigrant, literary Americanism, for her a condition of transformational possibility.

The cultural politics of such a program, of course, might be criticized as a reductive dismissal of Asian and other old-world cultures and lives. Much is sacrificed, here, for the sake of the vaunted arena of American interethnic relationality. Even the very range and heterogeneity of what Mukherjee calls her "chameleon-skinned" characterizations ("Immigrant") risks flattening or homogenizing differences. For backstories of home and family are thin, native languages make mere token appearances, and the predicaments of the present look much the same for these Americanizing immigrants, most presented in fast-paced, present-tense, up-to-the-minute prose, dense with pop-cultural references, place and brand names, and other detritus of 1980s American culture, in stories beginning *in medias res* and ending in sudden exits out the door and onto the American road. But beneath these surface uniformities, Mukherjee offers a rare and moving vision of a shared journey on the part of global migrants, a vision to be taken up in the 1990s, in different ways, in the crowd scenes of Chang-rae Lee's *Native Speaker*, and in the seven-protagonist structure of Karen Tei Yamashita's *Tropic of Orange*. Mukherjee's group portrait of the "middleman" cultural condition honors the will to self-transformation among the many who have left nearly all behind and staked their futures on possibility.

Interlingual Imaginings

Of the numerous recent Asian American texts that render the dynamics of multiethnic social worlds, many depart from Mukherjee in richly elaborating the intersection of multiple languages and dialects, in such a way that languages, as much as characters, enact a relational drama. An example is Japanese-Hungarian American Jiro Adachi's vibrant interweaving of speech forms from the linguistically mongrel immigrant neighborhoods of New York City in *The Island of Bicycle Dancers* (2004). Adachi's Korean Japanese immigrant Yurika Song, quoted in the preface as she attempts to make sense of the "too many different kinds of English" she hears on the streets of lower Manhattan ("Korean English," "American English," "Chinese English," "Spanish English," "Russian English," "Polish English," and "black English all over, even from white people and some Asians" [2]), comes to realize that

> [S]he too was learning her own kind of English. She had her grammar and sex-related slang that Suzie taught her, the bike English from the messengers, the store English customers spoke, and the words and phrases that she was learning from Whitey.... She was making her own English. She was growing a second tongue. There were words and phrases and attitudes for this New York life that she had no words for in Japanese. (70)

Adachi charts the immigrant's progress not through material accumulation or social rise, but in her "growing a second tongue" from elements of all the speech she hears around her. In a novel that rarely utters the word "America," the immigrant heroine names the new life she has found in New York, "English life": "English life gave her a friend like Whitey who, unlike friends in her Japanese life, had curiosity about things and people. He asked more and more questions of her that created more English life in her" (71). Yurika (whose name interlingually encodes discovery) transvalues hegemonic, global English as an anti-identitarian, anti-nationalist, radically open and inclusive medium in which to articulate her transformed sense of self.

The multilingual knotting that bespeaks the colonial history of the Pacific Islands is foregrounded in Jessica Hagedorn's 1990 novel *Dogeaters*, a satiric, kaleidoscopic portrait of the author's native Philippines during the Marcos era. To render the neocolonial Filipino condition, the plague of having been colonized in all but name by the United States, Hagedorn is lavish in her presentation of the creolized Tagalog-Spanish English spoken by her mestizo characters, and of their preoccupation with (and indigenization of) all things American: movies, pop stars, fashion, junk food, and shopping malls, of which they grow their own Filipino versions. Charged with a nervy energy, the novel celebrates the culture's expressivity even while exposing the nation's suppressed ills, most traumatically the violent terror tactics of the Marcos regime. Hagedorn's composition ironically juxtaposes family dramas of the corrupt and decadent rich with the sordid Manila street life of Joey (discussed in the epilogue), a male prostitute who is the son of a Filipina prostitute and an African American serviceman, and it multiplies inset texts and layers of self-conscious fictional fabrication to suggest the complexities of a historically hybridized, stratified, and contradictory society. Linguistic creolization is also at the heart of Lois-Ann Yamanaka's rendition of the distinctive talk of Hawaii, in several novels of which the best known is *Blu's Hanging* (1997), narrated in the voice of a young, pidgin-speaking daughter of a working-class Japanese Hawaiian family. Yamanaka depicts with affection Hawaii's variegated postcolonial ethnic mix, the layered and colorful speech this hybridization has produced, and the spirited resistance of pidgin speakers to its denigration as a legitimate tongue, but the novel has become controversial for an unflattering depiction of Filipino Hawaiians in particular.[33]

Gus Lee captures a classic Asian American immigrant situation of linguistic interstitiality, with the vivifying difference of Black English as the normative street speech, in *China Boy* (1991). This retrospective, semi-autobiographical, first-person narrative positions a skinny, motherless seven-year-old boy named Kai Ting between his refined, upper-class Shanghai heritage and the tough Panhandle neighborhood of San Francisco, oddly mixing glib humor and a deeply elegiac sense of the loss of China and Chinese culture, the life the family left behind. Dramatizing a Chinese American childhood within black territory, Lee's narration portrays the mixed, hobbled speech, the "ferociously hybrid street English" of a child caught among multiple languages and dialects (274), unfluent in any. At his mother's sudden death, Kai is left "between languages": "My Songhai was pitiful, my Mandarin worse. My English was fractured. My Cantonese was nonexistent" (50). The first words we hear him speak in the novel are "Flies, please," at a Panhandle diner, which wins the retort: "*Fries*! Crap! Boy, how long you *bin* in dis country? You bettah learn how ta talk . . . " (2). Communication failures and private losses are balanced in *China Boy*, however, by the narrator's spirit of comic appreciation for cross-ethnic affinity among transplanted peoples: "These families from Macon and Kiangsu met in . . . the rubble of sundered cultures" (14).

Leaving him orphaned in language, the mother's death also rips Kai from the future she had planned for him as a scholar in China, and from her protection in a rough U.S. urban landscape. When his avidly pro-American father soon remarries a blonde, racist, cartoon-evil stepmother, not only does she crush the bereft children's spirits by burning all the family photos and outlawing Chinese speech, Chinese food, and any mention of the beloved mother, but she also forces defenseless Kai onto the streets, forbidding him to return home before the six p.m. dinner bell, thus dooming him to a fearfully violent acculturation in the form of daily beatings by the local bullies, who are black. Though he strives in vain to become one with the locals so as to avoid being bloodied by them, Kai is eventually rescued by interethnic affiliation: first by the heroic friendship offered by a black boy aptly named Toussaint, then by a Chicano mechanic who literally lifts Kai out of a trash can after a beating and, momentously, persuades Kai's remote, uninvolved father to get him boxing lessons at the YMCA.

There, in a lovingly rendered world of cross-ethnic masculine camaraderie, Kai finds salvation in the form of a cast of tough guy former fighters who "would share their life gifts with me until I became an adult, for six dollars a month" (147). The mutuality of hardship and of solidarity across ethnic lines is of the essence in the YMCA life training that enables Kai to manage his grief for the loss of his mother and of his Chinese culture, and to manage a passage away from these symbolically feminized aspects of his past and into symbolic manhood (see Šesnić 94–97). His coaches—children of the Depression and WWII veterans all—"bore a unique durability," and also "carried the burden of not being Anglo-Protestants at a time when being different implied inferiority..." (147). The Y's ethos of the multiethnic solidarity of the socially inferior is key to Kai's thinking when his father tells him he must "Pick one. Be American. Or Chinese"—for the father, the choice of strength and modern technological progress versus backwardness, superstition, disorganization, and weakness—and Kai thinks to himself, "I pick Y.M. C.A." (213). The in-between boy chooses to affiliate not with one nation, one discrete and bounded culture, but rather with the masculine inclusion he finds in "the collective" of multiethnic boys (black, Jewish, white) who are his YMCA pals (256), and the mentorship he receives from a mixed fatherhood, Brooklyn Italian-, African-, and Filipino/Japanese/Chinese/French-American. For these coaches teach, as one of them puts it, that "we's all be da same... bruthas. Hollywood rich, dirt poor. Negro, Messican, Indian, Oriental, white" (284), or as Lee puts it on his Acknowledgments page (speaking of the YMCA of his own childhood), that there "all youth were of the same color, and every lad could be a hero." The brotherhood of "inferior" men substitutes a code of tolerant, multiethnic, hypermasculine physicality for whiteness, as a guarantor of every lad's right to American manhood.

This coalition forges its triumph in coaching Kai to an astonishing and unlikely climactic boxing victory over the street's terrorizing bully, Big Willie, after which he gives thanks to a "pantheon" of multiethnic "Fathers" (307, 319). And in the novel's last moment Kai is able to demonstrate a triumphant acquisition of new American fluency, as well, putting up his dukes and pronouncing a carefully perfected phrase to the cruel white stepmother—the meanest bully of all, a feminized embodiment of intolerant whiteness who violates the love of small children and hates "the invidious virus of cross-culturalism" (253): "*I ain't fo' yo' pickin-on, no mo'!*" (322).

Interethnic Romance Plots

The attraction of the plot of cross-ethnic romance hovers over contemporary Asian American fiction as the ultimate fulfillment of the interethnic encounter plot, and as a literary topos with a fascination in itself. Such literary romances always raise to some degree the special frisson generated by the interpersonal crossing of culturally symbolic borders; they may be as easily characterized by fear and fetishization as they are by special creativity and aspirations toward new understanding (Friedman, "Migrations" 279). But to be sure, romantic connections involving Asian Americans and ethnic others in the United States do not sound the cultural alarm bells rung by the literary pairing of black and white lovers, a popular theme in the history of American literature (and with a longer and earlier world history), and "a subject likely to elicit censure and high emotions, or at least a certain nervousness" (Sollors, *Neither* 4, 8). Drawing upon the central racial taboo of the culture, the black-white romance plot has tended to call up the drama and melodrama of tragic inequality and exclusion.[34] The literary topoi of cross-race romance and the mixed-race child in American literature are discussed in this study's epilogue, "Mixed Races, Mixed Children, Mixed Outcomes."

Interethnic romance in contemporary Asian American fiction, in my reading, is not really about the breaking of a racial taboo, or about the conundrum of the non-white hero or heroine whose race is a stigmatizing trauma and a barrier to love. Instead, such a romance tends to function as the barometer of the larger society's embrace of the Asian American subject, its welcome, or, by contrast, its inability to welcome him or her as a member of its family. The marriage of the formerly enslaved Chinese immigrant Lalu (Polly) to Charlie Bemis at the end of Ruthanne Lum McCunn's historically based novel *Thousand Pieces of Gold* (1981) resolves the problem of her acceptance of and by America, in a plot of marriage into Americanness that is a familiar immigrant narrative convention. But since the late 1980s, Asian American interethnic romance plots have tended toward greater ideological complexity. Often they are deeply occupied with the cultural differences and especially the geopolitical power imbalances that cross-ethnic lovers cannot help but drag with them into a relationship. Mukherjee's pairs in *The Middleman* are paradigmatic, especially a story like "Fighting for the Rebound," in which a white yuppie Atlanta stockbroker thinks to himself, "Some nations were built to take charge" (84), as he tries to quell the anger of his neglected Filipina émigré girlfriend, and gets a thrill when she accuses, "You don't know how to love," by silently adding, "*Sailor*" (83). In another story, "Orbiting," the Italian American heroine ends her narration awash with feeling for her Afghani boyfriend, a former political prisoner:

> I realize all in a rush how much I love this man with his blemished, tortured body. I will give him citizenship if he asks.... Ro's my chance to heal the world.
>
> I shall teach him how to walk like an American... how to fill up a room like Dad does instead of melting and blending but sticking out in the Afghan way. In spite of the funny way he holds himself and the funny way he moves his head from side to side when he wants to say yes, Ro is Clint Eastwood, scarred hero and survivor. (76)

Mukerhjee deftly conveys the ironies of a love impossible to disentangle from imperialist condescension.

The conflict between normative American and immigrant Korean cultural styles of emotional expressivity nearly destroys the marriage of Korean American Henry Park and his Scottish American wife Lelia, in Chang-rae Lee's *Native Speaker* (the subject of chapter 2). Cultural and class differences between a Chinese American husband from an immigrant family and Jewish American wife from an established, wealthy one prove disastrous in David Wong Louie's tragicomic novel *The Barbarians Are Coming* (2000) (discussed in the interchapter "Cross-ethnic Jewishness"). And foreignness sometimes persists, becoming a haunting kind of difference that cannot quite be overcome, as in the unexpected romance between a Korean student and a Southern white woman on the campus of Sewanee College in the 1950s in Susan Choi's *The Foreign Student* (1998), or—the tables turned, and the power of cultural rejection placed in the hands of the Asian American—as in Gish Jen's *The Love Wife* (2004), in which the marriage of a Chinese American husband and Euro-American wife is threatened by the lingering weight of his late mother's insistence on Chinese ways, embodied in the attraction of a visiting Chinese female relative.

In most of the wryly comic stories that make up Don Lee's *Yellow* (2001)—set in the invented California coast town of Rosarita Bay, site of multiple pan-Asian cross-ethnic plot encounters and romances—ethnic differences in relationships between the children of heterogeneous East Asian immigrants are muted and unimportant. For, Lee has said, he writes about "people like me, third- and fourth-generation, post-immigrant Asian Americans who are very much assimilated into the overall culture but who have residual ethnic loyalties (that make them ambivalent)," but "also face subtle acts of discrimination or stereotypes (that make them feel powerless or angry)" ("Question"). In the long title story, however, anger and powerlessness overtake the Korean American hero, Danny Kim, and race difference comes to mark his life through its warping effects, specifically, on romance between an Asian and a white person. Danny is an exception to the general rule, a beautiful, self-absorbed, white-resembling Other who, early in his tale, does recall a suffering tragic mulatto whose affair with a white lover is doomed by race. But Lee's plot later takes Danny in a direction usually not available in the tradition of mulatto romances, descending from the heights of romantic tragedy when he decides to give up cross-race melodrama and marry, in effect, his own ethnic American condition.

Lee writes Danny as an especially handsome but otherwise representative Asian American assimilist, a self-alienated everyman living under the tormenting visual regime of race. Danny "wanted to be exemplary, unquestionably American" (201), unlike his parents, whom he has seen suffer "the humiliation of being immigrants," and so without real intent, he distances himself from his "residually Asian family" (200), and ends up unable to account for "his vague, perpetual sense of anger" (202), blindly connecting it neither to the receipt of racial slurs and insults, nor to the constant irritation of being perceived through the screen of racial difference, nor, even, to having been driven away from his family.[35]

Nuanced plotting conveys Danny's deepening self-consciousness about his racialization, the ways others' perceptions of him shape his life. The climax of this trend is Danny's great college romance with a white woman, a love perhaps heightened by cross-ethnic frisson, but destroyed, too, because of ethnic difference. Danny destroys it himself through suspicion that Jenny cannot truly love him because of his Asianness; "Yellow" becomes at once a racial slur and a name for his own deep fear. At the end of the affair,

> [h]e marveled at how deluded he had been, for he had believed—abstractly, quixotically—that he *could* be white. Colorless. He realized he was doomed. No matter what he did, no matter how much he tried to deny it, he would never get past his ethnicity. It was untenable, and the knowledge broke him. (233–34)

The aftereffects of the failure of cross-ethnic love are disabling, leaving him permanently haunted by the racism he senses all around him. Living in Boston, "He constantly sensed the underpinnings of racial animus in the city, which was so plainly and historically stratified by class and color" (236):

> As the years went by, he grew more alarmed. Racial tensions were peaking.... A jingoistic, reactionary mood was consuming the entire country, and it scared Danny to death. He followed reports on the resurgence of the K.K.K. and white supremacy groups, racial assaults.... With all of this happening, then... how could Danny not bristle or feel threatened whenever he was asked "What are you?" or "Where are you from?"... He was born here, he spoke perfect English, he was as mainstream as anyone could be. Yet, in this country of immigrants, Danny, as an Asian, was always regarded as a foreigner, a newcomer, someone who was not a *real* American.... Every day he expected, at any moment, at any place, to be attacked. (238–39)

Once an ardent assimilist, Lee's hero is brought to a view that echoes that of Asian Americanist critics on the permanent deferral of full Americanness for Asian-origin citizens. In Danny's transformation, Lee presents the failure of Asian-white love as a traumatic rupture in the fabric of multiculturalist ideology.

The story's conciliatory ending does not attempt to recover the emotional heights of Danny's youthful romance, instead seeing him into a companionable marriage and family with the Korean American Rachel, a marriage that at first seems a misstep, as it lacks intimacy and passion. But over time this marriage comes to fit Danny exactly, as confirmed when he feels a "simple, pure joy" at the realization that "his son's face... was... becoming remarkably like his own" (255)—a mirroring free of the external, racializing gaze. Danny's ending also has him conquer fear in saving the life of a white colleague whom he had thought an enemy, thus overcoming (abjected) "yellowness" in both senses. Lee's story makes a notable gesture in rejecting the kind of resolution that might be implied by marriage to a white person, for the sake of marriage to another Asian American. Patricia P. Chu has argued, discussing Asian American revisions of the bildungsroman, that "Asian American texts tend to avoid the utopian 'well-married hero' plot, in which the... subject's moral and social progress is figured in terms of romantic choices that culminate in marriage," for these would signify a "reconciliation with the social order" and a "successful integration into the nation" that are not yet realities in Asian American life or literature.[36] One only has to think of a sequence of early Asian American fictional heroes—Chungpa Han of Younghill Kang's

East Goes West (1937); Carlos of Bulosan's *America Is in the Heart*; Ichiro Yamada of Okada's *No-No Boy*; Tam Lum of Frank Chin's *The Chickencoop Chinaman* (1972); the grandfathers of Kingston's *China Men* (1980)—to find ready examples of such unmarriageable types. Legally, racially and/or psychologically at odds with American national identity, recalling to varying degrees the legacy of "bachelor" communities and the vexed relationship of Asian American masculinity to heterosexuality (as discussed in the Asian/African interchapter), these are male characters for whom no adequate romantic partner is imaginable. Though the abortive romance with interethnic possibility remains a searing wound in Danny Kim's sense of Americanness, he actually does become a "well-married" Asian American hero, by making peace—eventually, years after marrying Rachel—with his own imperfect, unresolved Korean Americanness, a kind of Americanness that looks like him.

Lateral/Vertical: *Mambo Peligroso* and *Aloft*

The writing of novelistic protagonists from other ethnic or racial groups, a complex imaginative project familiar across many literary histories, has been uncommon in Asian American literary tradition, which from the beginning has undertaken above all to insert into American literature representations of its authors' own peoples and their historical experiences. In this final section of the chapter, I offer longer readings of two recent, sustained representations of American others by Asian American novelists, posing them as contrasting types of cross-ethnic figuration, following an argument by Amy Ling: "minority to minority" (which Ling calls "lateral") and "minority to majority" (for Ling, "vertical") forms of "cultural cross-dressing," which occur amidst "the inequitable reality of the United States." While minority engagements with whiteness inevitably contend with the distance and ambivalence created by power inequity, "the lateral crossings," Ling writes, "which involve the layering of other cultural traits onto those one already possesses, express solidarity with other groups who share a history of persecution and enhance/enrich the self" (232). The two novels considered below nuance this useful binary distinction, in both cases by means of an intimate, familial embrace of the other.

A novel that revels in the sublimely transforming possibilities of the minority-to-minority affiliation plot is Patricia Chao's 2005 *Mambo Peligroso*. Chao's own authorial trajectory as a first- and second-time novelist parallels this horizontal turn. Her first novel, *Monkey King*, is a within-the-family Chinese American drama about the legacy of incestuous sexual abuse. After the publication of this book, Chao traveled to Cuba for a writers' conference, and has since spoken of "My love affair with Cuba": "Cuba stunned me. I felt as if it were returning to a long-forgotten dream" ("Author"). Inspired by the trip, Chao's second novel imagines a heroine who does not merely love Cuban music and dance, like her author, but who is herself actually half Cuban; Chao pivots to create a protagonist both ethnically like and different from herself, who embodies her own powerful connection to an adopted culture. She has said of her heroine:

> Like Catalina, I'm a mongrel—she's Japanese Cuban born in Cuba and I am half-Japanese and half-Chinese and by birth American. Though she's Latina and I'm not, we both have Japanese mothers and have to deal with the issues of conflicting cultures. I drew on my own experiences to depict Catalina's story of falling in love with New York City mambo and the subculture that goes with it. ("Author")

The already "mongrel" author further mongrelizes her imagination and expands the geo-cultural range of the Asian American novel to develop a protagonist who can claim ethnic connection to the Cuban cultural scene that she loves.

While *Mambo Peligroso* displays its authentic *Latinidad* by the inclusion of a great deal of Spanish, beginning with the title and increasing in density toward the end of the book, when untranslated passages of dialogue become frequent, at the same time it highlights its author's cross-ethnic acquisition of that distinctive culture through its major preoccupation with lessons, with the plot of learning to dance mambo. When the heroine Catalina arrives for her first class at El Tuerto's dance studio, she watches the "mesmerizing" moves of the expert dancers and thinks, "*I will never look like that*" (22, 26). But "La Reina Mambera," the mambo queen who befriends the heroine, encourages her, saying, "Don't worry, you'll master the [steps]. You just have to get them into muscle memory" (172, 27). Dance, as a mobile medium of culture, is something anyone willing to work long and hard enough can take into his or her body, make a part of the self. Importantly, in the dance class, as Catalina notes at once, "Skin color ran the gamut" (19); racial heterogeneity characterizes both the cultures from which mambo derives and the culture of the New York City studio, where anyone can train her body to move (almost) like a Latina/o.

Though Catalina was born in Cuba, migrating to the United States illegally as a child, with her Japanese Cuban mother, the years have distanced her from Cubanness:

> Growing up in a white suburb, attending a Seven Sisters college, spending those years with her ex-boyfriend Richard the *über*-WASP—all that had bleached her to the point where she could hardly call herself Latina at all.
>
> *I am an American.* (18)

When she follows a flier to a mambo class, then, and becomes passionately smitten with the dance form and the world of its devotees, the reader understands her to have embarked on a profound return, from a bland, alienating kind of assimilation to a rich, emotionally compelling ethnic identification. The role of the Spanish language here is paramount; *Mambo Peligroso* could not achieve its rapturous embrace of the mambo life without the heroine's gradual remembering of her nearly lost Spanish, so that Catalina's dance-floor dialogues come to be conducted in that language and, fortunately, it all comes back to her in time for scenes of entirely Spanish sex. The most sublime moments in this English-language text, that is to say, are marked by Spanish as the moments of deepest entwinement, paradoxically, in both ethnicity and interethnicity. The complicated identity of Cubanness for the novel—the author's by affinity and the heroine's by national and ethnic origin once forgotten but now remembered—makes it a text that endorses, simultaneously, both ethnic roots and the enriching possibilities of "lateral" interethnic passage.

Chao resolves the possible contradiction by endorsing a de-essentialized notion of ethnicity that is much more a matter of culture than biology. When Catalina's Japanese Cuban mother lies ill in a hospital, "At rest her mother looked only Japanese; without language or gestures, there was no Caribbean" (257). Culture, then, is actively and bodily acquired and lived; Catalina's studying mambo is all about self-transformation, imaginative adoption of identity, learning to become whom she wants to be. And for Chao's readers (perhaps picking up the novel because they liked her first one, about a Chinese American family), reading *Mambo Peligroso* may give entry into a new way of life. Just as in dance class Catalina stands behind the teacher—positioned "in front, with his back to them"—and copies his footwork (20), one learns to embody culture, in this book, by imitating. The world of the dance club, the dance class, is race- and ethnicity-conscious, and mambo is shown to have its distinct Bronx and Cuban varieties, but cross-group borrowing, imitation, hybridization are at the heart of the scene. El Tuerto sends a student to watch the other major mambo troupes and steal their best moves; the novel in which he reigns as cultural master endorses the imitative acquisition of style.

Of course, copying and learning have to be done well, to have integrity. Late in the book, El Tuerto casts disdain on the "huge influx of new dancers . . . with a large percentage of white and Asian professionals," who "treat mambo like they treat everything else, something to be aced and then discussed at cocktail parties. *Look how at home in the third world I am*"; such dance students do not progress beyond a "Mambo Lite," for they miss a crucial lesson: "What they will never understand is not only do you have to have talent, you have to let the dance and music change your life. *Become* your life" (275). The kind of interethnic art thus modeled by *Mambo Peligroso*—which bears danger in its title—is no shallow cross-ethnic borrowing, but art that risks total reinvention of identity.

The vital presence of music and dance in the novel instantiates another notable form of risky crossing: the crossing of art forms. Chao's text is a striking experiment in the attempt to capture dance and music in words. Her extended rendition of dance steps and rhythmic patterns is probably unprecedented in Asian American literature, and as the reader struggles to follow these, the novel vividly articulates its imaginative stretch, the multiple new moves it makes to invent its horizontally affiliative, mestizo textuality. Its inclusion of a discography of Latin music rather than a bibliography suggests the larger transforming effect of cross-ethnic influence here.

Inevitably, the horizontal plot in this intensely bodily text drives toward sexual consummation, in the heroine's affair with the dance teacher, Tuerto. But the plot later turns, beyond mambo, to a further, romantic consummation with Cubanness in the relationship of Catalina and her first cousin Guillermo, whose forbidden teenage affair, once broken off (because of a pregnancy and abortion she never revealed to him), has left both sadly unfulfilled for a decade and more, though both have found other partners. A convoluted political subplot that sends the cousins on a dangerous mission to Cuba reunites them as lovers and returns Catalina to a sense of her true self, makes her feel "all those years in America that she had been dreaming, and now," in Cuba again at last, "*I am awake*" (220, 224). The lovers are fated to long separation again, however, when he is arrested. Catalina must leave Cuba, but this time she is left, at last, carrying a baby of Guillermo's that she will keep; symbolically, it feels to her that "*I brought Cuba back with me*" to New York (272).

What is most notable about the plot that makes Catalina mother to Guillermo's Cuban baby at last and yet keeps her in a suspended marital/romantic state as long as he languishes in a Cuban jail is that it leaves her "unmarriageable," in the best tradition of unmarriageable Asian American protagonists, in Chu's formulation. Catalina's is an unusual case: a woman of our less legally and racially restrictive era who nevertheless signals her unmarriageable condition when she finds the love of her life in her forbidden first cousin (and continues to do so through bad relationships with a bland white man and a dominating Latino). Even more than the failure of her romances with racially different types, the simultaneous intensification and prohibition of the romance plot by incest suggests a psychologically complex, unresolved national identification. As Jolie Sheffer has noted in a study of the tragic romantic heroines of turn-of the-twentieth-century Asian American writer Onoto Watanna (Winnifred Eaton), incest can work to "highlight the plot of the half-caste and her longing for a place within the nuclear national family," can be "a powerful fantasy of recognition and belonging ... [of] undeniable *inclusion*" (126, 128). For Japanese-Cuban-American Catalina, we might say that the prohibited love for cousin Guillermo represents a refugee's impossible dream of "reconciliation and psychological wholeness" with Cubanness (Sheffer 140).

On another level, the fact that Chao's heroine's true love is not only her first cousin but a prisoner who may never be released by Castro symbolically instantiates the traumatic separation of Cuban Americans from families and homeland; the near-incestuous and thus tabooed desire between cousins thus dramatically enacts the stalled, unfulfilled yearning for Cuban return. And yet, by staying forever in love with her forbidden Cuban American cousin, Catalina symbolically expresses the impossibility of her desire to be simply Cuban—for she has become American, and she is at the same time, in a more remote way, Japanese. Suspended among three identities, but no tragic victim of a hierarchical, national racial formation, as she might have been in Watanna's fictions, Catalina decides with a feminist and post-identitarian freedom that may even place her beyond the calculations of the marriageability index (if this is possible), that she can have it all: in the end she works out a "mongrel," alternative family without marriage, mothering her Cuban American son as well as the now-dead mambo queen's Dominican American son. Moreover, as Tuerto puts it, Catalina is soon "taking this roots thing too far," mirroring her return to Cuba by a concomitant closing turn to Japan, where she has never been: a copy of *Let's Go: Tokyo* is glimpsed and Catalina seems poised to begin a migratory, hybrid, post-national, post-marriage life among Cuba, Japan, and the United States, continuing to work for Guillermo's release but keeping a toehold in New York City (281). The mobile, multiethnic, transnational life-mode of dance is the book's ideal; roots returns are sublime, but absolute or final embrace of Cubanness or any other national, ethnic, or artistic identity is a bygone mode, which the heroine is sublimely free to dance right past.

Before the last decades of the twentieth century, when Asian American fictions represented European Americans, members of the white mainstream to which newcomers must try to assimilate, these were often rather remote, faceless representatives of an alien normalcy—the "taxi ghosts" and "newsboy ghosts," "demon" bosses and "blonde Jesus demonesses" of Maxine Hong Kingston's *The Woman Warrior* and *China Men*; the alternately idealized and virginal or traitorous and whorish white women of Bulosan's *America Is in the Heart*; the prostitutes repudiated for a beloved Chinese wife in Louis Chu's *Eat a Bowl of Tea* (1961); or, as late as 1986, the almost undifferentiated white presences who are bosses and landlords in Runyoung Kim's novel of mid-century Korean immigrant struggles, *Clay Walls*. There are exceptions: Younghill Kang's early- century fictionalized memoir *East Goes West* delineates with more detail the white woman, Trip, with whom the Korean hero is smitten, but even when she feels "close to me as my own," she remains "far away as the universe's utmost border." When he takes her on a date, Trip's "passive and somber expression" suggests to the hero that she is "wondering quietly to herself, just what she was doing in here with an Oriental, Chungpa Han" (341–42), quite as if she were wondering just what she is doing in his book; she ultimately disappears from town and so from the book, leaving no explanation. Here and there a memorable, vividly drawn white character stands out, like the eccentric, generous Mr. Carrick of Okada's *No-No Boy*, who builds a snowplow in a nearly snowless climate, just because he "felt [he] wanted to make one," and who offers the shamed Japanese American war resister a good job and a new chance.

But since the mid- to late 1980s, as Asian American fiction has increasingly presented negotiations with the white mainstream as the daily circumstance of Asian American lives, white characters have become much more common, both as normative figures of a social scenario and as fully drawn, particular, and remarkable presences, secondary and even primary characters in fictional worlds. Still, they are usefully read as cases of "minority-to-majority" cross-ethnic fictional imagination; unlike Chao's Latinos or Mukherjee's Asians and Caribbeans, these imaginings up the power scale are characterized by the traversal of a certain distance, by a sympathy charged with a critical regard from below.

Mukherjee's *The Middleman* features among its spectacular gallery of global migrant protagonists two stories, "Loose Ends" and "Fathering," narrated by white male American speakers, both Vietnam veterans, one somewhat and one severely emotionally unhinged. Their inclusion in the collection suggests that these vets have fallen into the status of the white approximation of displaced "middleman" figures, having traveled far and returned traumatically changed men to a changed country—and thus groupable with the Asian and other immigrants making their arduous way across America for the first time.

In Rishi Reddi's 2007 collection, *Karma and Other Stories*, Indian American protagonists live in a world thickly populated with white Americans, and must weather affronts and insults from those ignorant of their cultures. The story "Justice Shiva Ram Murthy" presents an elderly, widowed Indian judge, newly arrived to live with his daughter in snowy Boston, whose pride is assaulted by cross-cultural misunderstandings that Reddi draws with comic poignancy. Unwittingly, and contrary to Hindu practice, he ends up eating not the bean-and-cheese burrito he had meant to order but one made of beef, served to him by a gum-chewing young fast-food employee who is as offended by his rage at the mistake as he is by her inability to grasp his dilemma. In "Lord Krishna," a fourteen-year-old Indian American boy feels so isolated in Wichita, Kansas, that it is as if "he was looking through a large window at people in a parallel world, one that was familiar but that he didn't understand. Krishna could know these people, look through that window and wave to them, but he would never be one of them" (192). But Krishna is startled out of his safe remove one day when his teacher, a minister in the Church of Christ, is goaded by bored students to teach them about Satan, and hands out what he calls "pictures of the devil" he has culled from a range of popular cultural sources, including *Dungeons and Dragons*, *The Lord of the Rings*, heavy metal album covers, and a magazine illustration of a figure the hero recognizes from his devout grandfather's Indian home as the revered Hindu Lord Krishna. Some of Reddi's plots move through the window of separation into romance, as in "The Validity of Love," which weighs romantic possibilities for an American-born Indian woman, who closely observes her best friend's joyful acquiescence to traditional, parent-arranged marriage to an Indian but ends hoping for "the validity of love" with a white American ex-boyfriend, re-encountered in a supermarket; and by contrast in "Devadasi," when a frightening incident during a young Indian American woman's visit to relatives in ethnic strife-torn India makes the idea of cross-ethnic love seem an American delusion.

Jhumpa Lahiri's first story collection, *Interpreter of Maladies* (1999) centers on Indian Americans, but also features two stories that step aside to imagine with equal sympathy white protagonists, notably marginal, even vulnerable characters whose lives become, for a certain span of time, intimately entangled with those of Indian American characters. In "Sexy," a young woman new to city life is unsure how to feel about her affair with a married Indian American man, and in "Mrs. Sen's," a young son of a single, working mother witnesses the unhappiness of his Indian after-school babysitter, an immigrant wife. The gaze is reversed in Lahiri's magnificent final story, "The Third and Final Continent," in which the wonder that the elderly Indian American narrator finds in recollecting his life's traversals is somehow emblematized by the memory of his first American landlady, the astonishingly ancient and immobile, decorous but fiercely commanding 103-year-old Mrs. Croft, "the first death I mourned in America, for hers was the first life I had admired" (196).[37] Though Lahiri's white characters ultimately live across a palpable distance from her diasporic Indians, by investing them with the same simple dignity she gives Indian American characters and delineating them in the same, sparely elegant prose, she draws the two into encounters that brim with the suggestion of potential cross-ethnic mutuality.

A novel by an Asian American narrated entirely by its white protagonist would seem to merit separate attention. Chang-rae Lee's 2004 *Aloft* is told in the first-person voice of Jerry Battle, a near-sixty semi-retiree and hobby pilot of his own small plane, whose musings upon the Long Island he flies above portray him, at first, as an average, middle-aged, entitled, mildly sympathetic, suburban white guy, remote from the concerns of the characters who traditionally inhabit Asian American novels. The novel's first line reads, "From up here, a half mile above the Earth, everything looks perfect to me" (1).

But it soon becomes clear that the pleasure in these distanced pronouncements masks a more complex and sadder speaker than those words suggest, for Jerry's urge to fly comes in part from a desire for distance from all that troubles him below: "[F]rom up here... I can't see the messy rest, none of the pedestrian, sea-level flotsam that surely blemishes our good scene" (2), including everything from roadside trash to mortality itself. Indeed, he says, "the recurring fantasy of my life... is one of perfect continuous travel," the "knowledge that you'll never quite get intimate enough for any trouble to start brewing..." (202).

When interviewer Kenneth Quan remarks that this protagonist "sounds... like a kid," "skirting his responsibilities," the author agrees: "[F]or me... that's very American. Because he's endlessly a child, he doesn't want responsibility...." Jerry Battle, Lee goes on, has a different "perspective in how he fits into the culture" from Lee's earlier Asian American protagonists Henry Park and Doc Hata: "He's someone who feels he can say anything about anyone at anytime—he's very free. And why does he feel that way? Because of who he is and how he's grown up.... [H]e's never questioned his context in the same way that Henry Park and Doc Hata have..."; "the actual tonal differences" arise in part from "that liberty" (Interview). Liberty and irresponsibility, then, shape this white hero's declarations from "aloft." And yet readers come to discern in Jerry an irony born of a lifetime's education in disillusionment: "[T]he charming and the lucky and the talented" get to do what they love for a living, he opines, but "for the rest of us perfectly acceptables and okays and competents it's a matter of persistence and numbness to actual if minor serial failure and a wholly unsubstantiated belief in the majesty of individual destiny, all of which is democracy's spell of The Possible on us" (150–51). This multifaceted character—an overindulged but smart, self-excusing but self-aware, self-centered but generous, white critic of America's mainstream ideological habits—is a deeply interesting creation for Lee, author of two previous novels whose protagonists muse upon matters personal, social, historical from a distinctly Asian American angle.

An under-recognized mid-century African American fictional subgenre has been called the "white life novel." A study by John Charles discusses post-World War II novels centered on white protagonists by black novelists including Hurston, Wright, Baldwin, Petry, and Himes as demonstrating neither "racial false-consciousness" nor "acquiescence to white hegemony," but rather, "a radical claiming of cultural authority and civic entitlement," "a strategy for critical and creative action beyond the space of the injured other" (4, 6, 20–21). Writing whites, Charles claims, allowed the likes of Hurston and Wright to break out of the narrow sphere allowed them as black writers: "[D]rawing on the relative discursive freedom located in white bodies... enabled them to circumvent the publishing industry's continuing resistance to representing the full range of African American subjectivity" (6). Moreover, actually presenting whites sympathetically made it possible for these writers to "[assert] an identificational mobility and complex moral authority as part of a critical project that far exceeded what the dominant culture deemed possible or appropriate for black writers" (7).

In its deliberate crossing of boundaries to "do" a representative white man's voice, Chang-rae Lee's representation of Jerry Battle surely resembles white-life novels in crucial ways: it defies the publishing industry's (and the academy's) expectation of the limits on an Asian American author's subject matter, declaring the right to an imaginative range that extends beyond that of the minoritized Asian. Moreover, the narration in Jerry's voice might be read as Lee's rejection of ethnic marginality, his claim to speak with the kind of cultural authority typically owned by white men. Lee's Jerry Battle discourses knowledgably about aeronautics and the landscaping and construction business; engages in talk about ethnic and racial differences, women, and sex in varying degrees of respect, bewilderment, and crudity; and laments America's post-crest economy and changing values—"the steady downward trend of our civilization perhaps just now begun its penultimate phase of entropy and depletion" (292)—like a member of the old guard.

But of course the category of white-life novel cannot precisely fit *Aloft* for reasons of history and race difference; Chang-rae Lee writes as much more of an insider to white culture and social circles than did a mid-century black novelist like Richard Wright, having been raised and educated and employed among whites and in an era of much greater racial tolerance, and being Asian rather than African American, besides, a racial identity conventionally if somewhat absurdly understood to lie "between black and white"; moreover, Lee is married to an Italian American woman. The fact of his novel's white protagonist did raise critical attention, but mostly along the lines of this review:

> Whether you find the new book a joyous revelation, an ascent in Lee's career, or a betrayal and a wrong turn depends, I think, on how much you had invested in him as a spokesman for a particular ethnic experience.... I appreciate a writer who's not overzealously committed to any one ideology or group, who likes to confound expectations and who feels expansive enough in his spirit and ambitions to encompass not just his close kinsmen but the infamous Other. (Di Filippo)

In remarks about the novel, Lee indeed conveys a felt sense of license, beyond that available to Hurston or Baldwin, to play in an expansive and encompassing way across ethnic lines. Because *Aloft* is "more of a contemporary book and... a book about family," Lee has said, perhaps surprisingly, "it's a little closer to my own life" than are his earlier books, about Asian Americans. "I tried to think of all the characters," he recalls, "as how I would be if I were in their situation and gender and class. So I put myself into every character...." Musing upon the aging of his parents and parents-in-law, Lee "thought it would be interesting instead of writing about... a character based on my own father," to write a character who matched his Italian American father-in-law's "age, his ethnicity and where he lived—which is really all that I took from my father-in-law—and just try to think about who that person was":

> I had to think of a guy who's actually been a pain in the ass to everybody but try to make him likable at the same time. A guy you don't feel you should like but that you're charmed enough by him to keep reading and feel empathy for. (Interview)

Drawn to the empathic imagining of a privileged, white character because of his very difference, then, Lee felt at the same time a familiarly ethnic literary interest in reclaiming the full humanity of such a character from stereotype. He deliberately gave Jerry "thoughts that . . . go against the grain of what people expect of him, an Italian-American landscaper on Long Island," inventing a person who "has the same kind of feel and reach and depth that anyone else has" and is not "Tony Soprano or some 'goomba' who's kind of an idiot" (Interview). The writing of *Aloft* thus affords Lee an interstitial cultural position, a fluid imaginative mobility in which he feels a cross-ethnic empathy with the stereotyped, even while granting himself an imaginative range and freedom not unlike the "liberty" possessed by that average white guy, Jerry Battle.

The whiteness that Lee produces, then, is not a normative one, but "whiteness with a difference," in Charles's phrase, a difference often arising in white-life novels—as for Mukherjee's white veterans—through a white protagonist's suffering, a suffering that "serves a pedagogic function," "the white protagonist, and implicitly the white reader, undergoing a kind of moral reform that frequently includes a symbolic repudiation of his or her possessive investment in whiteness" (Charles 9). Jerry's whiteness is different in several ways: first, as readers do not learn until the second chapter, "Battle" is a revision of "Battaglia" invented by Jerry's Italian American father and uncles to make their lives easier a generation ago; Italianness is revealed as a cultural and experiential inheritance quite distinct from mainstream whiteness. Second, he is something of a disaffected middle American, "feeling distinctly outside of things" (174), an avid world traveler who looks back critically at precisely those aspects of America that outsiders most condemn: the consumerism: "[E]ven as I'm damn proud of my son Jack's wholly climate-controlled existence (despite the fact that we don't really talk much anymore), there is another part of me that naturally wonders how this rush of prosperity is ruining him and Eunice and the kids and then everybody else who has money . . ." (9); the solipsistic attitude, on a small and a national scale, of people who "think they can go anywhere and do anything, as if none of their actions has any bearing except on themselves" (281); and the impersonality of our social spaces: "because when you're walking along some quay or piazza or *allée* there's an openness and possibility and . . . intimacy with strangers which is near impossible on an American street or food court, the scale still hunched and human" (153). A particularly acute kind of assessment can be made in the voice of a white outsider who is his own culture's best critic.

But perhaps the most interesting form of his difference is the way that Jerry's whiteness is gradually shaded, over the course of the book, by ethnic differences and attachments, which begin with the origins of "Battle" in "Battaglia" and continue through sequential revelations of the ethnic distinctiveness of all those around him. We learn rather belatedly and sometimes parenthetically—("I should mention" [12])—about the ethnic identities of Jerry's loved ones: his girlfriend of twenty years, Rita, is a dark-skinned Puerto Rican; his "long-deceased wife, Daisy, was Asian herself and [his] children are of mixed blood, even though [he has] never thought of them that way" (29). "[W]e're an ethnically jumbled bunch," he remarks of his Korean-Italian American children and further mixed grandchildren (English, German, too), but Jerry admires the "grab bag miscegenation" of all those ethnicities "expressing itself in my and Jack's offspring with particularly handsome and even stunning results" (69, 77).

Moreover, from his daughter, Theresa, an English professor, Jerry has gained an analytical distance on normative whiteness; her vocabulary enables his insistently ironic take on his own sexist and patriarchal practices. Teased by her as "the last living white man" (28), he can mock his foreign travels as "rapacious, hegemonic colonialist 'projects'" and can add to a description of his late wife Daisy's beauty, "I realize I may be waxing pathetic here, your basic sorry white dude afflicted with what Theresa refers to as 'Saigon syndrome' ... and fetishizing once again, but I'm not sorry because the fact is I found her desirable precisely because she was put together differently from what I was used to" (107–8).

An evocative cross-ethnic relationship is Jerry's bond with Theresa's Korean American fiancé, Paul Pyun, an amusing figure for the novelist himself as he might be seen by an Italian American in-law:

> [A]pparently Paul is somewhat famous, at least in certain rarified academic/literary circles, which is great if true but also means that no one I've met on a train or plane or in a waiting room has ever heard of him, much less read his books.... *I've* read his books... and I can say with great confidence that he's the sort of writer who can put together a nice-sounding sentence or two and does it with feeling but never quite gets to the point.... I guess if you put a gun to my head I'd say he writes about The Problem with Being Sort of Himself—namely, the terribly conflicted and complicated state of being Asian and American and thoughtful and male, which would be just dandy in a slightly different culture or society but in this one isn't the hottest ticket. (74)

The satire on his own oeuvre and marginal place in the culture is a choice nugget in Lee's whiteface narration, and the meeting of these two refractions of self produces numerous other affectionate, wry ironies.[38] Perhaps inevitably, knowing Paul brings Jerry to the pithy heart of interethnic encounter:

> Paul is one of the few people who can always draw me out.... I don't know why exactly, though perhaps it has something to do with the fact that he's not like me at all, that we come from dissimilar peoples and times and traditions and hold nearly opposite views on politics and the world, and so have neither the subtle pressure nor the dulling effect of instant concord, an ease and comfort I've enjoyed all my life but find increasingly wanting now. Maybe I'm a racialist (or racist?) and simply like the fact that he's different, that he's short and yellow and brainy (his words, originally), and that he makes *me* somehow different, whether I really wish to be or not. (92–93)

Lee's hero admits he doesn't fully get the cultural changes going on around him—he has a "sharpening feeling that I can hardly understand anybody anymore, at least as far as pure language goes" (34). But his daughter has taught him, as he puts it, that "I should begin to re-envision myself as a multicultural being" (29), and things have evolved in his life to the point that it feels right to be made different—as learning mambo makes the true devotee different in Chao's novel. For Jerry, it feels right to be made more inclusively social; in a sense, to make his relations with others more "lateral," in Ling's terms. If he is a figure for the average white American, his desire to dismantle what has kept him elevated and privileged is a promising one, indeed.

As the trajectory of Jerry's plot "strips away the American myth of the lone, rugged individual to affirm the hero's dependencies on others" (Jaggi), it is crucial that these others are at once ethnically different and family members. Though it begins with a "solo flyer" (20), this novel ends with its speaker enmeshed in a web of "Other[s]," as he knows to call them (69), ensconced in an interethnic family. "How did our family get so damn Oriental?" asks Jerry's ninety-year-old father, and though Jerry has to admit that he has wondered "the same basic thing" (172), he is proud to be "father of such Diversity" (69) and displays a certain wisdom acquired in the experience:

> People say that Asians don't show as much feeling as whites or blacks or Hispanics... but I'll say, too, from my long if narrow experience (and I'm sure zero expertise), that the ones I've known and raised and loved have been each completely a surprise in their emotive characters, confounding me no end. This is not my way of proclaiming "We're all individuals" or "We're all the same" or any other smarmy notion about our species' solidarity, just that if a guy like me is always having to think twice when he'd rather not do so at all, what must that say about this existence of ours but that it restlessly defies our attempts at its capture, time and time again. (235)

Capable of admitting he cannot fully master and know reality, Lee's white hero ends up affirming above all "our capacities for tolerance and change" (331). Because of a tragedy and a financial collapse,[39] Jerry and his kids, their families, his aged father, and (sometimes) his returned girlfriend all end up living together at the end in his undistinguished suburban house, now being built onto and renovated to accommodate multiplicity. "[L]a famiglia" in the end is the answer, but in an expanded sense: "blood, relational, and honorary" (331). Lee's "white" novel gives us a man who comes to welcome the unwhitening of his life, or the dethroning of the meaning of that whiteness, who willingly gives up his privileged position "aloft," for a "life [that] stays thick and busy, on the ground" (330).

Most of the texts examined in the chapters, interchapters, and epilogue that follow traverse that ground in "lateral" forays into other peoples' lives and stories: those of African Americans, Jews, Latinos and Latin Americans, and people of mixed-race identity. It is an American ground rendered "thick and busy" with crisscrossing ventures, Asian American ventures to name and claim a home not in a fixed, white, monolingual, unmovable Gold Mountain America, but in an America continually remapped by cross-ethnic exchange and interrelationship.

Interchapter: Asian/African

Black Presences in Asian American Fiction

> [T]hat stirring, electric moment in *To Kill a Mockingbird* when the upstairs gallery of black folk stand up to honor Atticus Finch after the verdict goes against Tom Robinson, their expressions of epic suffering and dignity laying me low and then more generally instructing me that there are few things in this life as heartbreaking as unexpected solidarity.
>
> —Chang-rae Lee, *Aloft*

When the late critic Amy Ling distinguished between two types of "cultural cross-dressing," in an essay on Gish Jen's *Mona in the Promised Land*, she called the crossing of the Asian American-African American cultural border a "lateral" move; her "vertical" designation seems intended only for relations of minority groups with dominant whiteness. But the painful truth for the subject of this interchapter is that a "vertical" social hierarchy among racialized minority groups themselves, and the inequities, conflicts, and rivalries that have existed among them, challenges Ling's paradigm of ethnoracial crossings that enhance identity through solidarity and shared histories.

The violent abjection of African Americans over the course of U.S. history has made them a people that every immigrant group has readily understood to inhabit the lowest rung on the symbolic American racial ladder. For Asian Americans, entering into a racial formation not of their own making and seeking to survive and prosper in a new land, relations with African Americans have often been a puzzlement, raising ambiguous and shifting responses, on their part and the part of outsiders observing this particular pairing. While in some places and times, Americans of Asian origin have been regarded as equivalent to blacks,[1] in general they have suffered comparatively less social oppression and physical harm from the majority white population, and so carry a less traumatic psychic legacy (with exceptions including, foremost, the wartime Japanese American internment). More often, especially in recent decades, they have been considered as a group assimilable into whiteness and afforded the social advantage and thorny predicament of "model minority" status, which specifically rewards self-distancing from African American cultural values or social attitudes seen as threatening, including protest of inequity, or any form of radicalism. Class differences—and in extreme cases, urban economic rivalries—have in some cases driven a wedge between the groups. Yet, too, Asian Americans have in crucial historical circumstances made common cause with blacks, including both symbolic and activist political alliances.

This complexity of entwinement with African Americans is vividly developed in the tradition of Asian American fiction, in which, while they are not generally represented in the fictional foreground, a habit of cross-racial identification with blacks and a hope for Asian-African American mutuality have persisted, despite all conflict and division.

This interchapter offers an account of the history of Asian American fiction's engagement with African Americans and their culture as a contribution to the growing scholarly discussion of African-Asian American cultural connections. When I first began collecting examples of interethnic literary imbrication in the early 1990s, this particular lode had been barely mined at all by scholars. But since the turn of the millennium, the bridging of the histories and cultural production of African and Asian Americans is emerging as among the most vibrant areas of interethnic scholarship,[2] and, notably, the subfield of ethnic cultural studies that seems most determined to defy simplistic models of interethnic relations.

A Framework in the Making

In the foreword to Heike Raphael-Hernandez and Shannon Steen's landmark 2006 collection, *AfroAsian Encounters: Culture, History, Politics*, historian Vijay Prashad portrays a field of study on the verge of full formation: "what we have before us is a framework in the making, an archive almost ready to be theorized" (xx). This archive is the history of social, cultural, and literary relations between Asian and African Americans, framed by "AfroAsianist" scholars as two peoples who share not only the fact of (differing) racialized, minoritized American experiences and the mutual possession of long, rich, and sophisticated cultural and expressive traditions, but also a history of productive interaction.

This progressive emphasis is apparent when George Lipsitz writes (in a passage cited in part earlier), considering mid-century U.S. black nationalists' interest in Asia:

> Liberal narratives about multiculturalism and cultural pluralism to the contrary, race relations in the United States have always involved more than one outcast group at a time acting in an atomized fashion against a homogenous "white" center. Interethnic identifications and alliances have been powerful weapons against white supremacy. All racial identities are relational; communities of color are mutually constitutive of one another, not just competitive or cooperative. (210–11)

Bill V. Mullen takes "AfroAsian affiliation, cultural borrowing, and exchange" a step beyond relationality and mutual constitution, to a "model of transraciality that abolishes comfortable and discreet categories of 'racial,' 'ethnic,' or even 'disciplinary' modeling" (247). The conceptual radicalism of this developing field seems to have been implicit since its origins, which Prashad, author of the pathbreaking study, *Everybody Was Kung-Fu Fighting: Afro-Asian Connections and the Myth of Cultural Purity* (2001), locates in the "social justice ethos" of ethnic studies programs, rather than in the Cold War geopolitics of area studies ("Foreword" xv).[3] This is to say that "AfroAsian" studies have always been energized by a coalitional spirit, a reparative, anti-racist social urge. As Prashad puts it, defying the history of Asian and African Americans "long . . . pitted against each other as the model versus the undesirable" (*Everybody* x), "AfroAsian work tries hard to cultivate the epistemological and historical archive of solidarity" ("Foreword" xxi). And in the same vein, Samir Dayal looks toward a "heterotopia in which multiple and unpredictable interracial alliances are nurtured," "black-brown alliances" in particular (98).

At the same time, of course, this spirited turn to a more nuanced and dynamic sense of intergroup relations tends to reveal a complex, ambivalent, variable relation within the U.S. racial formation, having as much to do with phantasmal presences in the American psyche as with concrete histories. It is a connection marked at once by antagonism and alliance, deriving from "[competition] for scarce resources" alongside "similar if not identical experiences as racialized subjects as well as by the racial undertones of U.S. foreign policy" (Lipsitz 185).

To date, more scholarship seems to have been conducted on the African American side of the relationship, particularly on the ways that black thinkers and writers have engaged Asia and Asians in developing their own anti-racist work. Chronicling African Americans' inspiration by Asian and particularly Japanese nationalist movements in the World War II era (and beyond, to the decades of U.S. war in Asia), Lipsitz highlights the shaping influence of global politics on Asian/African American relations; for African Americans during the war, he claims, Asian "racial signifiers complicated the binary black-white divisions of the United States" (189, 210). Mullen argues that African Americans often regarded U.S. incursions into Asia "as a reflective mirror to assess U.S. racial conditions" and that this sense of solidarity has extended into their cultural production, for black writers have "recognized Asian and Asian American politics and culture as sources of their own dynamic, evolving, and innovative literary experiment" (246–47). Among cultural forms that connect Asian and African Americans, a particularly fruitful subject of inquiry has been the attraction of young black men to Asian martial arts, as "an area where nonwhite dominance is uncontested" (Ho 296; see also Prashad, *Everybody*).

Closer to the concerns of this study, the body of scholarship on Asian American political and cultural engagement with African Americans and their history and culture is growing rapidly. Substantial documentation has established the influence of black social justice movements on the late 1960s development of a pan-ethnic Asian American political identity and of the Asian American Studies movement, both "rooted in the support of community struggles against racial and class oppression" (Anderson and Lee 7). The very term "Asian American" was invented at U.C. Berkeley in 1968 by graduate student-activist Yuji Ichioka (later a distinguished historian), to name a group of students demonstrating for justice in the case of Black

Panther Huey Newton. An activist has recalled, "We had no [Asian American] role models for finding identity. We followed what blacks did.... Usually when you say Asian American, you are going to have some aspect of black experience too" (Rie Ayoma cited in Lipsitz 207).[4] Indeed, writes Frank H. Wu, "There would be no Asian Americans if black had not been beautiful" (xvii). As the era of Asian American cultural nationalism developed, African Americans were not only revolutionary models, but even nurturers of emerging Asian American arts, for Asian American men in particular. The four writers who were to become the editors of the groundbreaking *Aiiieeeee!* anthology of Asian American literature in 1974 (and its 1991 sequel, *The Big Aiiieeeee!*), Jeffery Paul Chan, Frank Chin, Lawson Fusao Inada, and Shawn Wong, met at a 1969 book party held by African American writer and editor Ishmael Reed, who had asked them to edit a special issue of his *Yardbird* magazine (Mullen 247). Subsequently, their own first anthology, the text that publically declared the arrival of Asian American literature, was published by the African American–owned Howard University Press. African Americans were always already there in Asian American cultural history, and the story of their shaping influence is now being written.

Thirdness

Just as social status for American blacks and Asians has been historically unequal, it must be acknowledged that, in the American racial imaginary, an "asymmetry" characterizes the symbolic relationship between American blacks and Asians (Daniel Y. Kim, *Writing* xvii), one that ironically tips the balance in the other direction. Among racial "others" in America, African Americans are, simply, mythologically primary, even as a diversifying population has strained the nation's traditionally binary racial self-image. For Daniel Y. Kim, Asian American cultural borrowings from African Americans suggest "the comparatively greater amount of symbolic value that African American culture possesses vis-à-vis other minority cultures" (xxvi). Moreover, in the literary sphere, a "sense of racial 'belatedness' ... frames the attempts of Asian American writers to write themselves into a literary landscape largely shaded in black and white" (126); the priority of African American literary tradition "enables as well as constrains" Asian Americans literary assertions ("Do I" 232).

More marginalized in the culture, then, but still compelled by their ethical compass to address the "Negro giant" whom Ellison detected beneath the floorboards of the stage of the American imaginary, Asian Americans find their cross-race affiliations complicated by the matter of their own unresolved racial positioning. Numerous scholars have written on this nameless, less fully articulated racial condition—Wong's "peculiar kind of Other (among other Others)," "'unassimilable alien[s],'" "permanent houseguests in the house of America" (*Reading* 5–6)—the position I have called that of thirdness, which tends to be located between black and white. Gary Y. Okihiro writes that the "marginalization of Asians ... within a black and white racial formation, 'disciplines' both Africans and Asians and constitutes the essential site of Asian American oppression," rendering their and other non-black racialized peoples "invisible" (62). "The nature of Asian American social subjectivity now vacillates between whiteness and color," writes David Palumbo-Liu, and put even more starkly by David Leiwei Li, Asian Americans are socially "[s]trangled between the authentic white subject and the oppositional black subject" (10).

This vexed position is rendered dramatically over the course of Asian American literary history, in which widely diverse and heterogeneous Asian American subjectivities are seen, again and again, as framed between the looming poles of blackness and whiteness. Japanese American poet David Mura, in "The Colors of Desire," recalls an episode from the Internment era:

> how my father, as a teenager, clutched
> his weekend pass
> passed through the rifle towers and gates
> of the Jerome, Arkansas, camp, and, in 1942,
> stepped on a bus to find white riders
> motioning, "Sit here, son," and, in the rows
> beyond,
> a half dozen black faces, waving him back,
> "Us colored folks got to stick together."
> How did he know where to sit?

The poem goes on to present the speaker as haunted by gruesome images of white-black violence, yet he asks of these scenarios, "[W]here am I, the missing third?" (4–5). One might wonder how anyone could long to be positioned within such frightening strife. And yet, insisting that they are not guests but in their rightful home, Asian American literary voices have consistently claimed a place in the midst of it.

Black Presences in Asian American Writing

Within just such settings of contradiction, ambivalence, and violence, Asian American fiction has long mused upon the question: what can Asian-African American relations be? Amidst a preoccupation with dominant, often hostile whiteness, a thread of connection to blackness tends to appear in brief moments of affiliation, unfulfilled plot segments, interludes of sympathy, of sensitivity to shared histories of minoritization and struggle. Such moments stand out all the more starkly against the backdrop of anti-black racism, of fear of and self-distancing from blacks, that informs immigrants' earliest lessons about America. In such instances writers point, across scenarios of violence and potential competition, toward the redemptive value of solidarity with African American people.

Early-century Asian immigrant writers, encountering blacks as an unfamiliar people, readily and sympathetically recognized them as fellow sufferers of parallel or worse oppressions. The Korean immigrant hero of Younghill Kang's *East Goes West* (1937) several times comes upon dispirited "Negroes" who confide in him. These include the butler Laurenzo, who drunkenly bemoans the misery of an educated "niggerman" who is prohibited from exercising his talents (284–86), and the student and "elevator man" Wagstaff (perhaps a lost Shakespeare or another Falstaff) who, discussing "his shadowy existence as an outcast in the white man's world," gives the hero his "first introduction to a crystallized caste system . . . here in the greatest democratic country of the world (297). In the "cosmopolitan" vision of this memoir, Stephen Knadler has argued, Kang "[calls] into question national narratives that would leave the 'Negro' and other people of color as outside the heterogeneous American scene in which the Korean might find a 'home'" (2). Among the many empathetic encounters with blacks and their stories in Kang's work, most astonishing is the harrowing nightmare that closes the book, the Korean hero's dream of sharing the fate of a group of black men who, stuck in a dark cellar, face a lynch mob armed with fiery torches (Kang 401). Few more dramatic renderings exist, in minority American literatures, of the terror of mutual victimization by white racism.

The radical social vision of Carlos Bulosan's *America Is In the Heart* includes African Americans only sparsely in the immigrant hero's experience, but it consistently positions Filipino American fellow-feeling for blacks as its gesture of ultimate social solidarity. The most prominent instance occurs in the central, inserted text of the speech reported to have been given by the hero's brother Macario, which reads, in part:

> We are all Americans that have toiled and suffered and known oppression and defeat, from the first Indian that offered peace in Manhattan to the last Filipino pea pickers. . . . America is in the hearts of men that died for freedom. . . . America is a prophecy of a new society of men. . . . America is also the nameless foreigner, the homeless refugee, the hungry boy begging for a job and the black body dangling on a tree. America is the illiterate immigrant who is ashamed that the world of books and intellectual opportunities is closed to him. We are all that nameless foreigner, that homeless refugee, that hungry boy, that illiterate immigrant and that lynched black body. All of us, from the first Adams to the last Filipino, native born or alien, educated or illiterate—*We are America!* (189)

Relentlessly dead, mutilated, the black figure in this assemblage is not humanized as are some of the others, his corporeality perhaps fetishized, even co-opted. Still, Bulosan, himself the victim of violent abuse by police and others in the United States, places the spectacle of that body unflinchingly before us in his democratic credo and does not distance his own, somewhat lighter-skinned and less often violently victimized people from it. The willingness to identify and affiliate with the tortured black body—emblematic target of white racism—makes Bulosan's a particularly strong expression of solidarity with African Americans and their history.

Corporeal identification arises in a gentler vein, in the book's memorable, penultimate scene, when the impoverished Filipino immigrant narrator repays an African American shoeshine man the ten-cent debt of his brother, who has asked him to do so in the final moments before he sets off to serve in World War II. The astonished shoeshine man takes the dime and invites the narrator to go with him to share a bottle of beer. As they pass the bottle, the narrator is moved by the resemblance of the black man's "toil-scarred" hand to the hand of his own, beloved brother Macario (author of the great speech), who, though expected to be the family scholar in the Philippines, instead suffered an American life that turned his hands, to the hero's sorrowed view, "hard and calloused," "ugly and twisted," "cracked and bleeding" (241). The black man takes his leave, turning to the narrator:

> I'm joining the navy tomorrow, so I guess this is goodbye. I know I'll meet your brother again somewhere, because I got my dime without asking him. But if I don't see him again, I'll remember him every time I see the face of an American dime. Goodbye, friend! (325)

Surely a Filipino face had never before been seen on "an American dime," always the site of an iconic national image.[5] In this scene of the poignant repayment of debts, of the fusion of the hands and surprising recasting of the face of America, the Asian is granted symbolic Americanness—through affiliation with the African American, rather than by racist subordination of him.[6] The scene's significant placement in the text plants potential brown-black solidarity in the moment just before the narrator's final vision of America as "a huge heart unfolding warmly to receive" him (326). In both of these examples, Bulosan's inclusion of African Americans draws upon their symbolic positioning as those most extremely marked and abjected by American racialization, to extend the political vision of his collective portrait of the Filipino immigrant masses in the boldest and most encompassing possible way, into that of an emergent American confraternity.

Mixed impulses toward African Americans and their potential relations with Asian Americans are recorded in John Okada's *No-No Boy* (1957). Black men on a street corner taunt a Japanese American World War II draft resister, who has just stepped off the bus at war's end, returned from jail, with "Jap!" and "Go back to Tokyo, boy." Okada's empathic narrator names this "Persecution in the drawl of the persecuted" (5), but his ex-con hero has a complicated response:

> Friggin' niggers, he uttered savagely to himself and, from the same place deep down inside where tolerance for the Negroes and the Jews and the Mexicans and the Chinese and the too short and too fat and too ugly abided because he was Japanese and knew what it was like better than did those who were white and average and middle class and good Democrats or liberal Republicans, the hate which was unrelenting and terrifying seethed up. (5–6)

A "place deep down inside" Japanese Americans and others can send up, alternately, savage, terrifying racist hate, or tolerance; there is no natural or inevitable cross-race response, but radically open possibility, including the chance for good to be nurtured. Later in the plot, we learn that "there's still plenty of good people around" when a black foundry worker named Birdie "really [suffers] for" and defends Gary, another Japanese American draft resister, until Birdie is victimized in Gary's stead (226). This "Negro who stood up for Gary" is recollected in the novel's last paragraphs among those who collectively offer the hero a "glimmer of hope," a "faint and elusive insinuation of promise" for American community and his place in it (250–51). *No-No Boy* understands Japanese-black tensions as moral problems, symptoms of a "savage" American society, potentially resolvable in a coming era of broader mutual understanding.

Entwined Masculinities, Shared Words

A more extended social and historical drama of interaction with African Americans is depicted in Peter Bacho's short fiction collection *Dark Blue Suit*, published in 1997 but reaching back to the '30s and '40s eras of Bulosan and Okada. These autobiographical stories offer poignant portraits of Bacho's Filipino immigrant father, his relatives, and comrades, "who came to this land long ago, when racism and violence, migrant poverty, tuberculosis, and despair should have killed them, but didn't" ("A Family Gathering" 142). The world Bacho describes reaches beyond the mainly bachelor generation of migrant Filipinos about whom Bulosan also wrote to other inhabitants of his gritty Seattle landscape, including white prostitutes and Chinese business owners. Most complex are the relations Bacho describes between his extended family and black Americans, with whom they felt a "natural" closeness, but from whom history would later separate them.

An elemental form of these relations is the adulation of black sports figures. For the poor immigrant Filipinos—as for so many poor American men, moved by boxing among all sports—black boxers like Sugar Ray Robinson are adored heroes. But notably, there are Filipino boxers, too:

> [F]aced with the heat of the fields and the filth and overcrowding of city hotel rooms, many young Filipinos in the 1930s turned to boxing as a way out, a way up. . . . The prize ring . . . provided that rare chance to be judged as an equal, which every Pinoy craved. The ring suspended society's norms, those rules that embodied a racial and social order favoring color over ability, class over potential. In the ring, a Filipino could beat a white man with his fists and not be arrested. . . .
>
> What [Joe] Louis meant to African Americans, Garcia, Dado, Santos, and Young Tommy meant to Pinoys. Every victory shouted equality from a forum of respect and public acclaim. ("A Manong's Heart" 110–11)

In these passages, Filipinos seem to face a form of racialization (perhaps because of darker skin color) that placed them nearer than other Asian Americans to the lot of African Americans, with a similar sense of dispossession—"In our neighborhood, blacks and Filipinos had shared a bond formed by poverty and bad attitude. We'd always run together—a natural match . . ." ("August" 62)—and a corresponding recourse to the organized violence of boxing, and to expressive culture as well, as Bacho suggests: "Filipinos always hired black bands . . . the horns made it raw and powerful, something white bands could never do" ("Rico" 28). The two groups also seem to share a machismo that places Filipino men out of danger of the symbolic emasculation that plagues other Asian Americans. "[R]espect," Bacho writes, was the purpose of his youthful devotion to boxing and martial arts:

> That's what mattered. In my world, you could never have too much. Respect—the most precious currency of the poor and colored. It couldn't pay the note, but it might buy a walk past older men who'd check you out. They'd nod. "You bad," the nod said. ("Second" 43)

At first glance, these passages portray an extensive interplay of black and Filipino masculinities in Bacho's Seattle youth. But in fact, the cultural flow goes almost entirely in one direction: the Filipinos—more recently arrived, fewer in number, assimilating to the minority dominant—adopting black music, black male somatic styles and practices, and black speech, in the effort to articulate their own experience and position within the structure of American race. Indeed, the ability of the young protagonist, Buddy, to speak a fluid ebonics is crucial to Bacho's presentation of this interethnic identification. Buddy says to his black friend, Aaron: "'Shoulda tol' me, brotha'man,' I said slowly, 'fo' you gave it up'" ("August" 57), and explains, "Bloods spoke that way; Filipinos, too. That's how we grew up.... And although we had both become bilingual—over the years we'd learned how to speak to whites—when we got back home and together, we fell into our language of choice" (57).

But this assimilation into blackness begins to fail just as Buddy's youth ends, with the coming of black liberation, when the assertion of a public, political African American identity could no longer allow the inclusion of ambiguously colored others:

> The sixties hit the neighborhood hard; people started to draw lines and call each other down, just on race. Mostly, the conflict was black and white, but where did that leave me? ("Second" 43)

> Their anger, black anger, the fuel that drove the revolution—and the response: white fear riding three cops to a car. But what about us, neither black nor white, who lived on the same block and shared the poverty? Did the revolution spare observers? ("August" 54–55)

In the story "August, 1968," Buddy's black friend, Aaron, comes to warn him of danger: in the recent racial violence in Seattle, he saw other black friends fatally beat a "Chinaman named Ron," for no reason except, as they put it, "That punk Chink... Ain' one o' us" ("August" 61). Instead of being grateful for the warning, Buddy is enraged by the "maddening nonchalance" of Aaron's delivery of it and begins to scream, "[Y]our friend, he's gonna take me out and it's cool 'cause the fuckin' revolution's on and I ain' black, and it's payback for oppression I had nothin' to do with!" (62). He then surprises himself by calling his friend "'Nigger!'... using that word for the first time" (63), and gets this chilling response: "'It's nigga,' he scolded.... 'Listen to yo'sef talk, man, ' he said evenly. 'Can' even say it right. You soun' like a damn white man'" (63). Furious to find himself placed on the other side of the race line in a world turned completely binary, Buddy has suddenly spoken a damning white word; his black friend, once his comrade in racialization, makes an accusation about the sound of his "talk" that can only signal the friendship's end. There is nothing left for Aaron to say but, "'I'da backed you, man.... Against anyone," and, "Brother no more" (63).

This story of the diverging talk of brothers reads like a parable about the vagaries of multiethnic life within the grid of the U.S. racial formation, of the way lives can be aligned or sundered because of the changing historical meanings of racial identities. For the developing Filipino protagonist of Bacho's stories, the period of love, respect, and dialogue with black men forms a cherished life chapter and a lost, much-missed experience of cross-race "brotherhood" for two peoples whose courses parted, ironically, just as the possibility of liberation from subaltern status first arose, to take disjunctive paths toward public self-definition.

This paradoxical predicament of longing for unity with those more violently repressed, more viscerally struggling, recurs in Asian American men's texts, one aspect of a deeply vexed engagement with black male models of masculinity (and "masculine" cultural nationalism). For in the absurd psychosexual calculations of the American mind, African American masculinity is, as James Kim has put it, "the benchmark against which other masculinities are proven" (157), and, as Elaine Kim has written, "Asian men have been coded as having no sexuality, while Asian women have nothing else ("Such Opposite" 11). The history of Asian American male emasculation has been well developed by scholars,[7] and the complexity of masculine identification in scenarios involving Asian and black men has recently received critical scrutiny.[8]

The vexed Asian-African masculinity knot emerges nowhere as powerfully as in the creative and critical writing of playwright, novelist, and essayist Frank Chin. Chin, it must be noted, has come under a deserved hail of criticism from feminist and other critics, in part for his masculinist literary visions, but even more for his baldly derogatory, polemical essays on other and more popular Asian American writers, including Maxine Hong Kingston, David Henry Hwang, and Amy Tan, especially in his essay "Come All Ye Asian American Writers of the Real and the Fake" in *The Big Aiiieeeee!*, which dismisses the above writers' work as "fake" Asian because insufficiently masculinist and nationalist.

In a fine, sustained reading by Daniel Y. Kim in *Writing Manhood in Black and Yellow*, Chin is said to borrow from the rhetoric of black nationalism so as to "[write] about the psychological structure of Asian American male subjectivity as it is injuriously shaped by U.S. ideologies of race, gender, and sexuality" (125–26). And yet, Kim finds in the work of Chin and of Ralph Ellison an ambivalent "interracialism that registers (though asymmetrically and unevenly) as identification and desire, as an uneasy libidinal charge that alternates between antagonism and solidarity" (xvi). Chin's projection toward both white and black masculinity of an aggressive, melancholic, sometimes violent and masochistic "interracial mimetic desire" (36, 126) is further troubled by an obsessive conviction that racism's crowning oppression is its attempt to feminize non-white men, to turn black men into homosexuals (xxiii). Thus Asian American masculinity in Chin must be aggressively homophobic even as it seeks, in the special sphere of literature, a certain rarified "homosocial intimacy" with writers of other races (39).

The locus par excellence of problematized Asian masculinity in Frank Chin's work, and a crucial text for considering Asian American imaginations of Asian-black cultural encounter and exchange, is Chin's play *Chickencoop Chinaman* (1972). Composed and produced in the era of Black Power and the Black Arts movement, this play dramatizes the outraged, mercurial psyche of a Chinese American male protagonist, Tam Lum, who, deeply alienated from a denigrated "Chinese" identity and furiously refusing to be an "honorary white" (37), cherishes instead his lifelong connections to black American culture and to black male role models, as does his friend and sidekick, the Japanese American Kenji, called "blackjap Kenji" (10). Written at a time when staged cross-race encounters were enormously charged and daring, the play presents horizontal affiliations in an embattled, at moments aggressively confrontational, dramatic scenario. As Kim puts it, Tam "prefigures the 'authentic' form of racial and masculine identity that Asian men ought to adopt if they are to emerge from the shadows cast by black and white men." Over the course of the play, Chin's hero is "presented as a kind of orphan" who must "work through the fixation with 'white and black heroes'" as potential fathers, must "mark their loss to him as appropriate love objects and move on" (Kim, *Writing* 185).

A poignant figure, then, even in his furious, absurd, self-dramatizing monologues, and in his antic chicken-clucking ("Buck Buck Bagaw" [51]), Tam reads, from the vantage of thirty-some years, like a would-be Black Power hero, longing to make a declaration of emergence into "voice" as powerful as that of late '60s-early '70s African American literary and popular cultural speakers (in, say, James Brown's 1968 hit "I'm Black and I'm Proud," or the Black Arts poetry of Amiri Baraka, or a little later [in an antithetically feminist vein] in the "black girl's song" of Ntozake Shange's 1975 play "for colored girls who have considered suicide/when the rainbow is enuf" [Shange 4]).[9] But the problem for Tam Lum, I would venture, is that he is unable to name the proud identity he wants to declare; this hero has not yet arrived at a conception of an Asian- or Asian American-ness that he could call either "powerful" or "beautiful." His pal Kenji remarks to the "possible Eurasian" female character Lee (3), "so what if I don't mess with other Orientals . . . Asians, whatever. . . . [Y]ou make everything I do sound ugly, man, like I hate myself" (21), and complains that Lee has "put me down!" by "[b]ringing in this goddam tatami grassmat Japanese bullshit and knockin the legs off the table," for "I'm not Japanese! Tam ain't no Chinese!" (22). But neither man can say, affirmatively, what he is, short of Tam's crazy, animal caricature of a self-naming, the "Chickencoop Chinaman."

Orphaned and inadequately named, this hero pursues a connection to black father figures that ultimately comes to naught. He demonstrates a certain anxiety that his strong attachment to and imitation of black men might suggest homosexuality (Kim 189–90), above all in the repeated, nostalgic recounting of episodes of urination with black men; Tam and Kenji's shared moment with the boxer Ovaltine Jack Dancer was "the greatest piss we ever took in our lives" (41). But beyond this anxiety, however, and even amidst the melancholic tonality and psychic structure that characterizes the whole desirous/combative engagement with male blackness here, I would point to a different, rather exhilarating element of the play: the astonishingly hybrid interethnic speech and physical movements of the protagonist and his blackjap buddy. Though continually problematized in the dialogue, the creative spirit of racial crossing in Tam and Kenji's insistence on their right to speak and move and act like black men, to love black music, to be a "blackjap," in part redeems the abortive quest for a newly articulable identity. Chin's defense of hybrid speech and somatic and cultural styles might be read not just as a failed, immature Asian Americanness, but as a breakthrough affirmation of interethnic hybridity, in defiance of the kind of separatist identity politics suffered by the hero of Bacho's stories. If the once-shared piss emblematizes a briefly glimpsed, longed for masculinist, homosocial, interethnic sharing of culture, Tam and Kenji's high fives embody a lived transraciality.

The matter of speech is particularly fascinating here. Chin develops a compelling portrayal of Chinese Americans as verbal orphans, logically driven toward hybrid speech. Tam declares: "I speak nothing but the mother tongues bein' born to none of my own, I talk the talk of orphans" (8); "I am the natural born ragmouth speaking the motherless bloody tongue. No real language of my own to make sense with, so out comes everybody else's trash that don't conceive" (7). Black and white speech seem to be the two poles on the available language continuum, in relation to which orphan Asian Americans must develop their speech. A stage direction reads, "*TAM goes through voice and accent changes. From W. C. Fields to American Midwest, Bible Belt holy roller, etc. His own 'normal' speech jumps between black and white rhythms and accents*" (6). Thus, Tam's normal locutions include lines like, "You ain't shittin me, you ain't signifying, you don't know what I'm talking about?" (47). Comments a black character, "The way you talked, why, I took you for colored over the phone" (40).

Though the female character Lee responds to the men's black performativity with lines like, "It's sick of you to make fun of blacks . . . the way you walk . . . your talk . . . giving five. Who do you think you are?" and, "I hate people making it on the backs of black people" (13, 19), Kenji retorts, in several lines:

> "I think you're wrong . . . About Tam, I mean. And me faking blackness. . . ."
> "Ovaltine Jack the Dancer was our hero, you know. We met him."
> "Maybe we act black, but it's not fake." (19)
> "I'm not imitating no black people. I'm no copycat. I know I live with 'em, I talk like 'em, I dress . . . maybe even eat what they eat." (21)

Chin's Asian American men insist that doing black style is not making fun or co-optation—they assert their right to act like the people whose life they share: "My place . . . right in the heart of the black ghetto. Just like home" (9)—the salient point being that a black home may be as much "like home" as they can get in America. Moreover, recourse to blackness makes perfect sense, asserts Tam Lum, for those whom assimilationist pressure never allowed to claim Asianness in the first place: "I mean, we grow up bustin our asses to be white anyway. . . . 'Don't wear green because it makes you look yellow, son'. . . . 'Don't be seen with no blacks, get good grades, lay low, an apple for the teacher, be good, suck up, talk proper, and be civilized'" (26). For Tam, no dignity and no sense of manhood lie in Chinese American model minority performances, caricatured in a dialogue with an absurd, racist figure of the Lone Ranger:

> RANGER: "China Boys, you be legendary obeyers of the law, legendary humble, legendary passive. Thank me now and I'll let ya get back to China town preservin your culture!" (37)
> RANGER: "I'm the law, China Boys, it's a curse I'm givin ya to thank me for, not a blessing. . . . kiss my ass, know thou that it be white, and go thou happy in honorary whiteness forever and ever, preservin your culture, AMEN."
> TAM *and* KENJI: "We don't wanta be honorary white." (37)

In the face of this abysmal account of Asian Americanness as conventionally imaginable in his moment, Chin creates an emergent Asian American as a principle of furious insistence on flouting the race rules, on acting and talking like whomever he wants to be—some kind of American on his own terms, neither Chinese "preservin his culture" nor white, nor fake-black, but some new mongrel American that he cannot yet name, except by recourse to a cross-species moniker of his own invention, who speaks in a chicken cluck, "Buck Buck Bagaw," that may be a cartoonish version of that cry of pain and fury, "Aiiieeee!" Beneath all this noise, the outrageous cross-race performance carries on, at a lower frequency, a suggestion of an unfulfilled desire for a fully interethnic American life, invoking a more productive, syncretic mode toward which the play—taking just a few steps beyond Bacho's lament—can only gesture with wistful longing.

Written two decades later but set two decades earlier than *The Chickencoop Chinaman*, the bittersweet comedy of Gus Lee's *China Boy* (1991) is a great deal more sanguine about the possibilities of multiethnic exchange and even fusion. In chapter 1, I discussed *China Boy*'s affirmation of the salvational multiethnic masculine solidarity of the YMCA, in the life of a Chinese American boy from the tough streets of San Francisco. But Lee's novel is also concerned with the Chinese-black interface in particular (see Šesnić) and memorably portrays the coexistence of these two groups as migrant peoples who landed as San Francisco neighbors:

> The Handle and Chinatown were neighborhoods that revered customs drawn from continents far distant from North America, whose features now were memory. Both neighborhoods were filled with people who had arrived en masse—not as single migrants.... Both neighborhoods had a strong spiritual sense, a different musical culture, unique foods, and unappreciated patois. Everyone had black hair, brown eyes, and darker skin that the majority.... And everyone in both 'hoods seemed so chronically poor that poverty had become an integral expression of local culture. (243)

Lee's portrayal of black and Chinese Americans must be unequalled in American literature for its attempt at an equalizing, even-handed comparison of the two groups. Indeed, although his young hero Kai Ting's daily trial is the avoidance of severe beatings by black bullies, the novel never presents blackness itself as the enemy or problem. On the contrary, blackness is, at the outset, the elusive goal of the hero's quest: "I was trying to become an accepted black male youth in the 1950s—a competitive, dangerous, and harshly won objective. This was all the more difficult because I was Chinese. I was ignorant of the culture, clumsy in the language, and blessed with a body that made Tinker Bell look ruthless" (4). It is black culture to which Kai must work to assimilate, black language he must learn to speak. And his eventual "*pound* "ing of the black bully Big Willie by no means inscribes an anti-black impulse in the book (321), for Kai is surrounded by black supporters in this effort, chiefly his loyal best friend, Toussaint, and Toussaint's mother, a loving mother-substitute who swabs away his blood. But it is a transracial, manly development that Kai goes to the YMCA to acquire, in the training of boxing masters African, Italian, and Asian American, so as to overcome the power of Big Willie. The binary Chinese-black problem and the black threat in this sense are overpowered by multiracial, masculine unity; the novel ultimately refuses ethnic binaries, overcoming them with multiplicity. Still, it must be said that Kai's joy in his growing fluency in the black vernacular provides the final coup and reinforces the centrality of a longed-for Asian-black fusion, when he can at last spit out, "*I ain't fo' yo' pickin-on, no mo'!*" to the mean, white stepmother (322) in beautiful, borrowed ebonics.

Beyond Black and Yellow Men

Perhaps what is most intriguing in the contemporary Asian American fictional engagement with African Americans, including the three novels considered centrally in the chapters that follow, is a phenomenon characteristic of the increasingly interethnic imagination of fiction across the American ethnic spectrum: the destabilization of racial binaries. I refer here not only to the black/white racial binary, but also to the black/yellow. That is, contemporary Asian American fiction tends to represent blacks along with Asians in a wide human spectrum, like that of Gus Lee's YMCA, which not only makes the black/white binary cease to seem natural and eternal, but also points toward a lessening of the sway of race as a social determinant. More and more, in Asian American fiction's outreach to black characters and black culture, binary opposition is undone, and ethnic difference is refracted through multiple encounters with others.[10]

Presented amidst a multiethnic throng, the African American hero Buzzworm, in Karen Tei Yamashita's *Tropic of Orange* (discussed in chapter 4), is a character designed to surprise: a "[b]ig black seven-foot dude, Vietnam vet, an Afro shirt with palm trees painted all over it, dreds, pager, and Walkman" (27), who "tapped your worst phobias. Seemed like he was who he was just to offend you" (25), but who happens to listen to the radio in Korean, Spanish, and any other language available, who serves his ethnically mixed community as a free-lance "*Angel of Mercy*" (26), and who maintains friendships and alliances with Latinos, Asians, characters of all the stripes that Yamashita's wildly heterogeneous social vision includes. In Jiro Adachi's *The Island of Bicycle Dancers*, Korean-Japanese American Yurika finds herself in an ethnically diverse New York City social landscape that suits her desire to escape from the mutual race prejudice she has known among Japanese and Koreans. Bored and lonely at the Korean family grocery where she works, she falls in with the foul-mouthed but genial and multiracial fellowship of Manhattan bike messengers who visit the store. Among the bikers, who are described as "black, white, brown, all kind" (49), she is drawn both to Hector, a messenger with "splendid caramel-colored skin" (1), and to another known as Whitey. As the latter name suggests, the novel is highly attentive to variations of skin color, but remarkably, its newcomer heroine intensely experiences the individual attractions and qualities of both men without attributing social meaning to their colors. Yurika might be said to be positioned within a familiar Asian-black-white racial triangulation. But the novel's broadly heterogeneous, multiethnic social world, its visual attention to variegated skin coloration, and its affirmation of "a future where the streets were filled with" people "like Yurika, people not fully part of one culture or another but smack in the middle of two or three" (33), prevents any binary or triangular dynamic from developing, instead presenting racial difference as enormously various, and destined to become as infinitely so as human individuality itself. Such figurations of African Americans amidst multiplicity might be seen to work toward relieving them of their anomalous status, the symbolic burden they have long carried in literature as in life, toward envisioning a generally more fluid and open social and cultural life, a life that could make even Chin's Tam Lum feel free.

The example of Yamashita's Buzzworm suggests a certain ease and freedom in representing African Americans that tends to be found in contemporary Asian American women's writing, in particular. Looking back to texts written before the current rise in interethnic representations, we can note Asian American women showing a minor but steady strand of cross-ethnic solidarity with African American figures, a sympathetic engagement which, if less developed or central to their texts, is also mercifully unburdened by the kind of agonistic competition, the love-hate relationship, that afflicts male Asian American writers confronting the differential masculinity complex discussed above.

Readers may remember the timidly spoken solidarity with African Americans on the part of the vocally challenged Chinese American female narrator of Maxine Hong Kingston's 1976 novel, *The Woman Warrior*. "'I don't like that word,' I had to say in my bad, small person's voice that makes no impact," to a boss who calls a bright color "Nigger yellow," and "'I refuse to type these invitations,' I whispered, voice unreliable" in generically feminist as well as anti-racist protest to another boss, who insists on holding an event at a restaurant in violation of a CORE and NAACP boycott (48-9). For this refusal, Kingston's narrator is fired, a sacrifice that compounds her significant effort in overcoming a speech anxiety that the novel portrays as distinctively a Chinese American girl's, so as to declare unity with more readily vocal African American public protest (48). Black-Asian solidarity is imagined in a dramatic, historical setting in the encounter of a male African American ex-slave and a Chinese American woman sold into prostitution on the Western frontier in Ruthanne Lum McCunn's *Thousand Pieces of Gold* (1981). When the ex-slave informs Lalu (Polly), "You ain't no slave, honey. . . . They is no slaves in America, not fo' ten years" (138), he becomes in effect her emancipator.[11]

African Americans hold a slight but special place, too, in the narrative of Runyoung Kim's *Clay Walls* (1986). Over the several decades of this Korean American saga, the Chun family has little significant interaction with white Americans; the young heroine Faye Chun declares toward the book's end, "I could never be one of *them*. . . . I really have no need to be" (298). But African Americans in their Los Angeles neighborhood are intimately known friends, rivals, and even models of Americanness, their "jive talk" and "swagger" taken up by the boys if only in defense against them, and—though forbidden by the protective Korean American mother—secretly tried out by the good-girl heroine Faye under her breath: "Whatchu mean, man?" (198). The influence of the young black man Lucerne Luke proves dangerous, involving one brother in theft and a criminal charge, and Faye shrinks from his sexually explicit banter. But a black girl named Bertha proves a lifelong friend. Though in youth Bertha's mockery of Faye's obedience to her mother elicits the explanation, "She was colored and did not understand Korean families" (190); in this plot almost entirely concerned with intra-ethnic Korean relationships, Bertha's recurrent reappearances always come as a joyful surprise for Faye and bring her a feminist model of female vitality and agency. Bertha shows loyalty and care by coming to "say goodbye," in confused sympathy with her Korean friend when the Japanese Americans are evacuated during World War II (263); she enters boldly into sexuality while Faye remains at home under her mother's wing, longing to live in the wider world; and she shows Faye the way to independence and participation in the war effort through an assembly-plant job. When later glimpsed in a newspaper photo, Bertha "looked beautiful" accepting the posthumous medal of her "war hero" husband—Lucerne Luke, whereby the choices of both members of the couple are redeemed. Faye praises Bertha as "the only girl I knew who took hold of life and made things happen" (284).

Alongside the affirmations of such plot-level solidarity, Asian American women writers have sometimes self-consciously adopted linguistic modes and literary styles and genres from the African American repertoire to shape their own self-articulations. Though poet Marilyn Chin has written in a mock self-epitaph that worries the ironies of her American identity, "She was neither black nor white" ("How I" 82), in another poem, "We Are Americans Now, We Live in the Tundra," she adopts the African American mode and metaphor of the blues as an ironized expression of her ambivalent Chinese American condition. The speaker faces China to "sing her / A blues song; even a Chinese girl gets the blues, / Her reticence is black and blue" (4–6). These lines recall the black/Asian vocal dialectic of Kingston's text, here the expressive content of a dramatic, black mode of vocal art analogized, perhaps surprisingly, to that of traditional Chinese silence, even as Chin's American "blues" mock-mournfully cries, "Farewell my ancestors," and offers a generic lament for the end of all things Chinese: "the extinct / Bengal tigers" and the non-mating "giant Pandas" (19, 7–8).

In an explicit acknowledgment of debt in the area of literary language, Japanese Hawaiian novelist Lois-Ann Yamanaka has credited the example of African American women's writing in Black English for enabling her to become a novelist in Hawaiian pidgin. She cites a writing teacher who introduced her to the work of Ntozake Shange and Thulani Davis, among others: "Her therapy for me was that I read a lot of African-American women who were writing in dialect":

> That's when I came to terms that pidgin was not an ignorant language, that I was speaking a dialect and that my feelings and thoughts were so connected to the language that in order for me to write truthfully, I needed to connect to that voice. (Takahama)

The example of African American women's literary expression has become a standard in ethnic American letters, both for sheer affective power and for the linguistic affirmation of ethnic identity. Carried across ethnicities and dialects, this model becomes emancipatory for Asian American women's own emergent expressivity.

Lessons on Class

Recent Asian American fiction has become remarkably explicit about both the desire for cross-race relations with African Americans and the obstacles to such connection. An example is the bold, earnest interethnic social experiment devised in the novel examined at length in chapter 3, Gish Jen's *Mona in the Promised Land,* which explores camaraderie with African American characters (classed by Ling as a "lateral" crossing). Chinese American teenager Mona joins her Jewish American friends in attempting, charitably and naively, to house Alfred, a temporarily homeless black coworker and the cook in Mona's father's pancake house, in one friend's huge, suburban house while the parents are away, a venture that evolves into a semi-communal, '70s encounter group among Jewish, Asian, and African American youth, who try to befriend and live with one another, with results alternately comic and revelatory, but ultimately, sadly doomed.

When Mona and friends take it upon themselves to investigate race, they unwittingly come upon the barrier of class difference, which Alfred helps them to understand is an intractable mediator of relations between himself and them. "You know the difference between you white folk and me?" he asks. While Mona thinks about protesting her inclusion in the group "white folk," "'See,' he says,"

> [Y]ou white folk look at the calendar, and at the end of the year comes Christmas-time, and at the beginning of the year comes a whole new year, maybe the year you pack your white ass off to college, maybe the year you go off traveling somewhere nice. Me, I look at that calendar, and at the end of the year there's flapjacks, and at the beginning of the year there's flapjacks, and when I die, man, they're going to cover me with flapjacks, and put the butter and the syrup on top, and they're going to write on the tombstone, He done burnt only a couple of jacks his whole life, and that's when the stove was broke and burning like a hellhole. (154)

There may be no comparably long excursus on the racialized American class system by a black character anywhere in Asian American literature, and few speeches this long by a black character, period. In *Mona in the Promised Land,* a cross-race encounter generates something approaching real dialogue and real mutual learning. This forthrightness in discussing the lived effects of race and class difference causes friction, however, when Jen's heroine crosses a crucial line, allowing her cross-race and cross-class loyalty to a friend to come before family loyalty: she admits to Alfred et al. that her parents would never promote him in the restaurant because he is black.

This causes a predictable family estrangement. Helen, Mona's Chinese immigrant mother, is outraged at the notion that social justice or any other value comes before the value of family: "How could you say that to outside people? . . . What kind of daughter talks that way? . . . [P]arents are racist, parents are not racist, even parents are Communist, a daughter has no business talk like that. You talk like that is like slap your own mother in the face!" (249–50). Moreover, Mona's mother is represented as embodying the racist modes in which a model minority citizen is instructed, precisely the Asian American self-concept beyond which Mona is attempting to progress. Helen is incensed, for example, at being invited to join a campaign for a new clinic where birth control and venereal disease treatment would be available for free. To the offending clinic organizer, Helen politely responds, "We own this restaurant. . . . You should see our tax bracket," while ushering her out, and later exclaims to her daughter, "Can you believe that woman? What is she talking about? Venereal disease! Birth control! She wants to lump us with black people!" (119). Helen and her husband, Ralph, incidentally, don't want to be minorities, because "they're just as good as anybody, why should they ask for help? Also they do not want to have to riot" (52); put even more bluntly, by Mona, "there's another reason her parents don't want to have too much to do with blacks—namely, that they don't want to turn into blacks" (118). Their vulnerable social position, as Asian Americans, is threatened by association with those of the lowest class and racial status.

And to tell the truth, even in a situation of relative class parity, middle-class or wealthy Asian characters—even Mona herself—are shown to be disinclined to identify fully with similarly positioned African Americans. Jen's plucky, anti-racist teenaged heroine, in the thrall of her sister's impressively multitalented, black Harvard roommate Naomi, thinks of her as a "Renaissance woman such as Mona would have envied mightily had she not been black" (169); even Mona understands blackness as an unenviable, a damning social condition. A similar line is drawn in Don Lee's story "Yellow," where shared affluence among the token few is shown to enhance fellow-feeling but not to guarantee solidarity at the risk of one's own status. The protagonist, Danny Kim, a Korean American management consultant competing for partnership at a prestigious Boston firm, feels "a kinship with prosperous blacks, a silent brotherhood of tokenism, and was ashamed of himself when he tolerated his colleagues' racist jokes and comments" (237). In such moments of distancing from African Americans, we see the social vulnerability of Asian American characters preventing cross-race solidarity, even in the upper echelons. As I will argue in chapter 3, though Jen's *Mona in the Promised Land* commits itself more completely than any previous Asian American novel to experimentation in cross-ethnic solidarity, and though it celebrates in this regard some rare successes, it finds its limits in the unyielding class and race formation that does not yet free African and Asian Americans to meet on terms of complete openness and mutuality.

Black Mimesis

Perhaps class more than race divides Yamashita's hero of the 'hood, Buzzworm, from her Japanese American female character Emi, a chic and media-obsessed TV producer whom Buzzworm calls an "Asian Princess" (167). The two seem so remote in style and upbringing, politics and values, that they could not possibly cooperate. But when the novel's absurd and disastrous events reach their fateful climax, Buzzworm's care for her brings Emi to voice her appreciation: "Who'd a thought you and I'd get this close?" (253), and even to make a gesture of cross-race healing, in Emi's astonishing deathbed imitation of a resonant African American historical voice, that of Los Angeles beating victim Rodney King: "If *we* can just get along, maybe all our problems will go away" (253). Here parody and tribute mix, but through the dissonance, it is above all the profound saturation of U.S. culture with the prophetic voices of African Americans struggling against racism that creates the moment, and its suggestion of potential future solidarity.

This mimetic incident (discussed further in chapter 4) is emblematic of a kind of literary encounter with blackness that seems likely to become more prevalent:

engagement with the blackness of the culture that has become mutually the property of all Americans, as suggested by Ellison's comment (quoted in chapter 1), "Whatever else an American may be, he is also somehow black." For Asian Americans, as for Americans of all backgrounds, contemporary cultural production increasingly incorporates black cultural forms as part of a hybrid American inheritance—so well mixed, sometimes, that the African American origins of various elements are not necessarily recognized, and in which black styles themselves become increasingly hybridized by diverse global influences. It may thus become harder to detach some, particularly younger Asian American literary and cultural self-presentations from a youth idiom dense with black speech and musical styles, as in the considerable phenomenon of Asian American hip-hop.[12] A memorable example is the performance, in Renee Tajima-Peña's documentary *My America, or, Honk If You Love Buddha* (1996), by two Korean American Seattle brothers calling themselves the Seoul Brothers, of macho, in-your-face rap lyrics about the sexual prowess of Asian men, while one wears a Malcolm X "By any means necessary" t-shirt.

In the heterogeneous contemporary cultural output of Asian Americans, then, we may still find literary and popular cultural texts—especially male-authored ones—in which the black connection is a relationship of agon (a variation on which will appear in the next chapter, on Chang-rae Lee), and are likely to find texts in which that connection is vexed by discrepancies of class. But while, amidst the burgeoning interethnicity of our culture, visions of race become less binary and Asian-black relations more often embedded in multiplicity, and at the same time, paradoxically, this heterogeneous mix of culture is more and more saturated with black expressive and musical influence, we may expect to see a continuation of the trend of unembarrassed black-influenced aesthetic production and more and freer visions of interplay among Asian and African Americans, enmeshed in an ever-more variegated multiethnic, global matrix.

2

"With Darkness Yet"

Chang-rae Lee's Native Speaker*, Blackness, and the Interethnic Imagination*

In Chang-rae Lee's 1995 novel *Native Speaker*, a Korean American named Henry Park lives out an acute self-consciousness of his minoritized identity—and the lifelong performance of a good Asian boy it has required of him—by working as a spy, with a New York City bureau of ethnic chameleons trained to report on their own kind. His job requires that he continually adopt new personae in "a string of serial identity," so as to infiltrate the lives of a variety of New York Asians, "the whole transplanted Pacific Rim" (33, 17). Others in the office, depending on their stripe, do the Africans, the Latinos, the Eastern Europeans—all the newest American immigrants. The boss is a predatory white man who saw a "growth industry" in this immigration wave and cultivates ethnic spies to capitalize on it (18). Henry and his coworkers are never told who has commissioned them, but know the client is usually a foreign government, a multinational corporation—some bad guys who want the goods on a "well-to-do immigrant supporting some potential insurgency in his old land, or else funding a fledgling trade union or radical student organization" or "simply an agitator. Maybe a writer of conscience. An expatriate artist" (18).

The ethnic treason required by this work suggests the depth of bad faith in which this Asian American hero dwells, an alienation deepened by his estrangement from family, language, and culture. But the novel, despite its hero's abjection and the prevailing tone of malaise, is a remarkably poignant and beautiful one, its spy plot set amidst Henry's first-person narrative of a lifetime of losses: his embittered relationship with his father and early loss of his mother, his estrangement from his wife, and above all, the death of their seven-year-old son, who haunts the book. It is through the spy plot, however, that Henry's quest centrally proceeds, for he must choose his truest public face when assigned to bring down a man who embodies a great ethnic American civic ideal, the Korean American politician John Kwang, who dreams of uniting all the city's peoples in the "family" of his candidacy. When Henry takes on the role of volunteer in Kwang's mayoral campaign, the novel takes an ambitious turn beyond many ethnic fictions (and first novels), as the meditations on self and family open out, not only into chameleon performances of identity, but also into the question of an ethnic individual's role in the wider, multiethnic public sphere.

This chapter examines *Native Speaker* in the context of contemporary ethnic American fiction's interethnic imagination. Many elements of the novel are of course rooted in Asian American literary tradition—an acute first-person portraiture of a striving subject in a hostile American social world, dramatic generational conflicts within the immigrant family, a struggle with acculturation and compulsory language acquisition and performance. But as Lee has put it, in an interview cited in part earlier:

> [*Native Speaker*] is a response to what was . . . becoming expected of Asian-American writers—which was that we write these very circumscribed family stories, within-the-house kind of stories, where there's also a keen intergenerational conflict. . . . I wanted to widen the stage in which my character was going to act. I wanted an occupation for him in which he'd have to get out in the world and see others. . . . dealing with different immigrant populations . . . different languages and different forms and stages of English. . . . I wanted to put him in harm's way, or at some kind of risk so that he would have to put himself on the line and speak. . . . ("An Interview" 6)

As Lee's spy-protagonist invents and reinvents himself amidst the manifold currents of life in New York City, his narrative's energy rides the interethnic social and imaginative axis, in diverse plot encounters and in borrowings from ethnically different literary precursors. The novel's ambitious interethnic vision places Henry Park amidst the conflicting imperatives and attractions of whiteness, Koreanness, blackness, and the heterogeneous, diasporic urban crowd.

Some of Lee's most memorable passages, indeed, are his lyrical invocations of an interethnic sublime. An ambivalent poetics of the crowd is central to the life of this novel. Henry is at moments a Whitmanesque rhapsode among immigrant New York masses, cataloguing and admiring the "platoons of Koreans, Indians, Vietnamese, Haitians, Colombians, Nigerians, these brown and yellow whatevers, whoevers, countless unheard nobodies, each offering to the marketplace their gross of kimchee, lichee, plantain, black bean, soy milk, coconut milk, ginger, grouper, ahi, yellow curry . . ." (83). But at other moments, polar opposites of these resplendent, global crowd scenes, the novel evinces a horror of massed humanity, as in the scene of the tragic death of Henry's young son, smothered in a children's game, at the bottom of a pile of white boys. *Native Speaker*, I would argue, raises to view the ambivalence of the interethnic vision in our contemporary ethnic literatures. I begin this study's extended close readings with a novel that casts a conflicted, even an elegiac gaze at the multiethnic ideal, so as to deflect the prevailing reception of interethnic readings as so much happy multiculti celebration, and to demonstrate the more precise and serious attention that interethnic fiction deserves. I mean to show how alive contemporary fiction is to the fraught histories of racialization and intergroup relations in the United States, and to what degree its exploratory, affiliative imaginings are entwined with uncertainty, foreboding, even grief.

While relations between Asian Americans and whites dominate the foreground of the book, in this chapter I open with a different and perhaps unexpected relationship: the obscure but charged relationship to blackness. I propose that grappling with the place of blackness—both the novel's relationships to African American precursors and its handling of African American characters—in this large and ambitious text can help illuminate the ambivalent interethnic imaginary of the text as a whole, as will be seen in later sections on the novel's treatment of whiteness and of multiethnic crowds.

Reading *Native Speaker* one first encounters an assertive link to blackness on the cover, which shows the stark black, white, and silver-grey tones we have learned to associate with books by and about African Americans—particularly those that portray race conflict—with the subtle, strategic addition of a signifying red, for the East.[1] A large, black-outlined Asian face dominates the background, its mouth covered by a small, black and white photograph of an Asian child in a cowboy suit and hat, awkwardly aiming a toy gun. While the child is playing white (cowboy, Indian killer), the book is in a sense playing black; this cover places the hero iconographically dead center in America's heart of darkness. It is nothing new, of course, for Asian Americans to be understood as naturally "between black and white" in the structure of American race, or for this strange position of "thirdness" to be represented as an agonistic dilemma. But I would argue that Chang-rae Lee's engagement with African American culture, like that of the other contemporary writers centrally considered in this book, complicates the reductiveness of the "third" designation, rendering the position "between black and white" a space for creative, assimilative, sometimes contradictory articulation and exploration, in which the impulses toward both ethnic self-definition and cross-ethnic contest ultimately give way to an interethnic identificatory mode, a condition of multiple and complex affiliations.[2]

A book blurb by Frederick Busch reads, "From the wounded love of Asian Americans for their nation . . . Chang-rae Lee has composed a moving, edgy new blues." But what have the blues brought to Lee's wounds, or his wounds to a new blues? What does it mean for a Korean American book to be so black and blue? And how do we understand the place of blackness, of whiteness, of Koreanness in Lee's encompassing American vision, his hybrid revision of the Asian American novel?

The Place of Blackness

The first African American precursor we can't help but think of when we pick up *Native Speaker* is Richard Wright, the title of whose 1940 *Native Son* employs an irony similar to Lee's. For Wright's hero, Bigger Thomas, though born here among us, is a native son his homeland does not own or embrace, who grows up impoverished, disenfranchised, hopeless of making himself at home. Lee's Henry Park is also a native of the United States and is a gifted speaker, but he is not a native speaker of the English language, the indispensable currency in the immigrant's pocket. Instead, Henry is a native speaker of what he speaks, the story of his life,[3] told in exquisitely careful, school-acquired English, with some recourse to the Korean that is his first language. So the stark contradictions of the hero's condition in *Native Son* are evoked—or, I'd like to say, inherited—with a difference, for an Asian American hero. The second precursor is Ralph Ellison, who gave us a character whom race makes "invisible" and whom it drives underground. Few characters in American fiction between Ellison's hero and Lee's Henry Park have worn their offending racialized faces with as extreme an existential angst, or developed as sophisticated, poignant rhetorical revenge for what is projected upon them. You made me the strange creature I am, say Ellison's and Lee's shadowy protagonists to white America, and you provoked me into writing you this elegant, outraged book. Ellison's hero explains in opening: "I am invisible, understand, simply because people refuse to see me"; they see instead "my surroundings, themselves, or figments of their imagination—indeed, everything and anything except me" (*Invisible Man* 3). As a result, he tells us near the end, "I was never more hated than when I tried to be honest.... I've never been more loved and appreciated than when I tried to... give my friends the incorrect, absurd answers they wished to hear" (432). And he closes, famously, "Who knows but that, on the lower frequencies, I speak for you?" (439).

Here is Chang-rae Lee's hero, near his beginning and ending:

> I am an amiable man. I can be most personable, if not charming, and whatever I possess in this life is more or less the result of a talent I have for making you feel good about yourself when you are with me.... I am hardly seen. I won't speak untruths to you... or odious offerings of flattery. I make do with on-hand materials, what I can chip out of you, your natural ore. Then I fuel the fire of your most secret vanity. (7)

> I and my kind... will learn every lesson of accent and idiom, we will dismantle every last pretense and practice you hold, noble as well as ruinous. You can keep nothing safe from our eyes and ears. This is your own history. We are your most perilous and dutiful brethren, the song of our hearts at once furious and sad. For only you could grant me these lyrical modes. I call them back to you. Here is the sole talent I ever dared nurture. Here is all of my American education. (320)

Both Ellison's and Lee's nuanced forms of Caliban's retort depend upon a racialized trickster's knowing proximity to an oblivious white "you." The distance between Ellison's "I am invisible" and Lee's "I am hardly seen" suggests the somewhat lesser social dispossession suffered historically by Asian Americans, in comparison to African Americans. Yet perhaps *Native Speaker* surprises us with its "furious and sad" account of Korean American experience, with the degree of suffering and outrage it expresses from an "interstitial position in the American discourse of race" (E. Kim, "Home" 270).[4] The phrase, "your most perilous and dutiful brethren," offers a withering critique of the "model minority" stereotype, even while it claims a degree of intimacy to whites far beyond what we find in Ellison. But the two texts surely have in common the stamp of what Anne Anlin Cheng has called "racial melancholia," an irresolvable grief that is fundamental to racialized American identity. In Cheng's psychoanalytic reading, the relations of U.S. whites and nonwhites comprise a "complex process of racial rejection and desire" that results, for the minoritized subject, in consciousness of "a lost, never-possible perfection, an inarticulable loss that comes to inform the individual's sense of his or her own subjectivity" (xi). Cheng finds *Invisible Man* "a seminal text for theorizing invisibility *as* a trope for the melancholic incorporation of the self-as-loss" (127). "Self-as-loss" is a resonant phrase for the quality that Ellison's narrating persona seems to have bequeathed to Lee's, for Henry Park's lamentations for his lost son, mother, father, and marriage seem to point, further, to a loss at his very core, unspoken amidst the daily business of impersonating other selves. Cheng does not discuss *Native Speaker*, but I would call its hero, Henry Park, one of the fullest exemplars of racial melancholia that the canon of Asian American literature has yet yielded.

It is striking, then, that *Native Speaker* strongly links its grief to that of African American forerunners. And yet, negotiating its differences from them, Lee's novel makes no overt claim to a relationship with African American precursors, instead signaling its affiliation with blackness silently, as it were, symbolically through the title and suggestively in its echoes of Ellison. We may well suspect an agonistic course of inheritance, here. But if we look for allegorical enactment of such agon on the level of the plot, we see the hero's paternal conflict with Korean and white father figures only, not black ones. In what follows I will argue, then, that *Native Speaker*, keeping a melancholic distance from African Americans, strategically avoids a face-off or any significant plot engagement with black America. That is, Lee's plot acknowledges "the real violence and tension" between New York City's Korean American and African American communities (149), but ultimately decides not to go there, not to risk a Korean-black confrontation that might well devour the book. Thus, though one of the first Korean American fictions to take on the urban multiculture, *Native Speaker* treats black-Korean discord as an ongoing noise in the background, choosing silent invocation of rather than live interaction with African Americans. Examining this uneven attention to blackness within the novel's psychic economy—the contrast between a strong but muted literary tribute and avoidance of engagement in the plot—can help us grasp the ambivalent texture of this Korean American novel's interethnic vision.

*

Notably, Lee rarely presents African Americans in the hero's immediate experience; instead they are actual or potential antagonists of the novel's two Korean father figures. Henry's father, a grocer, argued daily with black customers about shoplifting, was once robbed and beaten by black gunmen, and "In the end, after all those years, he felt nothing for them. Not even pity. To him a black face meant inconvenience, or trouble, or the threat of death" (186). Henry recalls:

> To hear those cries now: the scene a stand of oranges, a wall of canned ham. I see my father in his white apron, sleeves rolled up. A woman in a dirty coat. They lean in and let each other have it, though the giving is almost in turns. It's like the most awful and sad opera, the strong music of his English, then her black English; her colorful, almost elevated, mocking of him, and his grim explosions. They fight like

> lovers, scarred, knowing. Their song circular and vicious. For she always comes back the next day, and so does he. It's like they are here to torture each other. He can't afford a store anywhere else but where she lives, and she has no other place to buy a good apple or a fresh loaf of bread. (186)

Even as this passage evenhandedly stages the "most awful and sad opera" of the Korean American/African American rivalry, giving dramatic force to each role in their mutual "torture," it freezes the performers in an archetypal, economically structural conflict that transpires elsewhere than on the main stage of the hero's plot, in a theater he apparently has been able to pass by without entering, perhaps especially as he has risen in education and class status. Race conflict is happening, the novel suggests, but our hero stands apart from it, observing its awful sadness.

Henry Park's narrative engages urban Korean-black tension more centrally and currently, however, in the plot of Kwang, the wonderfully imagined politician—"Handsome, irreproachable. Silver around the edges. A little unbeatable" (23)—whose embrace of the vast metropolis that he dares to imagine united makes him a remarkable figure:

> Before I knew of him, I had never even conceived of someone like him. A Korean man, of his age, as part of the vernacular. Not just a respectable grocer or dry cleaner or doctor, but a larger public figure who was willing to speak and act outside the tight sphere of his family. He displayed an ambition. . . . I hadn't yet envisioned as something a Korean man would find . . . worthy of energy and devotion. . . . (139)

Devoted to his own family, Kwang "loved the pure idea of family as well, which in its elemental version must have nothing to do with blood" (146). He calls his staff and constituents "a family," and makes each person whose hand he shakes feel "that you were the faintest brother to him" (279, 138). Through Kwang's populist candidacy, Lee interrogates the limits of American affiliation. Can family feeling extend beyond blood ties; "can you really make a family of thousands?" (326). Over the novel's course, Korean-black troubles raise the greatest challenge to Kwang's inclusive vision. He continually seeks concord, conferring with black church leaders; mediating talks over black-led boycotts of Korean-owned stores; and appearing at deathbeds and funerals of victims on both sides of the violence. And in a key speech, he pleads with New Yorkers:

> [L]et's think together in a different way. . . . Let us think that . . . it is not a Korean problem. That it is not a black problem or a brown and yellow problem. . . .
>
> The problem is our acceptance of what we loathe and fear in ourselves. Not in the other, not in the person standing next to you. . . . No! No, no! . . .
>
> This person, this person, she, that person, he . . . they're like us, they are us, they're just like you! (151–52)

Kwang's remarkable speeches, evoking in their humane, empathic vision our memory of Martin Luther King, Jr., place an impassioned plea for black-Korean (and multiethnic) unity at the heart of *Native Speaker*. And yet, oddly enough, Lee offers us no major African American character; indeed, only one African American actually speaks in the novel. The black members of the spy bureau do not figure in Henry's plot. Kwang's electoral opposition is the white mayor and his party machine; the public conflict with New York City blacks does not ultimately generate a challenge to his candidacy. And when Kwang's headquarters are firebombed, responsibility is found to lie at home, not with the African American community. When an antagonist does arise to spur Kwang's inevitable fall, he is a Latino, a campaign volunteer named Eduardo, a son of Dominican immigrants who in a salient plot twist turns out to be Henry's double, a character fighting precisely Henry's demons. Parallel to Henry in terms of his family history of immigration, labor, and acculturation struggles, Eduardo (though a Dominican might be dark-skinned and of part-African ancestry) is, crucially, never positioned socially as an "African American," but rather as a Latino immigrant, and thus is marginal enough to the novel's main concerns to be a notable but not scene-stealing sacrifice. In an early scene, the Latino volunteer is the recipient of this sardonic tribute from Kwang's media strategist, the Polish American Janice Pawlowsky:

> "You're the only real thing, Eddy".... She looked at me. "Henry and I, we were secretly Reagan Democrats. Selfish cowards. Admit it, I will. I know you Koreans."
>
> "Never," I said.
>
> "See?" Janice told him. "You're the best thing we have. Our party loves you, Eduardo. To death."
>
> "I love the party," he answered tepidly. "I love the party." (91–92)

My point is that the "real thing" the Democratic Party loves to death might well have been an African American, but had Lee created a treasonous African American campaign worker (Kwang seems to have none), the entire emphasis—even the meaning—of the novel would have changed, indelibly seared by Korean-black strife. Instead, Lee keeps this particular conflict simmering in the background of his "edgy new blues" for the multiethnic city.[5]

What does this choice suggest about the political imaginary of Lee's Korean American novel? One reading might consider it in light of the politics of Kwang, who refuses to sensationalize the exaggerated discord that makes "the easiest 11 P.M. drama" on the local news (192). "It's a race war everyone can live with," he comments mordantly, "Blacks and Koreans somehow seem meant for trouble in America" (181). Suspecting that this script serves the interests of the powerful, Kwang will not perform it further for their satisfaction. Chang-rae Lee, too, can be seen to resist contributing to or exploiting this particular interethnic spectacle.

But in a different vein, we might read the avoidance of overt engagement with blacks on the model of traditional Korean expressive silence, so resonant in Henry's psyche and story. When he discovers late in the novel that Kwang is guilty of a grave crime, Henry refrains from reporting it, as a "final honoring to Kwang, my last offering, which is the sole way of giving I have known in my life: an omission, solemn and prone" (314). Perhaps Lee similarly omits outright conflict between Koreans and blacks as an honoring of and an offering to the African American cultural tradition from which he inherits so rich a fund of expressive resources. Though his plot sets up the possibility that Lee's own people and this other people could be real opponents in a contest for American dignity, cultural capital, or other resources, he steps away from the confrontation, allowing it to dissolve into nothingness, a distraction, a false clue to the novel's mystery. Lee will not make blacks into enemies, originators of the structure of racialized urban U.S. economic conflict, though he also will not erase the historical reality of recent violent clashes between Koreans and African Americans.

Lee's vision, then, requires delicate management of this and other historical contradictions, so as to keep hope of interethnic mutuality alive while narrating the sad course of a youthful acculturation to racialized American logic. As Jelena Šesnić has put it, "Lee both engages the sinister aspect of the ethnic/racial roster in American society based on the way . . . subjects are interpellated [within] . . . racial stratification and tries to transcend its constricting models" ("Histories" 99). The novel's rich chiaroscuro, its highs and lows, inscribe a fidelity to this nuanced engagement. At the same time, to note that *Native Speaker* embeds its hero in a symbolic, literary alliance with African Americans while downplaying plot relations—good or bad—with black characters, is to suggest that the novel employs strategies of repression not entirely unlike those cogently analyzed by Toni Morrison in the canon of white American literature. For Morrison, literature by white Americans has long denied the shaping presence of African Americans, but "[e]ven, and especially, when American texts are not 'about' Africanist presences or characters or narrative or idiom, the shadow hovers in implication, in sign, in line of demarcation" (*Playing* 47). A reader might well say that African Americans are absent from the foreground of *Native Speaker* because the novel simply isn't "about" them, but as Morrison puts it, "certain absences are so stressed, so ornate, so planned, they call attention to themselves; arrest us with intentionality and purpose, like neighborhoods that are defined by the population held away from them" ("Unspeakable" 24). In an extraordinary passage that suggests how deeply Lee's *Native Speaker* knows—yet needs to avoid fully addressing—the role of African Americans in Korean American psychic "neighborhoods," the hero recalls his immigrant mother in his suburban youth:

> I remember thinking of her, *What's she afraid of*, what could be so bad that we had to be that careful of what people thought of us, as if we ought to mince delicately about in pained feet through our immaculate neighborhood, we silent partners of the bordering WASPS and Jews, never rubbing them except with a smile, as if everything with us were always all right, in our great sham of propriety, as if nothing could touch us or wreak anger or sadness upon us. That we believed in anything American, in impressing Americans, in making money, polishing apples in the dead of night, perfectly pressed pants, perfect credit, being perfect, shooting black people, watching our stores and offices burn down to the ground. (52–53)[6]

The "ornateness" with which the text here frames and circumscribes its knowledge of violent, urban rivalry with blacks contributes to the shock of the images. To be sure, Lee's hero himself does not voice the racist hostilities, locating them instead in the behavior of his parents, at a generation's remove. Still, the strange contradiction between yearning toward and self-distancing from blacks is a salient element of the novel's portrayal of the Korean American condition within a layered, multiethnic landscape. What can it mean to pay literary tribute to the people from whom one must at all costs separate oneself, in the "great sham of propriety" that is the performance of assimilation to whiteness? To place oneself in the literary line of those whose demise, even, may be required by one's ethnic performance of Americanness?

Such maneuvering certainly recalls Irish, Jewish, and other European American immigrants' self-distancing from blackness in the upward climb to the status of whiteness, a subject developed by Morrison, Michael Rogin, and others.[7] Yet the specificity of the reference to violence here marks a difference. For Lee's novel was written in the aftermath of violent incidents involving Koreans and African Americans in U.S. cities of the early 1990s, including several murders of black shoppers and Korean shopkeepers, and most vividly, the 1992 L.A. riots that followed the acquittal of the police officers who beat black motorist Rodney King,[8] a recent history that brought intense media and public attention to the troubled relations among minority populations in the poorest and most violent U.S. urban neighborhoods. Scholars have castigated the media's scant consideration of the historically overdetermined causes of the riot.[9] For Korean Americans in particular, the events of *sa-i-ku* (April 29) left many bewildered to find themselves both victims of violent looting by Latinos and blacks, and abandoned by the (white) police who for three days ignored their calls for help. While the press tended to cast them in the light of oppressors and vigilantes, Elaine Kim describes Korean Americans' "initiation into becoming American": "Korean Americans [have been required to] take on this country's legacy of five centuries of racial violence and inequality, of divide and rule, of privilege for the rich and oppression of the poor," and "assigned a place on the front lines" ("Home" 220).

This painful history complicates *Native Speaker*'s impulse to append itself to the mythically central minority American condition. As suggested earlier, the allusions to Wright and Ellison symbolically position Korean Americans in solidarity with the marginalization and oppositional identity of African Americans. And yet, despite the cynicism and chagrin with which the novel regards Asian-white relations, the plot places Korean Americans as a group in overt hostilities with African Americans only, while it portrays them performing before whites an assimilist "perfection" that masks a subtle antagonism—recalling, ironically, the Invisible Man. Its hero locked in ambivalent proximity to whites, *Native Speaker* refrains from approaching the people it invokes as literary fathers, a distance haunted by longing, by guilt, and by violence.

Surely there is admiring imitation of African American styles of masculinity in Lee's echoes of the cool, removed rhetoric of Ellisonian critique, and surely black men are invoked as well as in the scene in which Henry and Kwang attempt to joke together "like regular American men, faking, dipping, juking" (179). The phrase "regular American men" is yoked, interestingly, to what seem to be specifically black masculine cultural practices. Though "juking," according to the OED, is what one does to the music at juke joints, and "faking" and "dipping" carry associations with musical improvisation and picking pockets, the three terms suggest more readily the artful strategies of football players, boxers, and basketball players.[10] This muted tribute to our Africanized culture is mediated by histories of the denigration of Asian American and the fetishization of African American masculinity. Indeed, the problem of Henry's masculinity might well be described by the title of David Eng's *Racial Castration*, which examines how "the Asian American male is both materially and psychically feminized within the context of a larger U.S. cultural imaginary" (2). Having rejected his Asian immigrant father's ways of being a man, Henry does not develop a stable Asian American masculinity for himself, but rather practices an emptying out of the self in favor of chameleon performances of others.[11] This version of the Asian American man's racialized emasculation is all the more perverse in that it is explicitly required by the corporate vision of a white man, his banally sinister boss, Dennis. Henry thus "achieve[s] his masculine identification," in Šesnić's words, "under the aegis of [a] . . . corporate-sponsored 'ethnic identity' . . . a virtual, symbolic, interchangeable mask that can be donned at will" ("Histories" 103).

But the figure of John Kwang offers a promising, alternate masculine model for the hero, as well as "a redemptive potential to engage primarily his own racial identity and subsequently other positions" (Šesnić 103). In Henry's relationship with this substitute father, Lee chooses—in contrast to the anguished searches in Frank Chin's writing for white and especially black father figures—a yearning toward a Korean father who embodies the tantalizing possibility of a Korean American masculinity the hero might actually want to own. Yet it is significant that Henry's homosocial bonding with Kwang is mediated by black American masculinity and, moreover, that Kwang and Henry engage in their "blackface" play ("faking, dipping, juking") just as the undercurrent of rivalry in their relationship intensifies. In the suggestive nexus of the hero's relations with this Korean father figure and the book's relations with blackness, then, distanced imitation—Derridean *differance*, if you will—stands in for any real achievement of intimacy or masculine identification.

To return to the problematics of Asian American masculine identification with black men, we might consider in what form *Native Speaker* manifests "triangulated racial desire," in James Kim's theory an "ambivalent desire for a racial other circulated through a system of three terms" (165). Examining the dynamics of violent, white male fantasy about black and Asian male bodies in the Hollywood martial arts film *Romeo Must Die*, Kim argues that the film's "yellow male figure" is constructed so as to mediate "white male fantasies" and "anxieties" about the black male body (162–65). I would suggest that in Lee's novel the Asian American protagonist is the subject rather than the object of such desire: Henry desires both to be white (to assimilate) and to resist whiteness through identification with blackness (so as to attain masculinity as well as to resist whiteness in the modes of black men). But while the former desire is the impossibility upon which the U.S. racial structure and racial melancholia rest, the latter is frustrated by the reality of urban black-Asian hostility. In a sense, this Asian American hero must give up his desire for blackness, must sacrifice a potential black affiliation, because of the white assimilation imperative. The failure of desires for—or to be like—blacks adds another dimension of melancholia, I believe, to Henry's racialized condition; this is to say, building on Cheng, that a racialized subject can suffer loss not only in his or her abjection relative to normative whiteness, but also in the failure of his/her longing to unite with others in marginalized conditions. Indeed, I would identify

Henry's silence before African Americans, and the novel's odd distance from a people to whose literary expressivity it is indebted, as above all as a melancholy, a grieving silence.

Among the many losses *Native Speaker* mourns, then, is a lack of relationship with, or recognition of kinship by, African Americans. Indeed, Daniel Y. Kim has argued that Kwang's impassioned addresses to black listeners, ("Know that what we have in common, the sadness and pain and injustice, will always be stronger than our differences" [153]), inspired in part by Kwang's own awed, youthful witness to African American activism, evince a distinct "political yearning," even a "political fantasy" in the novel:

> What is being conjured in . . . these rhetorical performances is the image of an avowedly liberal or progressive Asian American public figure speaking to an audience that is significantly African American and engendering in them a sense of cross-racial identification and solidarity. . . . in the same way that, in an earlier era, black figures captivated the political imagination of the first generation of Asian American activists. (240–41)

Actively and optimistically through the public figure of Kwang, then, and passively and pessimistically through the melancholy observer Henry Park, Lee articulates a powerful longing to connect Korean and African American aspirations, even to bring blacks to recognize their mutuality with Korean American people.

Readers witness the failure of that recognition in one plot moment in particular. Whenever Lee's Korean American characters discuss relations with African Americans in the novel, they do so in broadly political and economic terms, as a structural phenomenon that a belated Asian American has little chance of changing. "It's still a black and white world," Henry laments, and Kwang replies, "It seems so, Henry, doesn't it?" "[S]oon," he notes, "there will be more brown and yellow than black and white," and yet "the politics . . . barely acknowledge us" (195–96). Henry observes that "African- Americans didn't seem to trust [Kwang]" as a rule (142), and Kwang notes that black politicians approve of him only when he follows their agenda, but when he offers other ideas ("special enterprise zones or more openness toward immigrants"), "I'm whitey's boy" (194–95). "[T]here must be a way to speak truthfully," he laments, "and not be demonized or made a traitor." Henry's reply: "'Very softly,' I said to him, offering the steady answer of my life. 'And to yourself'" (197).

Speech, of course, provides the guiding metaphor in this novel notably mistrustful of the communicative powers of speech. Henry often contrasts speech unfavorably with the more refined suggestions of Korean silence; and despite the word-smitten quality of his narration, he is prone to understatement and ambiguity. Amidst this general reticence, however, it is striking that Henry's one explicit statement on the limits of speech, in his response to Kwang, above, occurs in the context of failed communication with African Americans. Indeed, Henry speaks with a black person only once in the novel.

When Kwang stops on the street to mediate a dispute between a disgruntled African American customer and a Korean jewelry shop owner, and takes the owner aside to urge a compromise, Henry notices and ventures to remark to the black man that they share the same name—in a telling coincidence, "Henry" is displayed on the other man's shirt tag. But this bid for equalizing recognition receives little response, and so the hero "didn't say anything else" (184), not even when the black Henry criticizes the "cold" demeanor of the Korean shop owner: "I didn't try to explain the store owner to Henry, or otherwise defend him. I don't know what stopped me. Maybe there was too much to say." Abandoning, when dialogue fails, the potential for cross-race mutuality so obviously signaled by the doubled name, Henry goes on to say much—to his readers—about his father's relations with racial Others: how he "saw his customers as adversaries," hated to explain his high prices to wealthy Manhattan customers but "always did," while "[w]ith blacks he just turned to stone. He never bothered to explain his prices to them. . . . [H]e always let them know there wasn't going to be any *funny business* here" (185).

The near-impossibility of the hero's explaining himself to black people seems one endpoint to interethnic communication in this Korean American novel, while at the opposite end are Kwang's open-hearted political outreach to the African American community; the cross-race sharing of a name; and the extended literary tribute to black cultural texts. Thus, though *Native Speaker* at times registers a capacity for soaring interethnic vision, one might say that blackness marks the sad incompleteness of its hybridity.

A reading of Lee's novel as marked by frustrated desire for interracialism strongly recalls Frank Chin's play *The Chickencoop Chinaman* (1972), discussed in the Asian/African interchapter, as well as Daniel Y. Kim's account of the ambivalent, sometimes antagonistic "interracial mimetic desire" toward black masculinity in Chin's work. Clearly Chang-rae Lee has in Frank Chin a much more violently agonistic precursor in yellow male melancholia, especially in the resultant "racial self-loathing," a hatred of white men turned back upon the Asian American self; in Kim's paraphrase: "I thus hate you by hating the me I have become in your image. . . . [I] hate with a passion and a vengeance the assimilated identity that is [my] own" (*Writing* 200–201). Lee's Henry Park shows a similar pattern of powerfully mixed emotions toward white and black male figures and a similar entrapment in melancholic self-loathing, but I would locate a signal difference in Lee's avoidance of the homophobic (and misogynistic) plague that taints Chin's writing. Yellow masculine anxiety in Lee simply does not generate a need to denigrate gays or women[12]—indeed, Lee's treatment of the central female figure, Henry's wife, Lelia, might even be called a feminist one, given the authority of her presence, her choices, and her views in the hero's narrative. Moreover, the unabashed treatment of Henry's relationship with Kwang in the terms of "a kind of romance" (139)[13] represents a great step beyond melancholic, mimetic interracial desire and beyond homophobia. One might even venture that Lee places Kwang, a figure of viable Asian American masculinity, precisely in the symbolic position where one might have expected to find—where Chin would have placed—a black man (recall Kwang's echoes of M. L. King, his play at boxing with his young aides, his ease and familiarity with black men). Kwang in this sense notably offers to the hero a form of homosocial masculine bonding, which, because it does not rest upon the supposed superior masculinity of blacks or whites, is not feminizing for the Asian American male subject.

This Korean American father fails, however, both as a family man and as the father of a broader, national "family," and his tragic flaws (as well as the symbolic rejection of his "wide immigrant face" by the U.S. polity [343], in the forms of both the federal government and his own ethnic New York constituency) ultimately make him no more a solution to Henry's melancholic quest than are his actual father or any white or black father figures in his world.

It is striking, then, that what plot-level realism cannot bear out, Lee manages to affirm by other means. While masculine identification disappoints in the hero's plot, Lee sustains, in the realm of literary intertextuality, lively relations with a multiracial cast of father figures. He might be said, as Kim says of Chin and Ellison, to represent an "idealized" resolution of "hybrid homosocial desire" through this "complexly agonistic interplay of authorial voices," as well as by constructing in his writerly narrator "a *masculine* figure who speaks back from the racial margins, whose linguistic prowess lies in his deft capacity to repeat parodically and subversively the languages that constitute the center" (38–40). This account is suggestive for the less violently aggressive but still complex dynamics of Lee's repetition of Wright and Ellison, as well as of Shakespeare, Walt Whitman, spy and detective novelists, and so on. In the case of Chang-rae Lee, I would say that if literary allusion works to assert an Asian American masculine position amongst male masters, it is equally a means of sending out filaments of love, longing, respect, and brotherhood. In regard to black men in particular, I am arguing, it is in the less governed, dreamwork realm of intertextuality that Lee draws the sympathetic connections from which his plot demurs.

Henry Park's narrative encompasses both the rarest kind of empathic, interethnic identification and the failure of communication and of generosity under the alienating pall of racialization. To span such contradictions is, of course, one of the capacities of the novel as a genre; as Lee sends his Korean American hero into the multiculture, and the plot of ethnic identity quest into the broad social matrix of a globalized novel, he richly complicates our sense of an Asian American literary text's cultural positioning, and shows how nuanced and multidimensional such a novel's imaginative work can be.

Speaking to Whiteness

How can we place *Native Speaker*'s intricate orchestration of relations with blackness within its representations of a larger multicultural scenario? Certainly Lee's hero/narrator is more overtly preoccupied with whiteness, Koreanness, and the most recently immigrated American populations than he is with African Americans. Yet even in its engagement with whiteness the novel shows the shaping influence of its black literary precursors, which offer an array of strategies for critique from the smoldering margins. Prominent among these is the trope of the anonymous but clearly white readerly "you," whom Henry accuses (in a passage cited earlier) of shaping his melancholy story: "This is your own history. We are your most perilous and dutiful brethren.... For only you could grant me these lyrical modes. I call them back to you" (320). The very narration of his story to such a "you" becomes, simultaneously, a struggle with the dominant culture's authority to define him: "[C]all me what you will. An assimilist, a lackey. A duteous foreign-faced boy . . . [who has] already been whatever you can say or imagine, every version of the newcomer who is . . . fearing and bitter and sad" (160). Lee marks a key difference from the dominant conventions of mid- to late twentieth-century African American and Asian American fiction both, however, in giving white characters a central place in his plot. In the novel's foreground is Henry's marriage to a white woman, Lelia, a canny and intuitive character who gives English speech lessons to the impaired and the newly immigrated. "Unfortunately," she says, "I'm the standard bearer" (12). In their first conversation, Lelia remarks that she can tell that Henry is not a native English speaker, for he speaks too carefully, evidently listening to himself. The choice of such a partner, sympathetic but forever on the other side of the native/foreign divide that Lee's title articulates, is a loaded one for Henry, who as a child suffered the humiliation of selection for speech therapy ("raised by language experts, saved from the wild" [232]). A profound ambivalence, then, characterizes Henry's relations with whiteness as well as with blackness. Indeed, over the course of a book that begins with Henry's wife's departure, his troubled marriage is emblematic of Henry's unresolved relations with white America, his incomplete integration into the nation, in the terms Patricia P. Chu has used to describe the marriageability of Asian American bildungsroman heroes (19).

To be sure, *Native Speaker* is suffused with the malaise of an assimilist's desire. Like many ethnic American characters, Henry Park has an emotionally fraught relationship to the cultural traits of his immigrant parents that he sees as impeding his struggle to join the mainstream. He learned the Korean practice of silence from his work-driven, unexpressive father, a huge figure in the novel, who uses his authority to quell speech: "*Let's not hear one more thing about it. . . . This is what I have decided. Our talk is past usefulness. There will be no other way*" (64); and from his mother, for whom "displays of emotion signaled a certain failure between people," and who "possessed the most exquisite control over the muscles of her face," seeming "to have the subtle power of inflection over them, the way a tongue can move air" (31). The issue of silence in Asian American literature and culture has been a highly contested one. In *Articulate Silences*, King-kok Cheung reclaims silence from Orientalist projections, asserting that it is not simply a "pure Asian [attribute]," but also an Asian American survival strategy, "overdetermined by both ancestral mores and exclusionary forces in North America" (3, 20). Henry has contradictory feelings toward his own silence, which creates friction in his interethnic marriage: "When real trouble hits," says Henry, "I lock up," "the worst response" in the view of the candid and voluble Lelia, "who grew up with hollerers and criers" and so "can't hide a single thing . . . looks hurt when she is hurt, seems happy when happy" (158–59). His muteness after the death of their child, in particular, outrages her, seeming a failure to share the mourning. But Henry continues to honor his Korean training in silence, even as he internalizes her outsider's critique of his cultural difference: "I celebrate every order of silence borne of the tongue and the heart and the mind. I am a linguist of the field. You, too, may know the troubling, expert power. It finds hard expression in the faces of those who would love you most" (171). Indeed, he sometimes longs to recover the different expressivity of his parents' home, as when, speaking to Kwang, he finds that "our English can't touch what I want to say," and wishes instead "to call the simple Korean back to him the way I once could. . . . [O]ur comely language of distance and bows, by which real secrets may be slowly courted, slowly unveiled" (275).

I take exception, then, to a reading of the novel by Tim Engles that characterizes Henry as a character entirely colonized by "doxic whiteness" and "virtually sever[ed] . . . from the culture of his parents" (28–29), who blames Korean "emotional reticence" for preventing his "sympathizing with the pain of others," thus "allowing him to exploit minority targets for the shadowy clients of his employer" (30). In my view, Henry blames not Korean culture but the searing effects of the assimilation imperative for making him a self-alienated spy. This is clear in the vignettes of his youth, such as when he steps outside before dawn into a world seemingly "unpeopled save for me. No Korean father or mother, no taunting boys or girls, no teachers showing me how to say my American name," and then "run[s] back inside" to the mirror, "desperately hoping in that solitary moment to catch a glimpse of who I truly was," only to find "the same boy again, no clearer than before, unshakably lodged in that difficult face" (323). Such experiences train Henry for a spy's career:

> I had always thought that I could be anyone, perhaps several anyones at once. [The spy job] . . . offer[ed] the perfect vocation for the person I was, someone who could reside in his one place and take half-steps out whenever he wished. . . . I thought I had finally found my truest place in the culture. (127)

Finding one's "truest place" in the chameleon contrivances of espionage may allow moments of a certain subversive, performative freedom—escape from an assigned, minoritized role into performances of one's own design—but ultimately Henry knows this career path as self-annihilation. Similarly, he admits complicity in his own cultural alienation. When he becomes a father, "[t]he truth of my feeling, exposed and ugly to me now, is that I . . . was hoping whiteness for Mitt . . . fearful of what I might have bestowed on him: all that too-ready devotion and honoring, and the chilly pitch of my blood" (285). He even avoids reading to Mitt in his imperfect English, hoping "that he would grow up with a singular sense of his world, a life univocal, which might have offered him the authority and confidence that his broad half-yellow face could not." "Of course," he adds, "this is assimilist sentiment, part of my own ugly and half-blind romance with the land" (267). While acknowledging his part in these uglinesses, however, Henry places blame ultimately on the doxic standard itself, personified in that intimate antagonist, the readerly "you."

Rather than total colonization by whiteness, then, Henry narrates his combative cohabitation with it.[14] In a novel in which nothing is simply black and white, relations with whiteness, blackness, Koreanness, and every shade of being become matters of ambivalence and nuance, and narrative desire unfolds among multiple ethnic, cultural, and literary modes of affiliation. If whiteness holds the hero in its thrall in certain ways, he is also enthralled in a melancholy way by blackness, as well as by the shaping influence of his family and ethnic cohort, and, especially toward the novel's ending, by the heterogeneous "family" to which he knows he also belongs, that of the global, multiethnic city. This, *Native Speaker* shows us, is how an Asian American self is now made. Not merely black, or white, or a third something else, this novel's open-ended construction of Asian Americanness exceeds binaries and boundaries, alive to a variety of entanglements and loyalties.

Into the Multiculture

What makes *Native Speaker* emblematic of the contemporary interethnic shift is the way it offers the ethnic subject—the racialized, melancholic, "castrated" subject in a triangulated racial situation—a fourth way out, so to say, a fourth axis of desire: the axis of interethnicity, along which I would place several key relationships: Henry's relationship to his city, to his son, and to John Kwang. Beyond the spy plot, the love plot, and the immigrant family plot, *Native Speaker* is a rhapsodic tribute to the multicultural city of New York. Henry identifies with, even loves, the heterogeneous urban crowd[15]—the Whitmanian intensity and lyricism of his attachment suggestive, even, of a libidinal tie, which Freud tells us, can bind the members of groups as well as it does lovers and families (35). Erotic energy in this sense extends in the book far beyond Lelia and the child Mitt to diverse others across the metropolis, especially in Queens:

> Still, I love it here. I love these streets lined with big American sedans and livery cars and vans. I love the early morning storefronts opening up one by one, shopkeepers talking as they crank their awnings down. I love how the Spanish disco thumps out from windows, and how the people propped halfway out still jiggle and dance in the sill and frame. I follow the strolling Saturday families of brightly wrapped Hindus and then the black-clad Hasidim, and step into all the old churches that were once German and then Korean and are now Vietnamese. And I love the brief Queens sunlight at the end of the day, the warm lamp always reaching through the westward tops of that magnificent city. (346)

Even Henry's much less sanguine portraits of the city unfold in such lyrically mounting phrases and end with such disarming appeals to love or charity that they manage to cast rays of beauty over the grittiest scenes. In a passage cited in part earlier, he muses upon early morning laborers:

> [A]lways loading and unloading the light trucks and cube vans of stapled wooden crates and burlap sacks, the bulging bags of produce like turnips or jicama as heavy on their sloping shoulders as the bodies of their children still asleep at home. They were of all kinds, these streaming and working and dealing, these various platoons of Koreans, Indians, Vietnamese, Haitians, Colombians, Nigerians . . . selling anything to each other and to themselves, every day of the year, and every minute.
>
> John Kwang's people.
>
> They must have loved him. (82–83)

Lee transfigures the crowded, noisy scene of the mix of working people by the wonder in Henry's attention to them, by his rapt immersion in human multiplicity.

Even the specter of violence becomes an occasion for his fascination with the city's rich cultural mix. When the TV news reports a Cuban taxi driver shot dead in the Bronx, "the fifth or sixth driver murdered in the last two months," Henry watches the frightened cabbies interviewed on the screen, "recently arrived Latvians and Jamaicans, Pakistanis, Hmong," so different from one another that "there's nobody who can speak for the drivers as a group." He thinks:

> What they have in common are the trinkets from their homelands swaying from the rearview mirror, the strings of beads, shells, the brass letters, the blurry snapshots of their small children, the night-worn eyes. I wonder if the Cuban could even beg for his life so that the killer might understand. What could he do? *Have mercy*, should be the first lesson in this city, how to say the phrase instantly in forty signs and tongues. (246)

Evident Whitmanian tropes in these passages include anaphora ("I love, "I love") and parataxis ("these . . . , these . . . ," "the . . . , the . . . ,"); the parades of named peoples and the lists of the things they proffer or prize, and most compellingly, the God's-eye view that in each passage rains "love" or "mercy" upon it all. Surely Whitman's ghost walks with Henry in the New York both love. The will to mastery suggested by this channeling of Walt's encompassing outlook on the multitudinous American throng is unusual among "emasculated" Asian American fictional protagonists.[16] But if Whitman is precursor to Henry's rapturous summoning of the crowd, the epigraph from his poem "The Sleepers" that opens Lee's book connects him to Henry's inward, alienated mode as well:

> I turn but do not extricate myself,
> Confused, a past-reading, another,
> but with darkness yet.

This portrait of the darkened soul enmeshed in complexities past and present, estranged even from himself ("another"), well describes Henry's persona throughout much of the book. Like Whitman, Lee sets a brooding soul abroad in scenes of human vitality and strife, finding in crowds a now melancholy, now uplifting affiliation. But would it be overreaching to read Lee's choice of epigraph via Toni Morrison and find in this yearning loner's abiding place "with darkness yet" the quiet claim to one particular interethnic solidarity, even one special, inspiriting intimacy?[17]

Notably, the observing eye of the crowd passages tends not to light upon African Americans, but rather upon members of the most recent immigration waves. The trope of the multicultural crowd allows Lee's hero a fuller embrace of otherness than do any encounters with African Americans. Still, the black relationship is the site of the novel's greatest ambivalence, the greatest challenge to easy multicultural mastery, and so the filaments extended to darkness amidst the broader vista help us see that the novel counterbalances its attraction to the interethnic axis with acknowledgments of real failures on the level of the plot. The extra-ethnic literary affiliations—to the cool outrage of African American literature, to the expansive, inclusive gaze of Whitman—work to realize what the plot finds not yet possible. The truths of realism and the truths of shared, inspirited literary vision are both upheld. What the plot cannot make happen, Lee works to accomplish aesthetically, embedding a more idealist vision in his richly imbricated, allusive narrative texture.[18]

This accommodation of both a cynical and a utopian politics, of impulses melancholic and sublime, occurs even amidst the robust rhetorical sweep of the crowd passages, in which empathy is sometimes brought up short by the reductive urban glance: "these brown and yellow whatevers, whoevers, countless unheard nobodies," and in which the sublimity of diverse peoples' convergence may be undercut by the specter of their doing violence to one another. Indeed, the novel holds the trope of the wondrous crowd in tension with a real ambivalence about the experience of the crowd—and indeed of any group identification, for the individual. It may be, in fact, that a focus on categories like ethnicity and race is not subtle enough to illuminate Lee's vision of our lives among others, his meditative oscillation between the hero and his city, between the experiential and imaginative range of the self and the promise and danger of the heterogeneous crowd. Powerfully attracted to the energy and multiplicity of mass scenes, the novel also conveys a nearly elegiac sense of the preciousness of the individual, whom the crowd might render a nobody, or literally kill. In a moment when Henry is discussing Lelia—who has left him for a time—with a female friend who is at a pay phone, as they speak he can "hear the street behind her, the din of a thousand hurried movements, my wife maybe becoming just one of them, hidden and indistinguishable" (113). And again, as she wails and rocks her son in the moments after his sudden death, Lelia "sounded like someone else, an anybody on the street" (105). The anxiety about the loss of human uniqueness is especially intense in passages in which Henry seeks—almost obsessively—the language to recapture those who have died, such as his father, in his last days "a kind of aging soldier of this life, a squat, stocky-torsoed warrior, bitter, never self-pitying, fearful, stubborn, world-fucking heroic" (48), or his co-worker Jack's wife, Sophie, whose picture Henry studies for the "[i]ndelible . . . last clues to a beautiful woman" (26, 36).

Most indelibly remembered is Henry and Lelia's son, Mitt, whose death at age seven steeps the narrative in grief. Little is actually said about this enormous loss; instead the reticent Henry scatters vignettes of Mitt throughout his narration, invoking his existence rather than lamenting his absence, so that the unspoken loss of him comes to convey the absolute irreplaceability of a person. Describing the large loft apartment in which he and Lelia live, Henry pauses to add one detail to the setting: "I can still see Mitt running wind sprints back and forth down the length of the room, hear the patter of his socked feet, see him sliding the last few yards, twirling to a halt, some beautiful kid" (24). Through Mitt, Lee pays tribute to the undeserved gift of a person; the boy is "some wondrous thing" (285), "the clean and bright one—somehow, miraculously, ours" who "runs off with . . . [the other kids] shouting the praises of his perfect life" (100). Delivered in the wake of this perfect life, Henry's narrative seems an elegy for the perfect promise of human life itself.

Yet inseparable from the sense of lost possibility that Mitt embodies is the wonder of his blended genetic inheritance, displayed, as Henry puts it, in "his boy's form . . . so beautifully jumbled and subversive and historic. No one, I thought, had ever looked like that" (103). The treatment of Mitt's character suggests that the individual is precious in an ultimate sense because he/she is so elusive, beyond social categories or ethnic labels, beyond the reach of words. Individuality as Lee embodies it in Mitt—or in Henry—is something lived between and among nameable identities, richly shaped by, but incompletely described by, identification with any one group, defined instead by multiple and incommensurable influences, alignments, inheritances. The relationship of an individual to a group, in Lee's vision, is more elusive than we make it seem, not the simple mathematics of part to whole, and thus is a useful wedge to critique ethnic conceptualizations. What, after all, is "the truest place" of the individual, in the ordinary welter of life, amidst the tensions and juxtapositions of a multiethnic, globalized city? Should Henry understand himself foremost through the connection of blood, the ethnic definition of self learned at home, "that tie unspoken and unseen . . . that unbreakable connection telling your boy or girl that hers will never be a truly solitary life" (108)? A powerful ethnic rootedness inhabits the novel in the legacy of Henry's father, and a strong ethnic identification draws Henry to Kwang, most evidently when he actually plays the role of Kwang in a campaign rehearsal, or when others remark upon their likeness (92, 37, 89). But when Henry says of Kwang, "I am here for the hope of his identity, which may also be mine," he means to enlarge an ethnic connection into something more: "who he has been on a public scale when the rest of us wanted only security in the tiny dollar-shops and churches of our lives" (328). To be an individual on the model of Kwang is to be a proud ethnic who yet steps into the public realm with open arms, departing the security of closed spaces for the possibilities of cross-ethnic solidarity. Kwang's centered, compassionate, ambitious Americanness embraces all within the self—much like Whitman, containing multitudes; Kwang blends the ethnic and American (he is "effortlessly Korean, effortlessly American" [328]). Through him, *Native Speaker* can voice a sweeping interethnic idealism that never abandons ethnic roots. Even as Kwang aspires to "bring all the various peoples to the steps of Gracie Mansion, bear them with him . . . as the living voice of the city," Henry reflects, "He was how I imagined a Korean would be, at least one living in any renown. He would stride the daises and the stages . . . unafraid to speak the language like a Puritan and like a Chinaman and like every boat person in between" (303–4).

Kwang brings to Asian American literature the vision of an individual who, by speaking like his Korean self, can claim kinship to every new American. He carries his sense of family to the outer reaches of his empathy, urging a crowd to see in the faces of those who seem most different, "your close ones, whom no one else loves," and saying of the lists of his diverse supporters, "*This is a family*" (279). Kwang actually commits these rolls to memory, incorporating multiple identities in himself, as it were, and his campaign's success lies, in turn, in peoples' willingness to see him as the embodiment of their aspirations and to want to participate in his. Something like transubstantiation occurs in his charismatic candidacy: "He is in the language now. The buildings and streets there are written with him"; "if you know him you can know a whole people" (169, 334). If Henry Park embodies Americanization as alienation, coerced assimilation, invisibility, betrayal, and ceaseless, joyless performance, John Kwang is the American as site of a multiethnic symbiosis. In this sense, though an Asian character, he constitutes a stunning departure from traditions of the Asian American novel.

For if an individual can be reduced to an invisible spy and alienated mimic, or can expand to embody a whole city, perhaps the same is true of a novel, of an ethnic novel, which might remain, like Henry the spy, a shadowy looker-on at the sunlit commerce of the majority, or then again might, like Kwang, "stride the daises... unafraid to speak the language like a Puritan and like a Chinaman and like every boat person in between," turning English into immigrant heteroglossia and daring to encompass multitudes.[19] *Native Speaker* does both, offering Henry and Kwang as two ethnic modes, two possible faces of the same condition. But the course of Henry's involvement with Kwang changes his public face; from the moment that he walks into Kwang's office, undercover agent posing as campaign volunteer, his spy plot confronts the plot of public service, of advocating and envisioning for the multitudes. Gradually Henry forgets "the very reason why I was there" (198), and we see him shift from assimilist/spy to public citizen, identifying more and more with the immigrant masses. Thus a narrative that begins as an outsider's struggle against self-annihilation in the mainstream eventually challenges the very notion of the mainstream, daring an embrace of all margins. For what, we might ask, is the Asian American novel's "truest place in the culture"? The plot of Kwang makes us believe that it need not keep to the shadowy margins, but can claim a central spot on the public platform, that like him an Asian American novel can represent and serve all the people, without losing its sense of history and identity.

But as Henry says, recalling his son's wiggly discomfort with a new book at bedtime, "There is something universally chilling about a new plot" (140). Though Kwang takes the Asian American narrative into new realms of public vision, readers suspect early that his aspirations are doomed. Perhaps because someone is paying for damaging information on him, we sense that a powerful force will block this Korean American politician from transcending his marginalized sphere. And similarly doomed, it seems, is the plot of the mixed child, ended before the book begins. These two tragedies make Lee's interethnic vision itself, ultimately, an elegiac—or as Cheng would say, melancholic—one centered on what I suggest we read as the symbolic, fallen pair of Kwang and Mitt: one attempting to embrace multitudes and one born of interethnic embrace.

The figure of Kwang is gradually tainted by the revelation of several kinds of corruption on his part (including the ordering of an interethnic murder); though the I.N.S. plays a large role in his demise, he seems in part a victim of his own hubris.[20] Mitt, however, remains a pure personification of the failed interethnic ideal. Long after his death, Lelia ponders its reason: "Maybe it's that Mitt wasn't all white or all yellow.... Maybe the world wasn't ready for him.... Maybe it's that he was so damn happy" (129). And indeed, his death is a cruel inversion, even a demonic apotheosis, of Kwang's vision of multicultural human community—for Mitt is killed in a children's game called a "dog pile," smothered by a heap of white boys clambering atop one another in an animalistic ritual. These boys had earlier mocked Mitt's mixed Asian/Caucasian features and may indeed have "stay[ed] on him as long as they did" out of animus (105). Most chilling in Henry's telling of the event is the use of the pronoun "you," usually addressed to the reader: "You pale little boys are crushing him, your adoring mob of hands and feet, your necks and heads, your nostrils and knees. . . . Listen, now. You can hear the attempt of his breath, that unlost voice, calling us from the bottom of the world" (106–107). The novel here underscores its conflicted ethnic relations with its audience, its uncertain place in the culture, by positioning the alien readerly "you" as the actual agent of the mixed child's death, but also, just possibly, as a capable listener now to the sound of his unlost promise.

Native Speaker forces readers to acknowledge this symbolic death of the multiethnic ideal. Paralleling Mitt's death scene, Kwang's plot also ends with a vengeful crowd, which assaults him as he "crouch[es] down, like a broken child, shielding from me his wide immigrant face" (343). In these two tragic crowd scenes, the novel marks with severity the limits of its own interethnic hopes. Grieving for Mitt, Henry grieves for a better self, one who embodied the wish for a sublime union of peoples, Ellison's "ideal American character—a type truly great enough to possess the greatness of the land, a delicately poised unity of divergencies" ("Twentieth-Century" 26).[21] The downfall of Kwang, too, shatters dreams of collectivity, of the "family" he had promised to make of all the inhabitants of the great, global city.

But though Henry's family is broken and Kwang's dream of "family" fails, still, something survives the mass attacks: the yearning strains of interethnic narrative desire, carried by Henry's ongoing attunements and identifications. "I think I would give most anything to hear my father's talk again," he muses, "the crash and bang and stop of his language. . . . I will listen for him forever in the streets of this city." And he adds, "I want to hear the rest of them, too"; "I can never stop considering the pitch and drift of their forlorn boats on the sea," nor stop listening, in the sounds of any immigrant's "different English," for "the ancient untold music of a newcomer's heart, sonorous with longing and hope" (337, 335, 304). Even after the failures of family, the narrator's imaginative receptivity to the lives of disparate, displaced, striving individuals continues to gather them, to make them a potential people in his words.

Lee's ending brings this narrative of interethnic longing and lament to a beautifully imperfect resolution. As Henry moves toward public penance and psychic recovery, quitting the spy job and walking the immigrant streets in homage to those he has betrayed, he finds new work assisting Lelia's English speech classes for immigrant children in the public schools. While Lelia attempts to show the children "that there is nothing to fear," "offer[ing] up a pale white woman horsing with the language to show them it's fine to mess it all up," Henry in his masked role as the Speech Monster "gobble[s] up kids but . . . cower[s] when anyone repeats the day's secret phrase" (348–49). A secondary figure, not the authoritative English teacher but her silent, monstrous sidekick, Henry replays his lifelong alienation in the language and his refuge in masks, but now in a comic, redeeming vein. The focus is on children with their faces toward futurity; recalling Henry's childhood self, they also substitute for lost, perfect Mitt; when Lelia and Henry "hug and kiss each one" goodbye, "they are just that size I will forever know, that very weight so wondrous to me, and awful" (349).

In this luminous scene Lee preserves the memory of loss, while honoring the potentials of both individuality and the mixed crowd. Turning the lesson around on herself, the English teacher makes a name badge for each exiting child, and as Henry "press[es] it to each of their chests," "she calls out each one as best as she can, taking care of every last pitch and accent, and I hear her speaking a dozen lovely and native languages, calling all the difficult names of who we are" (349). This closing line evokes an imperfect but hopeful American community, a "we" made of "lovely languages" and "difficult names." It gives us a revised image not only of public education but also of the ethnic novel, no longer sites of compulsory assimilation but places of education into heteroglossia, where ethnic differences enter and are transfigured in a rising chant. Yet it still retains the melancholy of Henry Park's Americanization story, the story of a tongue that trained itself on repression and self-abnegation in order to enter the heady chorus. Playing the Speech Monster, Henry does not deny but ironizes his compromised, ambivalent relationship to America and the English language. Still, in the meanwhile of his incomplete, unrealized state of being, he finds a more fruitful way to inhabit his "truest place in the culture."

No doubt, from a certain critical viewpoint, our hero would seem markedly "castrated" in his masked (emask-ulated?) ending, working as helper to his white wife, rather than having created his own version of productive citizenship. But, a number of factors mitigate such a reading: while he has been a kind of speech monster all along, in the bit of clownery that graces the ending, Henry dons the monster mask in the service of releasing children like his younger self from their disempowerment (honoring their languages, calling them "citizens,"); further, when he de-masks, he demonstrates to them that an Asian American person can remain himself, even if working under societal restraint. Moreover, the reader surely senses that this job is a temporary one for Henry, that he will move in some better career direction before long. Interestingly, his indeterminate status in the ending allies him with Ellison's invisible man who, Anne Anlin Cheng argues, may seem in his non-activist, "open-ended" ending "the classic figure of melancholy," but can also be understood as engaged in "an active process of subjective negotiation with loss and dismemberment." Cheng "valu[es] not the indecision but the *space of contemplation before action that his melancholic condition affords him*," and she affirms the radical potential of a novelistic ending that arrives not at identity, but at "the nonexistence of identity," at "invisibility with its assimilative and dissimulative possibilities" (136–37). Lee's masked Henry, too, ends in a position of refusal to claim a new identity, of contemplative waiting, and meanwhile of serving a new and larger "we," the hero's personal resolution becoming less important than the gesture toward a collective, hybrid identity. Or perhaps we might say that Henry's participation in a motley, collective "who we are" *is* a significant personal resolution for a protagonist who begins the book attempting to come to terms with a "list of who I was" handed him by an accusatory white wife (1), a list that includes the items "emotional alien" and "*False speaker of language*" (5–6). After the extended self-examination of Henry's narration, it is notable that the "we" whom he is moved to serve and join at the end—in a final, perhaps at last freeing performance—is embodied in a group of children who, memorializing Mitt, portend a mixed and unmelancholic future, a diverse, equally entitled, vocally authorized citizenry.[22]

To point to the contradictions of this poignant ending is to emphasize again the contradictory nature of *Native Speaker*'s positioning of Asian Americans within a multiethnic vision, its complex and conflicted engagement with blackness, whiteness, and ethnic multiplicity. Henry would not be in that room without his assent to normative English and to Lelia's white liberalism,[23] and his finding an—at least temporary—place of comfort there says much about his imbrication in white American culture, a position it seems impossible to read as all good or bad. Similarly, Lee creates his new Korean American speaker by means of a revisionary engagement with varied traditions of American fiction (ethnic autobiographical fictions, spy novels, black "protest" novels, novels of urban politics, postmodern narratives of identity). It is one of Lee's many strengths to be able to work within ambivalent relationships and inheritances, presenting an Asian American subjectivity that resonates with multiple American histories and narratives, but that strikes its own fine sonorities, in counterpoint.

There is much, of course, for such an ethnic literary project to absorb from African American literature and culture, much about longing, resistance, boldness, and lament, and much, especially, about raw and gorgeous new blossomings of American language. But there is much that is different and distinctively Asian American here, too—the monstrous problematics of speech and silence, the disciplined performance of perfection, the socially in-between position congenial to a spy, the sharing of an imposed public identity with a large, heterogeneous group, and not least, the predicament of late entrance on a scene malformed by a tragic racist history, into which one may be drawn in ways that distort the sonorous music of one's heart. "This," says Henry Park, "is all of my American education," and this is how Chang-rae Lee educates the American novel, bringing to it a vision of the complicated terrain—crisscrossed by filaments of love, rage, dread, and honor—to which the newest Americans' children are now native.

3

Letters from Camp Gugelstein: Interethnicity and Jewishness in Gish Jen's *Mona in the Promised Land*

American Means Being Whatever You Want

When the teenaged Chinese American heroine of Gish Jen's 1996 *Mona in the Promised Land* departs from all literary convention by converting to the Judaism of her suburban New York neighbors, she brings the Chinese American novel into a comic hybrid with the tales of Jewish America. Jen, who grew up in Scarsdale, New York, and who has spoken of the influence on her writing of Jewish authors Roth, Mailer, Malamud, and Singer; Ozick, and Paley,[1] constructs a narration that interweaves the syntaxes and sensibilities of Yiddish and Shanghainese, and earns admiring blurbs from both Amy Tan and Cynthia Ozick—never before seen together on one page of acclaim. Charting a path to acculturation through Jewishness, Jen's heroine Mona Chang unwittingly travels against the heavy traffic, in twentieth-century American Jewish fiction, that rushed toward America in the other direction. This chapter reads Mona's embrace of Jewish American culture as an inventive claim to an Asian American identity that is open-ended, transformational, and fundamentally connected to the histories, identities, and futures of other groups of Americans. Asking what Jewishness has to do with this Chinese American novel's interethnic impulse, the chapter is followed by an interchapter that meditates more broadly on the borrowing of Jewishness in contemporary world fiction in English.[2]

Reading *Mona in the Promised Land* after Chang-rae Lee's *Native Speaker* (published just a year earlier), it is startling to realize that Jen's heroine grows up in the New York suburbs not many miles away from Lee's Henry Park, at roughly the same time. For while both protagonists are deeply engaged in the experiment of trying on alternate American identities, Henry seems to inhabit a dark and shadowy world irreconcilable with Mona's sunlit life. Perhaps the rosiness of narrative retrospect on youth in part makes the difference, for Jen's novel mainly recounts Mona's late '60s-early '70s suburban adolescence, while Lee concentrates on Henry's adulthood in mid-1990s Manhattan and Queens, with flashbacks to childhood. Still, these differing time frames do not fully explain the difference in the two novels' tones.[3] Jen herself has called *Mona* "very different in tone and feeling," from her first novel, *Typical American* (1991) the story of the immigrant parents of the American-born girl who will become the teenaged heroine of *Mona*: "The first book is more tragic-comic, while *Mona in the Promised Land* is more purely comic" ("So"). Immigrant stories necessarily contain a modicum of tragedy—as a character in David Wong Louie's *The Barbarians Are Coming* puts it, "An immigrant has no business even contemplating such a luxury as happiness" (289)—so that it is the immigrants' American children who can be conceived as qualifying for comic endings, and the writers of Jen's generation who can begin to imagine them. Jen has remarked: "People often ask me where the comic outlook comes from. Among other things it comes from my experience. I have seen so much social change in such a short amount of time, it seems miraculous" ("*MELUS* Interview" 218).

A couple of generations of writers have witnessed the same social change, and yet, there is nothing in Asian American literary tradition that can prepare one for the downright cheeriness of *Mona*. The angst of a century of struggling forebears, so striking in the roster of texts that make up a conventional Asian American Literature syllabus, seems remote from Jen's novel. Before *Mona*, I would contend, Asian American novelists had scarcely imagined the possibility of a "purely comic" second-generation story,[4] a story that breaks miraculously free of its anguished inheritance into a romance with individual freedom, into a perfectly Shakespearian multiple-marriage comic ending, and also into the birth of the next generation—a real rarity in Asian American fiction—and moreover, an ethnically mixed next generation, the hallmark of the endings of the three novels examined at length in this study.

I want to argue that *Mona* arrives at its unique tone, manages to be the joyful book it is precisely because of the way that it crosses these two ethnic traditions; its giddy energy is inseparable from the *jouissance* of boundary-crossing in itself. For it has to be said that the particular degree of rosy comedy Jen is able to achieve in *Mona* is probably unprecedented in either of the two traditions she yokes together. There is nothing quite like *Mona* written by a Jew either, not even among the present generation of comfortably Jewish and unabashedly hilarious texts that have marked the beginning of the twenty-first century.[5] Jewish American fiction generally hasn't aspired to the "purely comic," and I somehow don't imagine that it ever will.

Neither is *Mona* purely comic, actually, but in the marriage of these two impurely comic contemporary traditions, Gish Jen hits upon the possibility of something close to it. Her heroine, daughter of Chinese immigrants, is much nearer the pain of immigration than are her Jewish friends in the barely pseudonymous suburb of Scarshill, New York, though the novel reveals both the Chinese and the Jews as Scarred peoples. But it is Mona's good fortune to live out a plot of mid-twentieth-century Asian immigrant aspiration in a Jewish American setting much like the one in which Jen herself grew up: amidst a liberal community that has arrived at safety, affluence, and assimilation several decades ahead of her own family, thus enabling her to make their full claim to Americanness her own as well—perhaps even to surpass them in degree of confidence that America is hers.

At the same time, of course, the very fact that Mona feels impelled to convert signals identity trouble, the difficulty of resolving identity within U.S. ideological parameters that Mona shares with so many Asian American fictional characters. David Palumbo-Liu speaks of "the persistent deferral of the status of 'American,'" and "the essential, racial separation of Asians from 'Americans' . . . buttressed by a belief system deeply ingrained in the American imaginary which insists on the essential difference of racialized peoples" (1, 3). Yet much of the comic appeal of Mona's story lies in her creative way of inhabiting the condition of racial in-betweenness culturally ascribed to Asian Americans—the same condition that makes Henry Park a suitable spy. Spontaneously, unevenly transgressing racial and ethnic boundaries, Jen's heroine seems determined to harness the energy of difference itself through a bold cross-ethnic affiliation, taking up with another group marked by difference and converting to a religion that, to her mind, is all about inquiring into one's place in the world; embracing a cushioning, comic, affirming Jewishness that she understands above all as a personal, spiritual politics, a commitment to freedom and justice—for herself, and for everyone else she encounters.

But Mona's quest might be deemed suspect in the terms of recent critiques of the privileging of plots of individualist ascent in Asian American fiction. In *Asian/American* (1999), Palumbo-Liu calls this "model minority discourse," "a blueprint for the deliverance of minority subjects from collective history to a reified individualism" (415):

> [T]he logic of model minority discourse argues that an inward adjustment is necessary for the suture of the ethnic subject into an optimal position within the dominant culture. . . . [Such a logic] vindicates the dominant ideology while rewarding the subject with a particular form of individual well-being freed from both the constraints of collectivity (that is, "I am no longer 'labeled as Asian American,' I am an *individual*"). (397–98)

Similarly, in *Imagine Otherwise* (2003), Kandice Chuh argues against reading the plots of Asian American fiction in the light of "U.S. nationalist accounts of immigration and settlement where arrival and achievement of identity with America stand as celebrated narrative closure" (110). In that an Asian American "'subject' only becomes recognizable and can act as such by conforming to certain regulatory matrices," Chuh advocates that we read Asian American literature as a "subjectless" discourse (9–10), and practice a "critique of subjectification" itself rather than privilege a "desire for subjectivity" (151). Chuh means the notion of "subjectlessness" to "[point] attention to the constraints on the libertory potential of the achievement of subjectivity," for "subjectivity itself, alone, cannot remedy injustice" (9–10).

Both Palumbo-Liu and Chuh offer bases for a potentially scathing critique of *Mona in the Promised Land* and of its heroine, who certainly does follow a path of *bildung* in which she can become "herself" and escape some of the pain of her minority status by internalizing the norms of the "dominant ideology," the "regulatory matrices" of teenage life in a Jewish American suburb circa 1970. But I would argue that it is the genius of Jen's project to avoid the trap of the triumphalist model minority ascent to subjectivity by portraying dialogic, comparativist, intersubjective acculturation.

Mona in the Promised Land articulates the difference made by a differing, nonmainstream acculturation, and affirms not so much the cultural values of Judaism itself—though it does pay generous tribute here—but rather the ethical value, the beauty, and the liberatory potential, for the minoritized subject, of somewhere else to go on the way back to the self, of a way out of pain through cross-ethnic identification.[6] The sense of self achieved by Jen's heroine has everything to do with inclusion, interaction, and mutual responsibility, not to mention the pursuit of justice. While a critique of the processes of subjectification is surely useful here and elsewhere in Asian American literature, the two critical paradigms mentioned above, it seems to me, cannot do full justice to *Mona in the Promised Land*, a bildungsroman that comically modifies the traditional bourgeois Euro-American model along ethnic, feminist, and postmodern critical lines to portray the contested, dialogic, intersubjective development of a girl who questions the meaning of all the "matrices" that frame her own and others' possibilities until she arrives, willy-nilly, at her womanhood.

The differences of such a plot suggest just how profoundly interethnic influence can transform a received cultural narrative, can open an ethnic text into different mythic currents. "I can't say that being a writer is an extension of my being an Asian-American," Jen has remarked:

> Quite the contrary. My life as a fiction writer is directly related to my assimilation, particularly to the Jewish community in Scarsdale where I grew up. . . . That was a community that greatly esteemed fiction writing, which is how I first got interested in finding my voice and expressing myself.[7] ("So")

The impact of Jen's Jewish literary upbringing can be seen, among other places, in the differences of her heroine's expectations from those of many other Asian American fictional protagonists; Mona seems to think that the vaunted freedoms of America are hers by birthright. Oblivious, at least at first, to the different racialization of Asians and Jews in America—unaware that because Jewishness has recently come to be considered in the West a secondary characteristic modifying a primary whiteness, most Jews carry the privilege of easy assimilation—Mona sees no difference between her possibilities and those of her Jewish friends. While her immigrant parents respond to culturally alienating U.S. norms, and to their own treatment as aliens, by building a figurative—and literal—wall around themselves, turning the family home into "Fort Chang," as Mona calls it (269), the America that young Mona enters when she steps out the fort door is Jewish America, and from her Jewish neighbors and the texts of Jewish American culture Mona might be said to borrow a distinctively Jewish embrace of Americanization.

This is an ethos evident across a wide range of twentieth-century cultural texts produced by American Jews, who have been called as a group "the luckiest Jews who ever lived" (Leon Wieseltier quoted in V. Cheng 123). Exchanging the poverty, marginalization, and long history of victimization in their Old World lives for the possibilities of the United States, American Jews "flourished to a degree unprecedented in Jewish history" (Joselit 293), and became, among new Americans, "[o]ne of the most quickly Americanized of immigrant groups" (Seltzer 1). Viewing America "as moral alternative to corrupt Europe," American Jews were "enormously grateful for the benefits of America and became passionate lovers of its freedoms" (Wisse 65, 63), "firmly enthralled by American individualism and secularity" (Seltzer 15).

Of course, the Americanization of the Jews[8] was a process initially beset by profound obstacles and ambivalences, as attested by the angst-ridden texts of early Jewish American literature.[9] Ruth Wisse writes, "[S]ince their immigration coincided with the painful self-transformation from a tradition-bound people into a voluntary community, they had to weigh the advantages of acculturation against the dangers of national dissolution" (63). But for Jen's Mona, meeting up with the Jews in a much later, golden moment of suburban security and affluence, unaware of any such losses or misgivings and seemingly untroubled by her own potential loss of Chinese culture (how could she lose it when she still resides at Fort Chang?), her acceptance by the Jews feels like unambiguous arrival, ironically, just the kind that the Jews themselves aspired to achieve. And because the dual nature of Jewishness as both religion and ethnicity makes it handily and anomalously an ethnic minority condition to which one can formally convert, Mona is able to enter into the cultural imaginary of Jewish America.

In this imaginary, according to Andrea Most in her book on the Jews' invention of the Broadway musical, "the experience of being an outsider . . . comes to be defined by a narrative trajectory from exclusion to acceptance" (3). Most reads the Broadway musical comedy as "a celebration of . . . the marvelous freedom Jews felt in America to invent themselves anew" (10); key to the attraction of Jewish immigrants and their offspring to Broadway was "the power and possibility of performance for newcomers to American cultures" (Most 1). For Jen's Mona, too, the possibility that she could freely perform her way into Americanness is a matter of blithe conviction, a conviction that sets her apart from the mainstream of Asian American literary heroes.

Though Mona's plot continually plays out the tensions of her different racialization within the American episteme she shares with the Jews, I think that Jen's novel demonstrates that interethnic acculturation among the Jews makes a person quite unlikely to disidentify with the American dream (or to call oneself "subjectless"!). What other Asian American protagonist can we imagine gracing a book cover like that of the 1997 Vintage Contemporaries paperback edition of *Mona in the Promised Land*: a pair of Asian eyes peering out smilingly from within an otherwise seamless fabric of American flags? This cover plays upon the tension between Asian eyes—historically, bodily emblems of racist objectification par excellence—and the chief icons of America. But in this ironic composition, instead of embodying permanent alien status, those Asian eyes boldly, humorously make a place for themselves among the stars and stripes. Though Mona remains always visibly and inescapably different from her Jewish peers, she and her plot derive from the Jewish atmosphere of Scarshill the conviction that no one can take away her right to be whatever kind of American she can imagine herself to be.

But when Mona's mother, Helen, possessed of a different conception of personal identity, discovers the appalling fact of her adolescent daughter's conversion, she exclaims, "How can you be Jewish? Chinese people don't do such things" (45). "They don't?" Mona asks in momentary shame, but later rouses herself and spunkily argues her case: "You are the one who brought us up to speak English. . . . You said we weren't pure Chinese anymore, that the parents had to accept we would be something else." "American, not Jewish," replies Helen. "Jewish is American," declares Mona—in a breathtaking assertion of equivalence exceeding any such claim a Jewish American writer has yet dared.[10] Mona explains, "American means being whatever you want, and I happened to pick being Jewish" (49).

This remarkable moment for Asian American literature, in which a heroine can announce that "American means being whatever you want"—and by extension, that the Asian American novel can be whatever it wants—is made possible because Gish Jen "happens to pick" Jewishness, and thus can propel Mona into a fully claimed American identity through an unprecedented hybridization with a people who believe in their own, open, unlimited American storyline. Of course, as the plot unfolds for Mona, her Jewish faith in voluntary American ethnic identity is ironized; while for some white ethnics this has become a reality,[11] for this Chinese American girl, things do not turn out to be as simple as picking and choosing. Most obviously, she continues to possess facial features that mark her publicly as something other than American, long after the Jewish community has managed to pass into American whiteness. But the serendipity of Mona's freedom, in this particular time and place, to choose to cross group lines and claim the narrative of Jewish Americanization as her own—and of the inclination of her early 1970s Jewish friends, enjoying a moment of both full assimilation and the luxury of return to roots, to embrace and bring her with them—goes a long way to explaining the breezy confidence of this Chinese American female coming-of-age narrative. A book that revels in self-transformation, *Mona in the Promised Land* celebrates individual freedom to play with self-creation, in the specific form of intersubjective identification amidst ethnic others. Such borrowing, Jen has avowed, is essential to her sense of American identity:

> In this time of huge, public embracing of ethnic roots, I wanted to show how our lives are more complex than what we're born with. While our ethnic roots are very important to us, I think that anybody who is interested in their identity would do well to learn about the place they grew up in, and learn about its culture. We make ourselves in this country; even people who are racial and ethnic minorities transform themselves. The different groups have spent a lot of time rubbing elbows, rubbing off of each other, and while the melting pot model of assimilation was unhealthy . . . the idea of assimilation is still with us in ways that we don't necessarily have to be afraid of. We rub elbows with each other, and learn from each other, and this is a wonderful thing. It's not like we abandon our own roots, we just know more things and allow them to change our lives. ("So")

Having grown up rubbing elbows with the Jews, Gish Jen wrote first a "roots" novel about Chinese immigrants of her parents' generation, and then in her second novel, giving pride of place to the Jewishness that rubbed off on her literary imagination, went on to write about a Chinese household in the Jewish neighborhood of her own youth.[12] A character, then, loosely based on her young self, Jen's Mona comes of age in in-betweenness, paying comic tribute to both peoples that acculturated her, witnessing their differing struggles to resolve their relations within the national episteme. Sometimes Mona rides waves of unity with her Jewish peers; sometimes she senses that they don't understand her at all; sometimes she feels at odds with every group to which she might belong. As Susan Stanford Friedman puts it, Mona's "narrative moves back and forth in an intercultural *fort/da* as it negotiates between identity's fixity and changeability, borders and borderlands, and difference and hybridity" (*Mappings* 167). In the course of this eccentric *bildung*, the heroine makes her in-betweenness into a comfortable, comic dwelling place, a hybrid home.

What Means Switch?

From the opening pages, this novel's hybrid discourse makes vivid the spirit of interethnic commingling. Jen's richly conversational, gossipy narrative voice, always busy at ironic wordplay, places the Chang family in an indeterminate ideological space, a space where they must choose who they will be: "There they are, nice Chinese family.... Where should they live next?" (3). When because of the excellence of the public schools they "settle into a Dutch colonial on the Bronx River Parkway" in Scarshill, the narrator declaims:

> For they're the New Jews, after all, a model minority and Great American Success. They know they belong in the promised land.
>
> Or do they? In fact, it's only 1968; the blushing dawn of ethnic awareness has yet to pink up their inky suburban night. (3)

In what Jen has called a "very fun, very loose, very fast book" ("So"), the narrative voice playfully tosses together received phrases from popular and academic, biblical and high literary discourse to establish amidst a texture of ironized heteroglossia and ironic retrospect the self-conception and public image of this representative "nice Chinese American family," in a developing 1960s moment treated as comically earnest, naïve, and in-process.[13] As-yet-unarticulated ethnic in-betweenness is essential to the Changs' position. In the very first lines, Mona's parents' decision about where to live is rendered in terms of their metaphorical rejection of a cup of ginseng in favor of a chocolate milkshake, suggesting assimilationist tendencies unusual in Asian American fictional parents. But soon after, we see them reject the snooty articulations of a white, anti-Semitic real estate agent ("she! for one! would rather live elsewhere!") (3), in a distinctly Yiddishized expression of sympathetic identification: "This is such a nice thing to say, even the Changs know to be offended, they think, on behalf of all three Jewish people they know, even if one of them they're not sure about" (3). Beginning to position themselves, in the American scene, on the side of minority interlopers rather than WASP defenders of American borders, the Changs' emergence as characters is inseparable from the narrative's interweaving of colloquial American, American Jewish, and Shanghai Chinese American forms of speech. Sprinkled with

Yiddishisms and Jewish humor, but equally dense with references to Chinese cultural practices and inventions, food and standards of etiquette, addressing at least these two insider audiences at once, Jen's language signals from the outset that the process of making a life amidst this mix is what the book will be all about.

In the growing friendship between Mona Chang and her best friend Barbara Gugelstein, Mona is as likely to do a mock Yiddish syntax as Barbara is to do her best Chinese English. When she fears Barbara may have been injured, Mona calls, "Hey, Kugel Noodle. You vant I should call an ambulance?" and Barbara calls back to Mona, when the phone rings, "Please to go answer it . . ." (65). Partners in a new insiderism, children or grandchildren of the immigrants they imitate, these friends share the condition of belatedness to cultural purity, and, in the spirit of the book's moment—the late '60s, early '70s emergence of American youth culture—are experimenting in the hybrid aftermath.

Jen's expressively elastic narrative discourse achieves particularly rich ironies in recounting Mona's interethnic acculturation at junior high school. As the only Chinese American girl in a school populated mostly by Jews, Mona shows herself after a short time in the neighborhood as prodigious an adapter to the local culture as any daughter of immigrants could be,[14] and finds herself, in turn, "not so much accepted as embraced." "[P]retty soon," Jen reports, Mona "has been to so many bar and bas mitzvahs, she can almost say herself whether the kid chants like an angel or like a train conductor. At seder, Mona knows to forget the bricks, get a good pile of that mortar. Also . . . Mona knows that she is, no offense, a goy." But as special sort of goy, something on the order of a "permanent exchange [student]" (6), Mona lives the life of a resident exotic. Until one day, walking into her eighth-grade class, Mona is taken aback by the sight of a newer newcomer, an evidently Asian boy. Mona bravely tries out on the new boy the few phrases in Shanghai dialect that she possesses (her best are "*Byeh fa-foon, Shee-veh, Ji-nu*," meaning "Stop acting crazy. Rice gruel. Soy sauce" [5–6], apparently the words spoken to her most often in the family home). Having just arrived from Japan, Sherman Matsumoto "looks at her as though she's much stranger than anything else he's seen so far" (10), but the teacher, assuming a natural sameness between the two, gives Mona the job of Sherman's chief English and Americanization coach.

Conversation between Mona and Sherman progresses from simpler lessons ("This is a book"; "What is this?" "This is a chair" [12]), to lessons in acculturation, such as where to shop, and for what: for example, Mona teaches Sherman that bagels should always be bought from a bagel store; Lender's frozen bagels, she informs him, are "gross" (13). Before long, their exchanges move on to matters of ethnic and national identity, about which Mona gradually begins to sense that she and Sherman have starkly different ideas:

> As for the things he asks her, they're not topics Mona ever talked about before. Does she like it here? "Of course I like it here, I was born here," Mona says. Is Mona Jewish? "Jewish!" She laughs. "Oy!" Is she American? "Sure I'm American," Mona says. "Everybody who's born here is American, and also some people who convert from what they were before. You could become American." But he says no, he could never. "Sure you could," Mona says. "You only have to learn some rules and speeches."
>
> "But I Japanese."

> "You could become American anyway," Mona says. "Like I *could* become Jewish, if I wanted to. I'd just have to switch, that's all."
>
> He looks at her in alarm.
>
> She thinks maybe he doesn't get what means switch. (14)

A class of mine once spent a very productive half hour on the wonderful phrase that ends this dialogue: "what means switch," why it works, why it's funny, what Jen accomplishes with it. Perhaps the alarmed Sherman doesn't get the meaning of the word "switch," but as Mona seems dimly to grasp, what he truly doesn't get is the American belief in total freedom to transform and remake the self. Her own avid Americanism is grounded in that belief. But when in the phrase "what means switch," Mona mimics Sherman's and also her own parents' immigrant English syntax, we see how close this American girl remains to immigrant negotiations with a new cultural lexicon, how well she knows the complexities of switch.

The syntactical play in the phrase "what means switch" becomes a running verbal joke in the novel, perpetuated by the third-person narrative voice that delivers Mona's interiority to us, often comically mediating between Mona's mind and the mind of the zeitgeist. Whenever Mona treads upon the shaky territory of cross-cultural translation, she (or her intimate narrator) tends to fall into this mocking but affectionate version of her native tongue, the English her parents have always spoken around her. We hear Helen in such usages, for example, when confronting Mona with her grave lapse from proper Chinese behavior: "You are daughter. *Daughter*. Do you remember what is a daughter?" (45), or by contrast, when she refers to a family of Chinese American teenagers whom even she sees as too rigidly parented: they "have no idea who is Jimi Hendrix" (48). Similarly, to illustrate Mona's limited, groping knowledge of her Chinese heritage, Jen writes, "For if [Mona] ever had to say what means Chinese, it would have to include a predilection for peeling grapes in your mouth without moving your jaw—also for emitting the peels without opening your lips" (7). Here the comic example of a form of Chinese oral style that Mona cannot hope to replicate mirrors the difficulty of verbal translation, exemplified in the phrase "what means."

This "switched" syntax becomes especially useful when, a couple of years later, Mona actually does convert to Judaism and, assigned by her rabbi a huge pile of books to study, applies herself with a wry, immigrant daughter's self-consciousness to the learning of new definitions: "All about the holidays, for example, and what is a mitzvah—namely a good deed. Also what is rachmones, namely a type of mercy every human being should extend to others but sometimes doesn't" (35). And in the novel's epilogue, Jen finds telling use for this syntactically playful phrase about meaning to render the difficulties of cross-gender communication on the model of the immigrant linguistic gap; after Mona marries her longtime boyfriend, Seth, now an academic, she learns of his unavailability for childcare duties in marital discussions of "what means job, and ambition, and manhood" (298).

When my class attempted to get to the bottom of the phrase "what means switch," one very good student finally exclaimed, "I know why it works, but I just can't say it!"[15] The moment seemed telling, for in this phrase, I think, Jen has found an idiom to say something better than it can be said in any other words, something interlingual and intercultural, a perfect idiomatic encapsulation of the imperfect translations of interculturality itself. If Mona had thought "maybe he doesn't get what switch means," that wouldn't express the Shermanness of the getting or not getting, or the dimly perceiving Mona-ness, either; "what means switch" captures the cultural in-betweenness that is the territory of switching, less capturable in either language alone.

I belabor this point because in-betweenness becomes this novel's dominant condition, apparent in its plot premises, its characterization, and its language. Once Mona makes the big switch to Judaism, the comically jostling hybridity suggested by "what means switch" is borne out by the book as a whole, which embodies and affirms an in-between, in-process, multiply-determined identity. "The Changowitz," Mona's friends start to call her, like some kind of cross-ethnic cyborg (56).[16] Even the book's resident Jewish authority, the hip, young Reform rabbi who lets the Confirmation Class go barefoot and who mentors Mona in her conversion, concurs in the hybrid vision: "*The more Jewish you become*," he prophesies to Mona, "*the more Chinese you'll be*" (190).

This paradoxical formula emblematizes the novel's comedy of superabundance, of the plenitude of possibilities that arise from comparison and combination—in distinct contrast to the contest among conflicting, mutually alienated identities in *Native Speaker*. For Mona herself, by "switching," embodies the fullness of promise that Henry Park sees not in himself but in multiethnic crowds and classrooms—and that he once saw in his mixed-race son, object of the book's elegy for multicultural hope. As Jen's novel progresses, the rabbi's paradoxical wisdom seems to be borne out, Mona's pursuit of self-knowledge leading her through radical change to a reevaluation of what inheres. To her credit, Jen never completely accounts for the mystery of Mona's conversion—arising in part from adolescent rebellion against parents, and from wanting to be like her friends, but also from her attraction to the inquiring spirit of Judaism. Turning Jewish is only the first step in the larger process of Mona's education. For in this latter-day tribute to Jane Austen—an author Jen invokes several times, and a comic antecedent perhaps as important here as Shakespeare and Jewish cultural texts[17]—the plot of manners and morals follows the key choices of a bright, young woman, asking, how should she best conduct herself on the precarious brink of adulthood? What's her proper relationship to family, community, society at large? How can she make her way from the family home to the best new home she can muster, from the materials of the available "three or four families in a Country Village," Austen's novelistic ideal? ("Austen"). As it happens, in Scarshill all the villagers are Jewish, and so this young heroine's narrative must involve a cross-ethnic development: she must become "Mona-also-known-as Ruth, a more or less genuine Catholic Chinese Jew" (44), as a first step to becoming the completed woman the novel can make her.

Make Yourself at Home

The possibility of turning Jewish might never have arisen for Mona had not her young friends, like so many Jews of the countercultural 1970s generation, decided to turn Jewish themselves, that is, in a more committed way. As Jen has put it:

> I did set it quite pruposefully [sic] in the late 1960s, when ethnicity was being invented, because it occurred to me when I looked back on my high school years that I had been a witness to that process of invention, on the heels of the civil rights movement, when blacks were turning blacker, and young Jews were becoming more Jewish, partly because of the Six-Day War, but also following the model of black people, reembracing their Judaism in a way that was quite astonishing to the older generation: returning to temple, learning Hebrew, things that their parents had gone to great lengths to avoid. ("So")[18]

Drawn into the moment's heady energies by an actual shofar blast from Barbara Gugelstein, Mona tags along to assorted Temple Youth Group events, until one day, helping explain to the assimilated Jewish parents the meaning of the fall harvest festival booth called a *sukkah*, she is confronted by a parent who asks, "Don't you have a home?" and rescued by friends, who claim "This is her home, you turkey" (33). In short order, then, the question of an Asian American's status within the nation (Sau-ling Wong's "unassimilable aliens," "permanent houseguests in the house of America"; Mona's status as "permanent exchange [student]") is raised and then resolved, by the paradoxical assertion that she is at home with the Jews—saliently here, the Jews as seen in their wilderness dwellings, the open-air desert booths that annually recall the Exodus from Egypt: Mona is declared to be at home with the homeless, wandering Jews. "[T]wo days later," Jen writes, "Mona's still chewing the cud of this conversation. A stranger in a strange land, that's her, she concludes after two more days of rumination" (33). And thereupon, she approaches Rabbi Horowitz about conversion. In a fine paradox, Mona's decision to "switch" seems to arise from her insight that, inasmuch as she stands out from the Jews, the lone Asian among them, so she is like them. A "stranger in a strange land," like the Jews in Babylon, she will join the yearning exiles, and make their *unheimlich* home hers.

Ironies abound here, not least being the distinctly un-exilic flavor of the lives actually being led by these comfortable suburban Jews, about whom Mona has to wonder, when studying Jewish history, "Do her happy friends in Scarshill with their patios and lounge chairs really live at the mouth of a stone age tunnel? It was hard to make out at first, but now she can see it plain, their own express lane down the centuries" (36). Indeed, her friends are living a unique moment in Jewish history, which, since the expulsion from the Land of Israel in the second century A.D., had been understood as a prolonged condition of spiritual and political *galut* or exile. In accord with "the rabbinic strategy for enduring exile" over a couple of thousand years of landlessness, persecution, or at best, marginality, home for the Jews was traditionally located in "the fulfillment of Torah" (Eisen 50–51), in Jewish spiritual work and study, as they awaited the Messiah (a conception that has persisted alongside modern, secular Jewish ideologies). But America presented a different story, as Arnold Eisen writes in his book *Galut*: "[W]hat could exile mean when it smiled upon Jews with the benevolence of America?" (ix). By and large, American Jews decided that "America is far from exile, rather as much a home as Jews could hope for" (xii).[19]

Despite this unprecedented sense of arrival, and despite the struggle that was waged by parents and grandparents to get them to these leisured patios, the kids in *Mona in the Promised Land* have turned around and reclaimed a tradition that always was about remembrance of where one came from. Mona, studying to convert, sees the attraction:

> The Changs don't have their friends' instincts, or reflexes. They don't have their ready alert. They don't have their friends' institutions, or their ways of reminding themselves who they are, that they not be lulled by a day in the sun. Prescriptions and rituals, holidays and recipes, songs. The Jews have books, they have games, they have tchotchkes. They have catalogs. And soon, G-d willing, so will Mona. (36)

Adopting another people's practices of the conservation of identity, Mona Chang joins a group both obsessed with maintaining its distinctness and newly confident of its place in the national community. Unlike a character such as Henry Park, she finds release from her immigrant-family angst by finding something to join that will accept her, even while, paradoxically, it enables her own cultivation of memory and identity (insofar as the more Jewish she becomes, the more Chinese she'll be). For Mona as for the Jews, American Jewishness operates in such a way as to realize simultaneous senses of difference and of membership in collectivity.

This crucial commonality with the Jews on the matter of home and homelessness resonates throughout the novel. Late in the book, attempting to describe to a friend "what it's like to be not Wasp and not black, and not as Jewish as Jewish can be; and not from Chinatown, either," Mona concludes, "I'm never at home" (231). Indeed, Jen dramatizes in Mona a degree of existential homelessness surpassing that of her friends, the American Jews, suggesting the more determining effects of Asian American racialization, as she passes through a number of insufficient homes: Fort Chang, the Temple, her hippie boyfriend Seth's backyard teepee, Barbara Gugelstein's lavish mansion, Grand Central Station (where she involuntarily cushions the foot of a sleeping homeless woman), her sister Callie's Harvard dorm room, the empty Gugelstein house (as a place where she and Seth live as squatters), and her Aunt Theresa's California beach house (the site of Mona's marriage). In this sequence, "extravagant" mobility eventually turns "necessitous," to borrow the terms Sau-ling Wong uses in reading early Asian American texts; comfortably middle-class Mona begins by experimenting, but when she takes the experiments too far and alienates her parents, she is forced to move out, and for the first time her plot resembles those of struggling immigrant characters who must, of necessity, crisscross the country in search of a safe and viable home (Bulosan's *America Is in the Heart* is Wong's powerful example).[20] It is important that we do not ever see Mona established in a home of her own, or a marital home with Seth. The existence of such a place is assumed, in the epilogue's happy ending, but the fact that Mona and Seth are married at Theresa's house suggests progress still in-the-making toward a home of their own, a still-rather-exilic, still-unresolved relationship to the social compact of the nation. Theirs is notably not, however, a marriageless ending like the ones described by Patricia P. Chu, in her argument that the scarcity of marriages in Asian American fictions signifies the failure of individual quests for "reconciliation with the social order" (18). So, though Mona's long period of exile and homelessness shows her to share to some extent her forebears' alienation within U.S. national space, a homelessness not entirely curable by interethnic affiliation, her ending confirms that Mona stands as avatar of a new moment in Asian American literature, in which collaborative interethnic bricolage replaces a more conventional reconciliation with the United States as home.

As I will argue at the end of this chapter, Mona's is a marriage scene replete with compromises and revisions of the norm, one that comically accommodates her competing desires and senses of self. More to our purposes here, being set at Theresa's house, this marriage scene occurs under the sign of a line Theresa speaks to Mona, as the two swing together in a hammock she hangs in the backyard of Fort Chang, an appealingly fragile, open-air perch reminiscent of Seth's teepee and of the *sukkah* itself: "'One thing very important in life,' says Theresa, 'is to know how to make yourself at home'" (247). Herself an immigrant, Theresa makes a resonant statement for the underlying ethos of this novel and for contemporary Asian American literature as a whole. She suggests that one can and may make oneself the home America does not necessarily offer, or that the ethnic family home does not necessarily offer. That home may be extravagant, outside of the bounds of established homes, and given one's marginalized condition, it may be one in a series of temporary homes; but as embodied in Theresa herself, the best home may be the one carried on one's back anyplace one goes. In other words, the fact that assimilation into the nation is not quite workable, even if it were entirely desirable, does not mean that the only other option is alienation, abjection, homelessness (or subjectlessness).[21] Making one's own sense of home is asserted as a real possibility for a heroine seeking to create her own idea of a happy ending. Adopting Jewishness, then—an exilic tradition in which home has always had to be a practice of the mind and heart—might be understood as the best way this particular Chinese American heroine can find to make a home of her own.

What Means Jewish?

The consonance between the plots of homelessness and home-making among Asian Americans and Jews is one of many points of connection undergirding Jen's interethnic plot. But beyond the matters of similarity or affiliation, Mona's switch would seem to demand a question not quite articulated by Jen's characters: what means Jewishness in this novel?

Perhaps the first answers would have to do with the heroine's desires on the levels of spirituality and politics. Mona finds a certain appeal in aspects of Judaic tradition: she says she "like[s] it at the temple," where the rabbi "tell[s] everyone to ask, ask, instead of just obey, obey" (34), the latter a principle her parents derived not only from Confucius but from their adopted Catholicism. Upstart, individualist Mona prefers to either of these the Jewish traditions of intellectual inquiry and the pursuit of social justice that assist her entrance into the public arena as the early 1970s social activist she wants to be, along with the Jews busily asking, "[h]ow they can help, how they can fix, how they can contribute and illuminate; and how they can stay, forever and ever, Jews" (35).

Next would come answers on levels of which the heroine is not quite aware, such as the social advantages Jewishness offers Mona. A white ethnic identity,

Jewishness stands in the U.S. racial/ethnic hierarchy somewhat higher than Asianness, which is often said to fall "between black and white." It thus makes available to Mona an alternate social space for self-exploration and transformation. Insofar as the creed of switch and the welcoming haven of Jewishness affirm her right to acceptance and assimilation despite her racial difference, Mona's plot involves a fantasy of acquiring a chosen and invisible "ethnic" identity rather than a racial, inescapably visual one. This is the aspect of Jewish social identity most important to the plot of Philip Roth's 2000 novel *The Human Stain*, in which a black man passes not merely for white, as is novelistically traditional, but for Jewish, so as to win the freedom to make his life as he chooses. Jewishness in both these novels is an adoptable identity closer to the advantages of whiteness, for characters born into more socially restrictive minority conditions.[22] A not-quite-assimilated assimilation; an outsider's insiderness, perhaps a more accessible or performable form of whiteness; the Jewishness adopted in these novels is a confident *claim to Americanness despite ancestry*.

Looked at another way, with no other Chinese families in the neighborhood, no models before her, Jewishness becomes for Mona, ironically, a route to finding her own minority American identity. That is, turning Jewish is the best way she can find to turn ethnic American circa 1970, when she is too late to be Chinese, like her parents, and too early to be Asian American—an identity term that does not arise in the book until quite close to the end (when Ralph and Helen want to know "what in the world is an Asian American?" [301]). While Mona's parents "don't like the word *minority*"—for, as Jen comically puts their logic, "they were never a minority when they were in China, why should they be a minority here"—Mona reasons that "we are a minority, like it or not, and if you want to know how to be a minority, there's nobody better at it than the Jews" (53). The value of borrowing others' understanding of ethnic minoritization is clarified in one of the book's more elementally comic moments. When Mona and her friends first begin to "talk about what it means to be Jewish," Jen's narrator slyly reports, "so far as they've been able to tell [it] mostly seems to be about remembering that you are." But, as Mona later thinks, "out in the world of other people," she is rarely allowed to forget that she embodies ethnic difference, that she is Chinese. And "[s]o here's the question," Jen writes, "Does the fact that Mona remembers all too well who she is make her more Jewish than, say, Barbara Gugelstein?" (32). Jewishness here is abstracted ethnic self-consciousness, a special and perpetual attentiveness to the difference of one's identity, and to the long historical roots of that difference, despite one's evident cultural assimilation and economic well-being—a quality Mona begins to recognize in herself. Finally, as I argued earlier, Jewishness should also be understood as a key element of the book's structuring myth of American ascent. Along with Jane Austen and Shakespeare, the Jewish American cultural imagination opens for Mona's plot comic-heroic possibilities.

So, the question presents itself, does this Chinese American book become a Jewish book? I can't say that it doesn't. But a funny thing happened when I began to teach *Mona in the Promised Land* in my undergraduate classes. At first, it seemed the perfect, provocative last text on my Asian American fiction survey. Then it turned out to be just the surprising book to end The Contemporary Female

Bildungsroman, and soon after, the book to send them out laughing from Contemporary Interethnic Fiction. It was just a small step then, really, to carry Mona with me to the close of my very newest course, Jewish American Fiction.

It had seemed to me a beautiful experiment to see how this novel about a Chinese American girl's coming-of-age in Jewish American suburbia would serve to close a course on Jewish fictions. For I was convinced that Jen had written a novel deeply Jewish in feel, in aspects of its language and humor, in much of its "material" about American Jewish life and Jewish religious tradition, as well as in its novelistic influences. I wondered what the class would think Jen contributes to portraits of Jewish America, or to the notion of a "Jewish" text, what we could say Jewishness becomes, presented from the point of view of Chinese Americans, called in the novel itself, "the new Jews."

And I thought the class had gotten the point of my inclusion of this anomalous book in the course. But when the papers came in, some of my students—who spanned a wide ethnic range—surprised me by their willingness to unhinge *Mona* from what I considered its appropriate field positioning in Asian American fiction, and to read it as unqualifiedly Jewish, even to treat it as the culmination of the century-and-a-half of Jewish American literature that we had spent the term reading, and further, in more than one instance, to assert the completion, in *Mona*, of a literary full circle: Jewish American literature's return to the optimism of its early immigrant roots and to the production, for the first time since the mid-nineteenth century beginnings of our syllabus, of a vision fully celebratory of the liberating possibilities of America for the aspiring individual. This to me was an idea based on so astonishing a misconception, and yet at the same time, so oddly on the mark about the book's historical resonances, that it caused me to rethink my assumptions about *Mona*, Asian American fiction, and Jewish American fiction as well. It has left me convinced that Gish Jen's wonderfully adaptable, fertile comic novel about well-off suburban teenagers augurs a truly radical development in contemporary fiction: it takes us so far out into the territory of cross-ethnic hybridity that it really does exceed the reach of ethnic literary categories.

I say this as one who must admit to being, fundamentally, an essentialist when it comes to ethnic literary categorization. That is, despite all post-structuralist thought to the contrary, I still find it necessary, and probably not just strategically necessary, to be able to say about Gish Jen's work, "This is a Chinese American book that is very Jewish." *Mona in the Promised Land* unsettles my adherence to the categories more than any text I know. While in the strict sense it cannot be the culmination of a Jewish tradition simply because a Jew didn't write it, the novel beautifully extends and embellishes that tradition by marrying it, so to speak, to the story of the Chinese Americans, and in doing so, perhaps does culminate an important trend in Jewish American literature's own Americanizing trajectory: that is, its yearning toward the American multiculture. In this sense, it is emblematic of the interethnic imagination of contemporary American fiction.

But when I asked my students at the end of my first Jewish American fiction course, what Jewishness becomes in this Chinese American translation, they replied, with astonishing unanimity, that it becomes "cool." Cool? Not a historical burden or precious inheritance, not impetus for psychological struggle, spiritual quest, or social action, but cool? Jewishness has been a lot of things, over the course of history, but cool it has not usually been. In fact, I had been thinking that Gish Jen takes a rather big risk in gravitating toward the distinct uncoolness of suburbia, and of upper middle class Jews, instead of, say, the cool of a gritty, urban scenario and the hint of the influence of literary blackness one finds in Lee's *Native Speaker*. I've noticed, too, that in Asian Americanist conference papers and course syllabi, Jen's *Mona in the Promised Land* does not seem to be the novel that scholars choose to include (much more often included is her first novel, about Chinese immigrants, *Typical American)*, perhaps because people just don't know what in the world to make of this novel, perhaps because a happy 1996 text about suburbia, Jewishness, and middle class life does not provide quite the narrative arc they were hoping for, in historical accounts that begin with protracted immigrant struggle. That is, *Mona* may be less rewardingly read as the struggle of a resistant "bad subject" against the "regulatory matrices" of subjectification (Nguyen 144; Chuh 9),[23] insofar as the novel affirms the redemptive possibilities of American interethnic subjectivity.

But if my students claim that Gish Jen makes Jewishness cool, I figured, it must be true. And no sooner did I accept this dictum, than I began to see everywhere more evidence of the coolness of Jewishness in cross-cultural translation, and was left musing on the question of in what that coolness might consist. Surely *Mona*'s Jewishness seems cool in part, to my students, because of its close association in the novel with teenage rebellion and social experimentation. But I began to wonder if there might be some particular coolness accruing to Jewishness when included as one among many elements of postmodern culture and textuality. Perhaps the capacity of diaspora Jewishness to be distinctively itself while always also dialectically engaged with other ethnic or national conditions—that is, its close connection, even correlation, with interethnicity, is in itself cool. Rather than whether Jen's novel switches to Jewishness, then, I began to focus on its use of Jewishness to switch to interethnicity, and on how, in so doing, it animates both Chinese and Jewish Americanness as cultural conditions: they become dialogic, relational participants in a sphere of broader transethnic exchange. The interchapter that follows will discuss the contemporary cross-cultural coolness of Jewishness in the context of global postmodern reading practices.

Who Is This We?

Telling a story of adolescence, this novel is appropriately obsessed with issues of individual identity. Versions of the question, "who am I?" abound, as when Barbara tries on a necklace given by her mother and asks, "Is it me?" (to which her mother replies "What a question. . . . Who else would it be?" [211]), or when Mona reads a sex ed. pamphlet titled "*Introducing . . . You!*" (213), or has sex for the first time and marvels "that she owns a whole self inside the self that she knows . . ." (109). Continually reconsidered and reframed, identity is presented throughout the novel as eminently transformable. In the first chapter, "Mona Gets Flipped," Jen introduces a series of tropes—flip, choose, convert, switch—that echo throughout the text the presiding trope of transformation. Nearly every character at one point or another undergoes some sort of switch, notably besides Mona, sister Callie, who eventually turns more Chinese; Seth, who thinks he's turning Japanese; and Sherman the Japanese exchange student, who first turns into a telephone voice with whom Mona has a long-term relationship, but eventually turns out to have been an act, played out over several years by Mona's Jewish male friends, and finally revealed in a broadly comic, Shakespearean version of the identity-switch plot.[24] Observing the changes of those around her, Mona engages in dialogue with Seth and others about the boundaries of selfhood, including issues of manners, ethics, authenticity, and contrasting Eastern and Western notions of the circles of family, community, and the world.

Beyond the bouncy narrative of interethnic teenage development, then, Jen's novel opens out into a broader examination of relationships outside the family and the ethnic group. And what starts as a novel about Chinese and Jewish American teens seems almost inevitably to turn into a novel about the relationship of these groups to African Americans. Mona's parents, who through necessitous self-reinvention have become a good deal more Americanized than many parents in Asian American novels, are financing their house in a neighborhood with top-notch public schools (with the ultimate goal of sending their daughters to Harvard) by running, of all things, a House of Pancakes. And it's there, in conversation with the black workers who mostly staff the kitchen, that Mona's and Barbara's politics are transformed, and the book reaches out to ask questions about a person's responsibilities to the larger world. Ultimately, in the spirit of the 1970s, Mona and friends must discover for themselves the limits of identity, family, home, and community. And so, taking over Barbara's lavish, parent-free mansion for a few months one summer, they launch a grandly doomed experiment in American interethnic communalism—Chinese, Jewish, white, and black.

For it's not ultimately with Jews that Mona has to have a central encounter, as she works out the meaning of her ethnic Americanness. Jews, it seems, will pretty much acknowledge (and be acknowledged by) her as a more or less parallel people, inheritors of a parallel immigrant history. But the structure of race in America seems, like some physical force, to impel Mona and her Jewish friends to address African Americans, so as to work out their relationship to blacks and the central black/white racial binary of U.S. history. The novel includes two important black characters: the first is the fabulously imagined Naomi, Callie's Harvard roommate, a charismatic character who embodies the book's ethos of hybridity. Born into the black lower middle class, she has managed by the time we encounter her in a Harvard dorm to raise herself to the status of "Renaissance woman," who does *tai qi* and speaks Chinese better than Callie and Mona ever will, but also loves jazz and sweet potato pie, whose simultaneous groundedness in black culture and mastery of the arts of multiple others makes her a meta-ethnic. Though she mentors the Chang sisters in identity politics (*"You are yellow. . . . a yellow girl"* [170]), more important is the way she models for them a very personal, creative form of self-definition. A larger-than-life figure whom none of her peers can help aspiring to imitate, Naomi stands in Jen's novel as a sort of bodacious John Kwang (of Lee's *Native Speaker*): the embodiment, for the hero/ine, of an interethnic ideal.

In the second case of Alfred, the handsome, black cook at the pancake house, class and race differentials produce more predictable barriers to relations with Mona and friends. Alfred is kicked out by his wife when he takes up with another woman. Though the form of homelessness he thus suffers is bathetic, self-created, he becomes a social action project for Mona, Seth, and Barbara. One dope-hazed evening, the teens do some comparative ethnic history and come to the amazing conclusion that, notwithstanding historical traumas on all sides, in America today it is a harder fate to be black than it is to be either Chinese or Jewish. They are brought to confront rank injustice. Jen writes: "Where to go from here? Mona doesn't at first see why they should have to go anywhere, but then she recalls that she is Jewish" (141). And in the earnest self-consciousness of their Jewishness, the teenagers decide to do teshuva—return, repentance, repair. "[O]ut of the Jewishness of her heart," she offers Alfred refuge, first in Barbara Gugelstein's garage, and then in the Gugelsteins' house, the parents having gone away for the summer (144). This is a mansion of hilariously lavish scale, featuring not only a pool and tennis court, but also turrets, "a greenhouse with automated vent-flaps," attic servants' quarters, "hand-tinted murals of country scenes in France" (59), and a basement tunnel that Barbara claims was built as part of the Underground Railroad—or may actually be more on the order of a wine cellar or bomb shelter. But as Underground Railroad the subterranean tunnel becomes the racial unconscious of the book, "the heart of darkness," as Mona thinks, vaguely recalling a literary title as she steps through the creepy tunnel (61), and fittingly, it's through the tunnel that Alfred soon comes to transport himself in and out of the house, so that none of the neighbors spot him at the front door and call the cops.[25]

Mona and friends have in mind a limited and quiet stay in an upstairs servant's room—no lights at night, no radio, no TV—but Alfred develops instead a quiet resentment of all this imprisoning largesse, and is soon privately inviting a crowd of his friends to hang out daily, enjoying the peace and comfort of the den. Add to this his secret romance with Barbara's cousin Evie, who is staying in the house for the summer, and you have the ingredients of a big surprise. When all is discovered by Mona, boyfriend Seth, and Barbara, what evolves after some shock and awkwardness is a communal be-in affectionately known as Camp Gugelstein, in which over the course of an enchanted summer, Mona, Seth, Barbara, Alfred, and a cast of African Americans named Ray, Big Benson, Professor Estimator, and Luther the Race Man hang out together, listen to music, exchange the words of Martin Luther King, Gandhi, and Elijah Muhammad, and discuss "politics, or drugs, or the war," good hair and bad hair, "sports, or cars, or—a surprise favorite—car repair" (200). They play chess, mah-jongg, ping-pong, swim in the pool, even practice yoga, and experience a season of cross-race enlightenment made possible by the convergence of youth, affluence, suburbanness, an optimistic moment in history, and parental absence—this last creating the illusion that the reign of the social order has been suspended.

Downstairs, the Underground Railroad, but upstairs, "the most interesting people Mona has ever known" sit cross-legged, hold hands, and chant "*Ommmmm*" together (202–3). Camp Gugelstein becomes a charged space, a scene of utopian longing we know must surely cease to be the minute Barbara Gugelstein's parents come home from vacation. And we are not too surprised when tensions arising around race and class difference and the rule of private property send everybody packing even before that. But for a short while, this novel imagines a house of American multiethnic coexistence—haunted by violent histories to be sure, as well as by the history of cross-race freedom work (both signaled by the Underground Railroad)—but for one bright season, a home for the healing of mutual homelessness, and for multiethnic collaboration of a kind that feels new and auspicious to all the participants.

My sense is that Camp Gugelstein is the heart of the book, the space that the narrative was driving toward all along. It is the sort of "[scene] of intercultural encounter" that Susan Stanford Friedman has proposed as the very "motive for some narratives, removing us as readers from the oedipal and post-oedipal scenes of the dwelling (the localized family plot), and directing us to the intersubjective spaces of self-other interaction" (*Mappings* 141). For a key ideological shift in the novel is its gradual passage from the question, "who am I?" and matters of self-discovery toward much broader communal concerns—specifically, to the encounter of the luckier ethnics with African Americans—and toward the question voiced (angrily) by Mona's mother late in the text: "who is this *we*?" (295). Camp Gugelstein provides a space outside the Chang family home for the heroine to explore a fuller range of American engagements. With the Underground Railroad below and the satire on the dissipations of wealth above, this mansion is the (scarred) home of the multicultural American dream, the dream house of interethnic coexistence—or to borrow Sollors's term, of American consent. It is the place where, leaving parents and their histories behind, we can all hold hands in a circle, at least until Closing Day of camp.

Does it matter that these grooving teenagers are squatting in the house of the Jews? I think it does matter, because the house of the Jews in this book is the house of both American aspiration and liberalism; compared to Fort Chang it is a house of relative openness as well as of achieved success. Jewishness makes Camp Gugelstein possible; it's the terrain of meeting in the middle; a place where long struggle has achieved security and material comfort, but a place still capable of generating Barbara Gugelstein, liberal, generous, and oblivious enough about class to invite home all her coworkers from the restaurant kitchen. Of course the be-in is made literally possible by the odd absence of the parents, a seeming result of the self-indulgent lifestyle of the assimilist adults, as well as of the growing generation gap between them and their politicized, Judaicized teens. At the same time, it makes sense that Jewishness is there at the meeting of cultures, where Jewishness has always been located. Moreover, it seems fitting that Jewishness marks the intersection of home and homelessness. For it is a brilliant turn on Jen's part eventually to reveal, after Mr. Gugelstein loses his high-power finance job for essentially anti-Semitic reasons, that the Jews had not actually owned the fabulous house where the camp took place. Rather, they were just leasing; "It wasn't ever even really ours," as Barbara puts it (281). The dream house was not really the permanent property of the Jews after all. The ideal of enduring familial position and wealth, of secure ownership of the prominent place in community that it embodies, of America as no *galut* but the long-dreamed home, at last turns out to have been illusory, a thing that could easily slip from the grasp of the Jews. Then whose fabulous house is it? Later, while the renegade young lovers Mona and Seth camp out in the attic, it's an empty house a real estate agent can't seem to sell; it's nobody's house; it's the vacant, languishing-on-the-market American dream house, a would-be European ancestral castle (turrets, murals) that is mocked by the Americans who cannot make themselves at home in it (such as Mona's friends, and the disgruntled bygone servant who painted pornographic satires of the murals in the attic servants' quarters).

But in the summer of Camp Gugelstein, with the parents gone and with the 1960s generation Jewish girls Barbara and Mona in charge, Jen realizes the dream house's possibility as the house of American multicultural collectivity, a place where young Asian, Jewish, and African American people can together say not only "Ommmmm" but also "we," can together make a temporary home. Jen's ironic use of narrative retrospect may create satiric effects throughout the novel, but it is worth noting that the moment of the book's setting, and the adolescent characters, allow a text written in the mid-1990s actually to indulge in "naïve," utopian experiment once again.

After some weeks the bubble bursts; a silver flask of Barbara's father's—emblem of paternal property and privilege—is discovered missing, and Barbara feels she must confront the newer members of her crowd about a possible theft. It is over this crude eruption of white ownership and of racial suspicion that the black characters split, saying, "Let's get out of this hellhole"; and "[a] lot of racist bullshit coming down here" (205). And it's a sadder, wiser Mona, Barbara, and Seth who leave Camp Gugelstein. Seth laments, "I believed it would work"; "I was naïve"; "They considered me a racist bastard and I considered them my friends" (206–7). To make things worse, when the parents return they discover evidence of the whole escapade, including the fact that Alfred has been sleeping with cousin Evie; not only are Mona and Barbara grounded and Evie "packed home to Minneapolis" (219), but also Mona's parents fire Alfred, the cook, whereupon she calls them racists, bringing on deepening family troubles. Then the Gugelsteins lose the house itself; it all falls apart. "Was all that transpired such a bad thing?" the novel asks (206). Surely the implicit answer is "no"; this youthful experiment in collectivism pushed the boundaries of cross-race relations further than adults usually manage, before hitting up against the recalcitrant structure of U.S. race, class, and power. Jen would seem to affirm the value of this unusual cross-ethnic stretch among all parties by the continuation of Alfred and Evie's romance into the novel's epilogue—though that closing section, in its cartoonish tone and blithe wrap-up of all loose ends and relationships, might be said to gloss over too easily the real race and class fissures the novel had revealed.[26]

When the missing silver flask is found, it turns out that the thief is not a black man, but, "Fernando!" (288), a former cook at the pancake house who is mentioned only once previously in the novel, here again, as in Lee's *Native Speaker*, a Latino. This discovery further shames Mona and company; but thank goodness for the availability of the Latino, whose crime doesn't have any long-reverberating racialized meaning in the book. Alfred later reconciles with Mona and friends in enduring and comic ways. As in *Native Speaker*, the treacherous Latino here may be a casualty of a refusal to demonize blacks, even while the Asian American hero/ine makes a home in white neighborhoods and power structures.[27]

This novel of a girl's development makes one of the most deliberate, extended attempts in Asian American literature to come to terms with the Asian American relationship to African Americans. Mona doesn't *marry* any of them, though cousin Evie eventually does, but Mona's plot of education takes her directly into and through the house of this particular cross-race experiment and possibility, where like any Austen heroine, she learns crucial, humbling lessons that help turn her into a person more ready to establish her own home. Now, the function of African Americans as catalysts to the growth of the non-black hero/heroine's moral conscience may be a tired and predictable plot, familiar to us from colonialist texts, but Gish Jen knows that it is, and never takes tongue from cheek while narrating the whole adolescent experiment. Moreover, she writes funny, smart, individuated black characters who get some of the best lines, as when Alfred, responding to Mona and Barbara's attempt to impress on him the virtues of switching to Jewishness, tries to explain what they don't get—his unswitchable racialization and its relationship to class: "We're never going to have no big house or no big garage, either. . . . We're never going to be Jewish, see. . . . *We be black motherfuckers*" (137). Jen's black characters clear out of camp when they've had enough "racist bullshit," but until that point, they also enjoy a time of finding themselves, astonished, in a circle they had never sat in before.

When a student of mine remarked that "college is like Camp Gugelstein," a temporary place of multiethnic coexistence that doesn't exactly resemble the outside world,[28] I realized that my classroom in particular is even more like Camp Gugelstein, comically enough: sponsored by a Jew, taking place in hallowed halls not originally intended for denizens such as myself or many of my students (female, ethnic, non-white), in which we attempt to make the most of a short-term multicultural collaboration. Then, of course, it struck me, more saliently for this essay, that Gish Jen remakes the Asian American novel, too, to be like Camp Gugelstein: a place where all kinds of people can enter, be heard in the conversation, and even change one another's minds and words, if only for a brief space of time. What can the Asian American novel be? this study continues to ask. Jen's book demonstrates that it can "switch" itself into being almost anything it wants, but that one of the most important things it can be is a house of spirited multiethnic engagement, built upon a hill of scars.

For Better or for Worse

When Mona's mother asks, "who is this *we*?" she refuses to recognize her daughter's membership in any circle outside that of the family. Mona has cheerily come back after long estrangement to report that, "We talked to Alfred," who has decided no longer to sue the Changs for race discrimination in his firing (a suit he can support with Mona's own admission to him that her parents are racists). But her mother is not interested in a display of daughterly duty by one who has shown herself to be more loyal to a larger sense of "we." So it is enormously important for the book's negotiation of these competing circles that the ending manages to place Mona happily within several of them simultaneously. The final scene opens with Mona getting dressed on her wedding day, as conventional a vision as a female bildungsroman could conjure out of the storehouse of literary endings, but comically undercut, here, by several dramatic additions and omissions—most notably the addition of Mona's one-year-old daughter, Io, and the omission from the scene of her father and Mona's groom, still Seth after all these years of cohabitation, but apparently otherwise occupied as Aunt Theresa helps Mona dress in the book's final pages. His crucial absence not only takes pressure off the heterosexual romance plot to allow more focus on the heroine and her own sense of the moment to which her narrative has brought her, but also leaves room in the scene for another momentous embrace.

Though this novel had not seemed, all along, to be shaped in the mold of Amy Tan's *The Joy-Luck Club*—that is, it had not seemed obsessed with the essential mother-daughter dyad, as is Tan's best seller, along with some other recent Chinese American novels[29]—notably in this epilogue it comes to seem that Mona's long estrangement from her mother, Helen, who has not spoken to her daughter for years and has never seen her granddaughter, is the key unresolved element of the plot, the one problem that interethnic marriage and even the birth of an interethnic child cannot resolve. And yet, just as Mona is joking with Theresa about whether she should change her—and Seth's and Io's—name to Changowitz (303), who should come up the walk but her parents, and soon the language of the Anglican wedding ceremony is taking over Mona's thoughts about her mother: "For the way she's crying, anyone would think that Helen is the person Mona's taking in sickness or in health. . . . The way Mona's crying, anyone would think that she's being taken too—finally!—for better or for worse. *Until death do us part*, she thinks, and rushes forward . . ." (304). Marrying her mother at last, Mona seals her loyalty to her Chinese roots, or perhaps better, to her Chinese-mothered sense of self, even as she prepares to marry out. And the ensuing applause by the "fine little witness" Io (discussed along with the other children of interethnic Asian American novels, in this study's epilogue) signals the next-generational fruition that Mona's rooted passage into the multiculture has already brought into being. Given neither a Chinese nor a Jewish name, Io (whose name signifies transformation, though in a peculiar form[30]) seems poised to be more Mona than Mona herself: free by virtue of her hybrid pedigree to invent the meanings of her own future transformations.

Postscript to a Letter from Camp Gugelstein

We might speculate on how a youth like Gish Jen's—an adolescent stay in the house of the American Jews in the 1960s and 1970s—shapes an Asian American writer's view of American race relations. My sense is that "rubbing elbows" with the Jews may tend to make that view at once rosier (as argued earlier) and more ironic, both because the Jews have a long-standing, humorous, creative engagement with marginality, and also because any significant interethnic engagement seems likely to lend one the irony of a comparatist.[31] This spirit of ironic combination has traveled with Jen into her next two publications, the 1999 short story collection *Who's Irish?* and the 2004 novel *The Love Wife*, which together expand and deepen Jen's examination of lived interethnicity among contemporary American characters and families. The title story of *Who's Irish?* marries Chinese American and Irish American lives, its ending, like that of *Mona*, another lively upset of expectations for closing union, when the Chinese American grandmother of a mixed family decides to move in with her Irish American counterpart, setting up a surprising form of interethnic home. Another story, "Birthmates," sends an unhappily divorced, unsuccessful Chinese American salesman on an accidental booking into a welfare hotel inhabited mostly by African Americans. When he is knocked cold by roughhousing kids and nursed by a woman named Cindy, her intimate care causes him to rethink his position in life, including his notions of "*you folk*" and "*us*" (32).[32]

The ethnically mixed American family of *The Love Wife* is given luminous presence by means of an innovative narrative form: a novel presented like a play, in short, sequential monologues by characters located not on a stage but in a telling nowhere. As the Euro-American wife, Chinese American husband, adopted Asian-origin American daughters, and visiting Chinese relative retell dramatic incidents, dialogues, or private reflections, their voices meet and converse, interrupt and contradict one another, without their actually being able to "hear" one another's words. The fabric of their pieced-together narration creates the effect of a miraculously full presence of multiple perspectives, of an alternately oppositional and harmonious narration-by-heterogeneous-family, Jen's most powerful realization to date of an interethnic consciousness in fiction. The added strand of adoption has an especially anti-essentializing influence on this novel's meditations upon ethnic identity, which are wryly summarized in a statement delivered by the laughing, post-mortem voice of a Chinese mother revealed at the end to have been an adoptive mother: "Nothing is natural. . . . Nothing" (376).

In *Mona in the Promised Land*, although Jen's exuberant attention to ethnic others bumps up against unfulfilled ideals—sad limits in its relations with African Americans, and in the enduring racialization of American culture—interethnicity does not become just an episode in a Chinese American character's larger story, but remains a vital principle throughout the novel. Jen keeps both of the important black characters, Naomi and Alfred, in the picture in the epilogue, updating their histories along with all the other characters'—her fame as an author, his college degree—and solidifying Alfred's link to the Jews through his marriage to cousin Evie, and the family they produce. Moreover, Mona is shown to retain Jewishness as part of her identity to the end; we expect that Jewish sponsorship of her investigations into identity positions will continue when her most recent job is described as "researching ethnic cartoons" at B'nai B'rith (298). For Mona, then—and perhaps for her author—the view of the world from the big-windowed house of the Jews is essential to an ironic, always-in-process sense of the possibilities of becoming.

But why, we might ask in general, would non-Jews want to spend time at Camp Gugelstein? What could be the attraction of making oneself at home, imaginatively, at least, with the Jews? The interchapter that follows considers forms of imagined Jewishness in late twentieth and early twenty-first century fiction in English by Asian American and other non-Jewish writers.

Interchapter: Cross-ethnic Jewishness in Asian American and Other Contemporary Fiction

The preface to John Okada's *No-No Boy* begins with the announcement that from the moment the Japanese bombed Pearl Harbor on December 7, 1941, "everything Japanese and everyone Japanese became despicable" (vii). The paragraphs that follow this preface offer a sequence of responses to the fall of Japanese Americans on the part of four generic representatives of the American public: a college professor, now embarrassed to look his Japanese "star pupil" in the eye; a drunk, ranting about "sneaky Japs" though it is his Japanese landlord who "[picks] him up off the sidewalk and [puts] him to bed" that night (vii); a "whore," who feels sorry for and "suffered a little with" her Japanese American customers, whom she "really liked" (viii); and someone named as "Herman Fine," who gets the longest paragraph. Fine, who has "a truck and a fine sense of horse-trading," "bought from and sold primarily to Japanese hotel-keepers and grocers," who, he believes, often schemed "to cheat him out of his rightful profit." Okada writes:

> Herman Fine listened to the radio and cried without tears for the Japanese, who, in an instant of time that was not even a speck on the big calendar, had taken their place beside the Jew. The Jew was used to suffering. The writing for them was etched in caked and dried blood over countless generations upon countless generations. The Japanese did not know. They were proud, too proud, and they were ambitious, too ambitious. Bombs had fallen and, in less time than it takes a Japanese farmer's wife in California to run from the fields into the house and give birth to a child, the writing was scrawled for them. The Jap-Jew would look in the mirror this Sunday night and see a Jap-Jew. (viii)

Thus ends the sequence of individual responders to the plight of the Japanese Americans; Okada goes on to the "indignation," "hatred," and "condemnation" more generally directed toward them by the public at large. The fact that Herman Fine's response is the longest of those cited suggests it is the most interesting for Okada; then again, it is not the first, second, or third thought that occurs to the omniscient speaker of this preface, but rather the complex, climactic fourth. Certainly it is an intense response, equal parts sympathy and insult, self-pity, accusation, and empathic grief. A Jew like Herman Fine is represented as not particularly likeable or admirable, but as one who no doubt understands what the Japanese are about to suffer, and knows it as a condition that will match, replicate, echo that of his own people. The two might as well share a detestable name.

This sense of a distant but clear parallel between the lots of Asian Americans and Jews can be traced throughout Asian American fiction, though usually found without the more unpleasant elements of Fine's characterization. But the Jewish thread is a far slenderer one, in this tradition, than that of African Americans; nothing like the extended and evolving engagement with a black presence, traced in the Asian/African interchapter, can be found in relation to Jews in Asian American fiction (and Okada, too, later includes black characters in more important roles than that of Herman Fine). While African Americans turn up regularly in Asian American texts, if only in cameo roles, Jews are much less common, a fact that reflects the centrality of blacks in the national racial imaginary—a position that Jews (to their good fortune) do not hold in the United States, as they sometimes did in Europe. Instead, Jews tend to make appearances in Asian American texts as remote but comparable others, not intimately known but recognized as bearers of a parallel historical minoritization.

Thus, in the wide canvass of Carlos Bulosan's Depression-era saga of Filipino American struggle, *America Is in the Heart*, two or three Jews appear, singly amidst the crowds: a girl who accompanies Carlos to a Los Angeles Communist meeting when he experiments with the Party (266); another Jewish girl who appears in a brief vignette in Montana, to say the emblematic thing: "It is hard to be a Jew!" (242); and an energetic fellow patient in the tuberculosis sanitarium, the Polish Jew Sobel, who "could not be outdone" in his zeal to wheel the breakfast cart from patient to patient, "singing peasant songs" all the way (251). Such figures appear in Bulosan simply to expand the horizontal reach of his vision of progressive solidarity.

In the more comic world of Gus Lee's *China Boy*, among the multiethnic, working-class San Francisco boys training in the 1950s at the life-saving YMCA is Joey Cohen, about whom Lee's young hero Kai Ting thinks, in a succinctly definitive example of this tendency: "He was Jewish and seemed, in some inexplicable way, to share a social ranking reminiscent of mine" (202). The two happily share a communion through food, too, for Joey, unlike the other non-Chinese boys, of course "liked Chinese food," and the underfed hero eats the deli sandwiches sent by Joey's mother "with joy"; "They were delicious," and Lee writes, "Next lifetime, if I'm *really*, *very* good, I thought—I'm coming back Jewish" (240). But when Kai, searching for his spiritual home in America, and having tried "Chrishten Science. Rutheran. Pre-boterian . . . Episcoparian," and other faiths, asks Joey, "I join you church?" Joey is puzzled: "It's called a synagogue. You don't *pick* 'churches.' You have *one* faith. You keep it, and never change." But he promises to ask his father, and returns:

> "Dad says Gentiles can pick religions like groceries. Jews don't do that. You're born into it, or ferget it."
>
> I felt a great sadness. "Sorry," he said. (240)

And so how is it that this remoteness disappears, the distance is so easily crossed, and a whole novel can hinge on Mona Chang's ease in joining the Jews' "church," barely two decades later, on the opposite coast, and a few notches up the social scale? Huge cultural changes between the '50s and the '70s certainly played their part in this literary transformation, including ideas held by Jews and many Americans about individual freedom in relation to religious and ethnic heritages, as well as the difference made by sheer numbers—Mona lives surrounded by Jews in suburban New York—in the seeming common-sensicality of such an assimilation, and also by the ascendance of youth culture, which made self-reinvention every teenager's right.

But more important, perhaps, is an unquantifiable change in the meaning of Jewishness in the late twentieth century, its evolution into something culturally central, essential, something contemporary fiction of all sorts partakes of, almost by definition. African American novelist Leon Forrest, musing in a 1994 conversation on the need to "open your imagination up to the different sensibilities that are American," thus on the way that Saul Bellow, along with Tennessee Williams and Ralph Ellison and Toni Morrison, can all help us "talk about what it means to be an American," elaborates on Jewishness in a way that complements Ellison's own claim (cited in chapter 1) that "whatever else the true American is, he is also somehow black." Forrest remarks, "Jews have opened up the consciousness of this country. We are all part Jewish too. Certainly to be an American intellectual, you must be a Jew. That's all to the good" (298).

Forrest does not quite say, "to be a reader or a writer you must be a Jew," but this interchapter begins with the notion that the Jewishness of *Mona in the Promised Land* builds upon potent cultural meanings of literary Jewishness that deserve investigation. In what follows, I carry the example of Jen's novel into an examination of two more novels that exemplify the interethnic impulse in contemporary fiction, both of which balance Chineseness with mainstream assimilation even as they turn substantially and rather surprisingly in the direction of Jewishness: Chinese American novelist David Wong Louie's *The Barbarians Are Coming* (2000) and Jamaican British novelist Zadie Smith's *The Autograph Man* (2002). Louie's novel, with its Chinese American protagonist from an immigrant family, would seem the most immediately comparable to Jen's *Mona*, and indeed many similarities arise between the two. But non-Chinese, non-Jewish Smith's novel of cosmopolitan London life also melds Chineseness and Jewishness in the person of her ethnically mixed protagonist and in key structural and thematic elements of the book. At the risk of stretching a trope too far, I will ask, what means Chinese Jewishness in these recent texts?

The sociological fact of the increased recent opportunities for diasporic Chinese and Jews to bump elbows can in part explain the appearances of three Chinese-Jewish plots (those of Jen, Wong, and Smith) in novels published by young writers in English within six years. But the specificity of this particular interethnic attraction suggests richer cultural work going on, even as it resonates with familiar modern literary and cultural deployments of Jewishness as trope. On one level we encounter, simply, the high visibility of the Jews as symbol in Western culture, the strange way in which, to borrow historian Robert M. Seltzer's terms, this "small people" of the ancient world eventually became, through the influence of its sacred texts, "the matrix of the cosmic historiography that came to dominate Europe, North Africa, and western Asia after late antiquity"; "the powerful valence of the image of the Jews," as Seltzer puts it, led to their lasting position as "both a paradigm for many other small groups and a special case" (1). Alain Finkielkraut refers to the paradigmatic figure of "the Jew in the abstract, who functioned as a kind of standard measure for comparing all types of misfortune" (175). According to Vincent J. Cheng, "Jewishness . . . function[s] . . . pervasively as a trope, as an empty signifier that can be objectified into a figure for suffering, alienation, and victimhood," while at the same time, "'the Jew' has become a popular metaphor for modernist exile, cosmopolitan rootlessness, and alienation" (106), most prominently in the instance of Joyce's epic hero Leopold Bloom, about whose Jewishness much has recently been written.[1]

On another level, Jonathan Freedman's 2008 book *Klezmer America* argues persuasively for the central, generative role of "the Jewish precedent" in "the ways in which Americans imagined Otherness," in "the making of the American racial and ethnic imaginary" (6, 12). For Freedman, contemporary Asian American writers—Gish Jen is his "classic example" (292), but also Bharati Mukherjee, Han Ong, and Lan Samantha Chang, among others—evince a revisionary "working through of the Jewish American fictional example" (303), in the mode of a Bloomian anxiety of influence (291), struggling with and overcoming American Jewish precursors, particularly as regards the handing-down from one "in-between people" to another, of the dubious distinction of "model minority" culture (276, 303).[2] And making claims not of influence but of mirroring, Judith Oster's *Crossing Cultures: Creating Identity in Chinese and Jewish American Literature* (2003) posits deep "affinities" between Jewish and Chinese cultures and "a mutual recognition between Jewish Americans and Chinese Americans," upon which she bases a comparative study, in the hope that the two bodies of contemporary fiction "will illuminate one another" (5, 8). All of these analyses seem to me useful, but not fully to satisfy the question of what in particular can be said to be going on when contemporary novels by Asian Americans or a half-Jamaican Londoner centrally thematize Jewishness. I turn to a look at Louie's and Smith's novels to help flesh out a complex literary phenomenon in which Gish Jen's *Mona* participates.

Like Jen, David Wong Louie deploys a wonderfully satiric eye in his entanglement of Chinese and Jewish people and cultures. But though *The Barbarians Are Coming* begins in outright farce—the Chinese American hero's blind date, Lisa Lee, turns out to be not a Chinese-American, biological woman but a white transsexual—in his further adventures through the realms of mixed identity, the jokes are increasingly darkened by an underlying tone of tragedy, which surprises the reader as it comes to dominate toward the end. A crucial distinction from Jen's work is that Louie's is ultimately a far less comic sensibility, in the classical sense. Immigrant parents in his novel are not allotted happy endings; indeed, late in the book the hero's father, a laundry owner given unexpectedly nuanced biographical treatment in the center of a novel told largely by and about the son, meditates, "For the entirety of his American life, he saw now, he had been unhappy. An immigrant has no business even contemplating such a luxury as happiness. It was an American affectation, slipperier than Chinese luck or money lust" (289).

Both this father and one of the hero's young sons are dead, in quick succession, by the end of the novel, allying this work much more closely with the tragic sensibility of Lee's *Native Speaker* than with Jen's *Mona*. And similarly, Louie's protagonist Sterling Lung resembles Lee's Henry Park much more than he does Mona Chang in the intensity of his desire to distance himself from—even his repulsion by—Asianness: his upbringing, his parents, and all that makes him not a white American. He summarizes his plot as "my desperate attempt to overcome the unremarkableness of being a Lung, and create a family more to my liking," and admits "I embraced school because school wasn't home, European cuisine because Escoffier wasn't home, Bliss [his Jewish wife] because she wasn't home. My sons were the blades of scissors that were supposed to snip me permanently, and genetically, free from home, from past and present, from here and over there" (323). Trained as a French chef, Sterling resists above all things Chinese cooking, and so it is painfully ironic that—recalling Henry Park's false performances of a variety of Asians, his discomfort in his own skin, his wearing of the Speech Monster's mask—Louie's hero ends up playing a grinning, pidgin-speaking Chinese chef on TV, and ashamed before his sons for doing so. So, although its plot depends upon an extended entanglement with the lives of American Jews, *The Barbarians Are Coming* is not a novel that takes up the American Jewish ethos of happy, individualist acculturation, but rather, one that bears witness to Asian American alienation—or, to borrow the terms of Anne Anlin Cheng, David Eng, and Kandice Chuh, racial melancholia, racial castration, and subjectlessness—which here is unrelieved, perhaps only attenuated, by the project of attempting to make oneself at home with the Jews. The hero's interethnic relations with other kinds of Americans are deeply tainted by his unacknowledged grief and anger about his racialization and its damage to his patrimony. This book indeed seems to share the anxiety about paternity and progeny in Louie's first book, the story collection *Pangs of Love* (1991), which Sau-ling C. Wong treats as an inheritance from the Exclusion-era Chinese American "bachelor societies," transmuted into misgivings, produced by widespread acculturation and by ongoing racism, about "extinction" for a certain cultural nationalist notion of Asian American male identity (Wong, "Chinese/Asian American Men" 181, 187). More so than either Jen's or Lee's heroes, Louie's Sterling is a profoundly unmarriageable Asian American protagonist, in Patricia P. Chu's terms; the plot of his marriage to a Jewish woman—and even a subplot of his possible marriage to a woman from China—are ultimately blips on the screen of his unfulfillable quest for reconciliation with his Chinese father and Chinese American self.

At the novel's opening we find Sterling dominated by, almost bound in emasculated servitude to, the WASP upper class, in the form of the rich ladies of the Richfield Ladies' Club, for whom he works as chef. The ladies tend to treat Sterling like an exotic pet, the more daring of them stroking his black pony tail, while they urge him to perform his ethnic difference by producing the Chinese food he has no desire to cook. From his servant's home in the club's carriage house, the remoteness of the ladies' sheltered, leisured lives from his is absolute, and so it is clear that in the American racial hierarchy represented in the book (no one here is black), Jews present the only viable engagement with Americanness available to Sterling; he often slips seamlessly from thinking of characters as Jews to calling them "Americans," and his marriage to a Jewish woman is described as "my breakneck dash from [his parents] and into the arms of any willing American girl who would have me" (323).

While indentured to the WASPs, Sterling seems in his personal life to encounter Jews everywhere. They seem to be his natural companions: every former girlfriend he mentions has a Jewish name (Brenda Bloom, Rachel Berg); his only friend is the Jewish butcher Fuchs, and the woman he reluctantly marries, and with whom he has two sons, is Morton and Selma Sass's daughter, Bliss—icon par excellence of Jewish American dreams of happiness—who grew up in a mansion in a promised land called New Canaan, Connecticut. Unlike Jen's Mona and family, Sterling and the Lungs do not "know they belong in the promised land" (Jen, *Mona* 3); rather, this novel records the hapless attempts of a working-class Chinese American son to enter it through marriage with the Jews. For if Jews seem in one sense a parallel people to Sterling's own, at the same time their particular brand of obsession with mythified ethnic tradition, tribal continuance, and American success seems a grotesque exaggeration of his own people's, placed in the path of this Americanizing Asian simply to torment him further. Jewishness in this novel may be an available and welcoming form of white Americanness, an Americanness that "would have" him, but in its symbolic valence of route to successful Americanization, it is by no means a figure for perpetually innocent victimhood, as in the conventional formulations cited above. The Sass grandmother, who bears concentration camp numbers on her arm, is the most overtly racist figure in the book, and her son, according to his daughter, Bliss, works at making money solely "[s]o he can say, 'Fuck you! You put my family in death camps, but I am better than you. Look at my Cadillacs, look at my gigantic house, look at my children's straight teeth'" (138).

Still, Sterling at first prefers this Americanized father to his own remote, alienated, laundry-working Chinese one. He says of Morton Sass, on a Thanksgiving early in their relationship, "I love this man, his open heart, his willingness to bend my way, the vodka in his hand shimmers like silver," but he cannot stem a rising sense of anomie as he turns to contemplate Bliss's mother's realm:

> I look at Selma Sass in her apron, her liberalism reflected in the riches of the kitchen she keeps: the bulging bowls of fruit, Golden Delicious, Red Delicious, Granny Smith, Pippin, Empire . . . crystal dishes brimming with walnuts, pecans, almonds, hazelnuts . . . pumpkin, spaghetti, hubbard, acorn, turban squash for show . . . and the best ingredients money can buy for sides . . . Idaho russets, Carolina yams, Long Island corn, Cape Cod cranberries, Florida oranges. I can hardly recognize myself, an emergent madness surfaces on my face, lost as I am in such a magnificent jungle of goodness. (147)

Clearly a substantial part of the problem is that, as masters of America's bounty from coast to coast, the Jews ultimately cannot be Sterling's allies for simple reasons of class:

> I know then, in my most honest heart, that I don't belong here, absorbing their heat, eating their food, getting high on their good fortune. I've earned none of this. . . . It's my back-of-the-laundry soul clanging inside her beautiful house; it's my bigoted immigrant parents who'll remain, until their death days, bottom-feeders, washing and ironing for others, while her bigoted immigrant grandparents ran a tailor shop into a chain of department stores. (154)

There are moments when Sterling thinks otherwise; when finally married into the Sass family and father of their grandson, he says, "Now all is good! I'm one of them, baby Moses my permanent membership card" (186). But life under the terms of his power-broker father-in-law breeds a violent resentment bordering on disgust, as when, about to muscle Sterling into the new identity of TV chef, Morton Sass also makes the emasculating move of verbally claiming Sterling's son as his own ("my little Moses"),[3] and Sterling says, "Something about this man, the stubble that pierces his cheeks, the pits and scars in his skin that pulse and creep. He is distinctly old-world: fleshy-headed birds, blind faith, and leeches; pickled meat, blood sacrifice, ritual bones, salt-in-wounds retribution" (188).[4] The distance of this rather startling, not-quite-coherent prose assault on the historical culture of the Jews from anything imaginable in the world of *Mona in the Promised Land* suggests the difference I mean to delineate between the two texts. In contrast to Jen's affectionate insider's stay in the house of the Jews, Louie's is an outsider's satiric sparring-match with the category of American Jewishness. While the Jews in both novels are the obvious, available white Americans most easily joined or married by a Chinese American protagonist, in Louie's work the two identities are usually at odds with one another, and their melding is as undesirable and finally impossible as is full embodiment of one's inherited Chinese identity.

This difference becomes clearest in the very different fate of the interethnic children of this novel. The first, a baby secretly born to Sterling's father and a white woman in the early days of his immigration to this country, dies almost immediately after birth; clearly born in the wrong generation, when Asian American plots could not sustain hybrid progeny, this purple infant is the blighted fruit of his failed American hopes. Of Sterling and Bliss's two sons, the first, ironically named Moses, resembles his Chinese grandfather. Sterling is delighted then, when the second, Ira, looks nothing like Sterling's family: "No sign of Lung chromosomes remained. Natural selection. We had finally done something good together" (217), and further: "With Ira, whom everyone deemed pure Sass, I thought I had succeeded in erasing every trace of myself, committed genealogical suicide" (323). The astonishing degree of loathing Sterling feels for his Chineseness makes it impossible for him to understand or celebrate Ira as the embodiment of an interethnic ideal, as is the case with young Mitt of Chang-rae Lee's *Native Speaker*; rather, for Sterling, Ira embodies an aspiration to achieve total whiteness. Tragically, however, Ira like Mitt dies at a young age, in his case in a car crash caused indirectly by the failure of his parents' interethnic marriage; both boys die in a sense because of and to demonstrate the failure of interethnic desire. Ira's death and funeral provide the novel's emotional climax, and when in death he "seems to float like a little cloud, free of the rancor everyone confuses with sorrow"; he somehow does incarnate a lost hope very much like that of Lee's Mitt, despite Sterling's color emphasis: in his "bright white coffin," "[h]e is pure, and will always be" (319).

But at the gravesite, the two sides of the family, both mourning this lost possibility, are absolutely divided from one another in their mourning, and this division seems definitively to put to death any chance of real Chinese-Jewish blending. While the Lungs arrange a ritual food offering at the grave—"thick slabs of boiled pork belly, strips of glistening *cha-siu*... [o]ranges, sweet tricornered muffins, sponge cakes. And a giant whole chicken... (326)—the Sasses are aghast ("What's going on here? That's pork!" [327]), but attempt to adjust, in liberal fashion. Louie records in Sterling's narration a dance of mutual alienation and convergence, suspicion and commonality:

> I hear Selma Sass whisper, "Food is very important to Chinese culture." She's explaining us to the rabbi and the geologist. What viciously stupid talk: isn't food important to every creature that ever walked, crawled, or swam this earth? She continues, "They don't do anything without food. They're like us that way" (326).

Though similarity is glimpsed through the screen of difference, the two families stand unalterably separate: "Rabbi Ron says a prayer in Hebrew. At his insistence, the food has been cleared from the grave" (328). The two parts of Ira's family are last seen together as disunited, parallel mourners.

Louie's ending stages a reunion between Sterling and his surviving "Chinese" son, Moses, that partly recuperates the possibility of Jewish Chinese hybridity. But the emphasis here is less on the "horizontal" interethnic than on the vertical plot of ethnic generational transformation: as father feeds son "Chinese food" made of quintessentially American ingredients (saltine crackers, sweet condensed milk), he begins the work of repairing the wounded father-son story that traverses the novel, with the goal of more fully embraced American Chineseness. Demonstrating the profound ambivalence that can attend interethnic plots, *The Barbarians Are Coming* positions Chinese and Jewish Americans as, mutually, barbarians to one another. A stay in the house of the Jews, conducted by a melancholic Chinese American, may be only partly and painfully fruitful, may amount to not much more than an absurd and vexing passage on the way back to one's own familiar homelessness.[5]

It is harder to define the eccentric role of Jewishness in Zadie Smith's *The Autograph Man*. Though the work of this twenty-something London novelist exceeds the expected boundaries of this U.S.-centric study, I include it in this interchapter because its strong resonances with the Jewish engagement of Gish Jen's work signal a transnational web of imaginatively adopted Jewishness that bears reflection here, both because the Jewishness concerned is often, interestingly enough, American Jewishness, and because transnationality, one of the characteristics most identified with Jews throughout history, is a key quality of the economy of literary identification engaging Asian Americans, among many others, in our globalizing age.

Smith, whose wildly popular and ultra-cool first novel was *White Teeth* (2000), returns in this second novel to multicultural London. But this time the protagonist is not half English, half Jamaican, like the author, but rather half Jewish, half Chinese, one Alex-li Tandem, a melancholic twenty-something dealer in celebrity autographs, whose aimlessness has something to do with the death, years ago, of his Chinese-born father, but also seems simply the shared slacker condition of all of his friends; upon whom Alex-li muses, in poetic lines: "I saw the best minds of my generation / accept jobs on the fringes of the entertainment industry" (55).

This theft from Allen Ginsberg is the least of the book's adaptations of Jewishness. Alex-li's friends are all Jews, the closest of them a brother and sister who are black Jews originally from Harlem. The ten *sfirot* of the medieval Jewish mystical system called the kabbalah frame the book, giving names to the chapters (*schechinah*, *t'feret*, *binah*), and a diagram of the kabbalistic *sfirot*, which looks something like a dining table set for ten cross-connected circles, is prominently displayed near the opening of the book, with the faces and names of famous British and American writers and celebrities inserted in and around the circles (e.g. *Hochmah*, Wisdom, Virginia Woolf; *Hod*, Splendour, John Lennon; *Hesed*, Love and Grace, Fats Waller). Besides this there are plenty of running Jewish jokes, including the hero's obsession with classifying the world according to the binary system made famous by the American Jewish comedian Lenny Bruce in a routine in which all things are declared either "Jewish" or "Goyish." At the novel's opening, Smith posts a long excerpt as an epigraph, from which I'll quote a bit:

> If you live in New York City or any other big city you are Jewish. . . . If you live in Butte, Montana, you're going to be goyish, even if you're Jewish.
>
> Kool-Aid is goyish. Evaporated milk is goyish even if the Jews invented it. Chocolate is Jewish and fudge is goyish. Fruit salad is Jewish. Lime Jell-O is goyish. Lime soda is *very* goyish.

Smith's hero, Alex-li, is actually writing a secret book in which he catalogues the world's Jewishness and Goyishness as he sees it: "Jewish office items (the stapler, the pen holder); goyish office items (the paper clip, the mouse pad)"; and he walks the streets of London maniacally classifying; "Goyish. *Jewish*. Goyish. Jewish. Goyish. *Goyish* Jewish. *Goyish*!" (75). To be fair, the book and its hero later give up this binary obsession and move on to a more complex sense of things. But to the critic James Wood, writing in the London Review of Books, *The Autograph Man* epitomizes a contemporary trend toward what he calls "irrelevant intensity," an obsession not with truly important things but with random information, with the "comedy of culture," and a tendency "desperately [to semaphor]" nothing but its own "gross mimetic appetite." Alex-li, Wood writes, "seems quite ludicrously . . . deranged by his Jewishness. . . . Improbably," Wood goes on, "Alex thinks of his cat as goyish ('this goyish, humourless, pink-eyed fluffball')." "It is an obsession which seems essentially inauthentic, and which marks the novel precisely as one *not* written by a Jew." Indeed, Wood entitles his review of the book, "Fundamentally Goyish" (Wood).

I must say that I cringed for Zadie Smith when I read that title and that, in fact, though I liked certain aspects of the novel, I also began to develop a permanent cringe of embarrassment while reading the Jewishness/Goyishness sections (although not about the fluffy cat; that strikes me as self-evidently accurate). My embarrassment came from wondering if it could be that the author of this extended conceit never did stop to ask herself, "and under which of these categories might *my book* fall?" Zadie Smith really seems to think she has the capacity to write a book that is not "fundamentally goyish," that she can stride that divide, perform Jewishness as a legitimate part of her repertoire. Still, I would not be as quick as Wood to declare that she doesn't do so, that the whole thing is a travesty, a flop, a useless exercise in postmodern pastiche, designed to dazzle us with the ironies of our own multicultural literacy. Something Jewish *is* happening here, I think, though perhaps not in a fully realized, fully successful way.

For, sprinkling Jewish intimations of the divine throughout the vapid realist landscape of her novel, Smith produces, alternately with moments of pure bathos, suggestions of transcendent meaning. Threaded throughout the book is a poignant effect of yearning after God; if this is a less tonally Jewish book than Jen's *Mona*, it is a more spiritually Jewish one. Though graspable only in the diminished form of signs, a Jewish idea of immanent transcendence is always there nevertheless. This effect is most fully present in the book's prologue, which focuses on the hero's father, the thirty-six-year-old Chinese British doctor Li-Jin Tandem (originally Tan) who knows over the course of a summer afternoon that he will soon die of a brain tumor, the existence of which he cannot bear to relate to his wife or to his much-loved adolescent son, Alex-li. In the afternoon the prologue relates, Li-Jin drives his son and three friends to a wrestling match, a hideous and crowded event that he endures in order to spend some of his remaining time with his son, despite the excruciating headache.

Who can explain exactly why, dividing the prologue about Li-Jin into sections and marking each one, appears the name of God, the tetragrammaton, sometimes in the English form YHVH, and sometimes, oddly, in the Hebrew letters (Yod-hay-vov-hay) inside of a cartoon speech bubble, suggesting that someone is calling out God's Hebrew name (which no one is supposed to do)? In either form, the name here gives the appearance of somehow emanating from inside the page to its surface, mystically signifying God's presence, or a plaintive yearning toward God, or a seamless equivalence of the two. The effect is rather haunting. So that when on the last page of the prologue, in a post-wrestling match rush of the crowd, Li-Jin falls, apparently dying and seeing "Many, many people," but "No one familiar or friendly. No one to help. No one he knows" (35), the final emanation of the yod-hay-vov-hay in the speech bubble suggests Li-Jin calling out to, or perhaps just beginning to know, the one named by that repeated name, whose presence and even agency in this oncoming death the reader has received hints of all along. Li-Jin, who is not Jewish at all though married to a Jew, could not possibly have been thinking in Hebrew, but somehow his death is framed, in the book, within mystical Jewish parameters. Is this because, being a creature of a prologue, he is an ancestor of a questing Jew, in other words, granted cultural hybridity postmortem? Or does the author of this book genuinely mean to give Li-Jin's life and death, and everyone's life and death, sacred meaning, in Jewish terms?

Despite the novel's cross-cultural incongruities and its ironic play with names and autographs—the merest, flimsiest signs of presence—Smith's use of Jewish sacred forms and traditions suggests an abiding order, undergirding this disordered, over-full, jagged composition of a life. The hapless hero is at last brought back to rightness when he finally says Kaddish for his long-dead father, on the book's last page, or as Wood puts it, "The man who trades in false signs is finally led into synagogue to do business with the great transcendental signified Himself" (Wood). The more Jewish the hero becomes, the closer he comes to his Chinese father.

What is Zadie Smith doing granting this sort of narrative force to Jewish ideas? As readers of modern literature we are, of course, well used to writers drawing upon ancient narratives and symbolic systems to undergird their modern texts. The propriety of this process tends to come into question only when the material is borrowed from cultures not understood to be part of the author's legitimate inheritance. Thus nobody questions Joyce's right to use Greek epic, or even Jewish history and scripture, or Eliot's right to use the myth of the Fisher King; but rather, say, Eliot's use of material from the East, to which the West stood and stands in a relationship of imperial mastery.[6]

But what of borrowings in the other direction, bottom-up instead of top-down? Those terms seem inadequate to the complexity of the relationship between a Chinese American or a half-Jamaican Londoner to the historical culture of the Jews, particularly its fringe traditions, and yet some trace of this sense of the power relations would seem to color James Wood's charge that Zadie Smith's Jewishness is inauthentic. Surely we could say that for Smith, as for Jen and Louie, Jewishness is an available middle term, neither black nor precisely white,[7] nearly parallel to and thus easily and comically comparable to Asianness, even while the deployment of its sacred forms might be seen as an imaginative claim to its cultural authority.

Even if we grant Freedman's argument about the place of Jewish texts in American literary culture, and contemporary Asian American fiction's tendency to exhibit "the complex mix of ethnoracial envy and desire that informs aspirants to the cultural capital claimed for—and indeed achieved by—Jews" (308), the agon of this U.S. family drama cannot fully account for the imaginative leap of Zadie Smith, writing from post-national London. What can mean the switch to Jewishness from that location? If we are to read *The Autograph Man* as more than just a performance of Smith's ability to inhabit multiple cultural vocabularies, more than either shallow multicultural cross-dressing or a claim to the symbolic authority of Hebrew letters, we need to figure out by what logic she deploys Jewishness here.

Again, my interest is not whether Smith, Jen, or Louie have the *right* to appropriate Jewish material—it seems to me, when all is said and done, that an author makes his or her own right to do such things by doing them well—but rather why one would *want* to write Jewishly, when it would seem ever so much cooler not to; why, instead, would one want to contribute (as do Jen and Smith, and to a lesser extent Louie) to the contemporary literary project of making Jewishness cool?

To begin, it is apparent that the Jewishness under discussion in these cool-Jewish texts is something other than the cultural, religious, or ethnic self-understanding of Jews, but has become, rather, a malleable sign or site in the web of global, postmodern culture. As E. San Juan, Jr., has put it, describing the unequal relations of the global and the local amidst contemporary commodity capitalism, "Ethnic and racial markers become 'floating signifiers' with meanings dependent on who articulates them, for what purpose, under what circumstances of production and reception, in what place and at what time" (276). Our subject of interest thus may become not ethnicity per se, but what Jelena Šesnić has called "the processes by which a specific ethnicity ceases to be a self-understood identification and instead becomes a living, changing construct, such that may enter into cultural/representational contracts with others of its kind" (Unpublished paper, 13). What, after all, is Smith doing playing with Chineseness, here, as well, somewhat less important to the novel's structure, but still a key thematic presence and half of Alex-li's parental heritage, while none of the author's own?

Further, the oeuvres of these three novelists would seem to suggest that, amidst the contemporary web of such signifiers, it is no longer possible not to be culturally hybrid. Indeed, in Smith's second novel, painfully conscious of mortality, of the unknowability of the cosmos, of the lamentably partial truth attainable by all cultural systems and signs, she grants a special power, one that James Wood would not grant, to cross-cultural bricolage—borrowing, mixing, juxtaposing, crossing lines to commune with another people's truth—seeing in that artful fusion a potent source of the comic spirit, and of the potential for truth and beauty.

Jewishness as sign seems to have a special place, for Smith and Jen, in this hybrid vision. Surely part of the appeal lies in the way that Jewishness functions, at least in the West, as a figure for self-conscious difference from a surrounding, normative, "goyish" whiteness. And certainly the availability of Jewishness, even to "people of color" like Smith, Jen, and Louie, has something to do with its history of crossing lines, of adaptability across many regions and identities. As David Biale, Michael Galchinsky, and Susanna Heschel have written:

> The Jews are perhaps the longest-standing case of a group whose self-definition was always a part of a multicultural context. For much of Jewish history, what it meant to be a Jew was to be multilingual and multicultural and never to live in splendid isolation from interaction and struggle with other cultures. . . . to be a Jew, especially at this historical juncture, means to lack a single essence, to live with multiple identities. Perhaps the Jews are even emblematic of the postmodern condition as a whole. (Introduction, 8–9)

If Jewishness can exemplify postmodern hybridity, it does so in the specific form of diaspora; and as Michael Galchinsky has noted, postcolonial "theorists have begun to understand Jews' history and theories of diaspora as crucial to postcolonialism's attempts to subvert identity politics of all kinds. . . . transnational, hybrid, and fluid diasporic communities . . . can be subversive of the brutally homogenizing ideologies and practices of nations and empires" (186). In the work of authors like Smith, Jen, and Louie, the switch to Jewishness can emblematize their own hybrid, diasporic condition by proxy—a move that is especially anti-homogenizing. And insofar as Diaspora Jewish cultural production has been especially "syncretic, heterogeneous," as Freedman puts it, has been "a tradition of dynamic innovation wrought in the encounter between Jewish and gentile cultures that has the property of reanimating both" (22), perhaps these contemporary non-Jewish novelists affiliating with Jewish cultural forms invoke just this spirit of syncretism and mutuality.

Moreover, my sense is that all three of these novels draw upon the Jews' contradictory, ironic way of inhabiting modernity, of being unable not to trail an ancient and extravagant spiritual history with them into the sullied and secular present. Vincent J. Cheng speaks of a tendency toward a certain "Jewish chic" (107), which we have recently seen manifested in such pop culture phenomena by non-Jews as Madonna's invocations of Kabbalah, or even in the return by young American Jewish artists to a Jewish-centered avant-gardism in contemporary New York.[8] Cheng explains that Jewishness has attained the status of an enviable condition because, "[i]n a world haunted by a sense of millennial inauthenticity and by a pervasive anxiety about identity," Jewishness "is imagined to still obtain and exist in the modern world—a cultural atavism and essence in conflict with contemporary globalism that has somehow not yet disappeared" (107). As Finkielkraut puts it, non-Jews may "envy their collective memory, their intense sense of belonging . . . the inherent transcendence that makes them more than mere individuals. . . . To people such as these prisoners of the egosphere, Jews seem blessed by history: part of their being is not of the self but transcends it, partakes of a vaster group and greater temporal scheme" (92, 94).

For Finkielkraut, those likely to envy Jews are "sullen members of the majority culture [who] have the white bread blues" (94). If it does not make sense to say the same of the diasporic or ethnic American writers discussed here, imbricated in the blues of their own greater historical narratives, we might still see that embracing Jewishness in these novels has the common effect of enshrining an—however ironic—sense of history at the core of selfhood. Whether Jewishness is presented as a path to social commitment, to Americanization, or to healing the brokenness of the world, it brings a certain intensity of self-consciousness, a self-consciousness that memorializes tragic, diasporic history, within an essentially comic vision. Jewishness, then, works to figure the irony of being ethnic in postmodernity. When Smith and Jen wear the mask of Jewishness, they affirm what is redemptive in the fate of shlepping through the hybrid postmodern world remnants of the old ways of seeking after meaning. Whether wrestling with Jewishness, like Louie, or like Jen and Smith making Jewishness cool, they inscribe an ironic appreciation of the psychic residue of one's own distinctive and eccentric world-traveling heritage. At the same time, we might also say that for Jen, Louie, and Smith, the switch to the exemplary condition of Jewishness seems in itself an exemplary form of postmodern interethnic identification, of freely borrowing others as models of cultural self-positioning. In the interethnic zeitgeist of the present, elaborating identity through the encounter with difference may be a powerfully expressive representational strategy, evoking what it is to be a bearer of a historical culture in a globalized, hybridized world.

Above all, the switch to the subject of Jewishness in the contemporary interethnic novel suggests that Jewishness has evidently become part of the collective global inheritance, something one can now acquire through books, something fun to play around with, something that seems readily detachable from the exigencies of either orthodox religious observance or Israeli national policy, an elastic and accommodating, even welcoming, condition for any experimenting individual. Perhaps this ultimately has something to do with the well-known text-centeredness of Jewishness, the fact that Jewish identity is centrally derived from reading books, both traditionally and even in contemporary life, when Jewish selfhood has continued to be derived from texts now located at a certain remove. While, for Leon Forrest, one becomes "part Jewish" by entering into American literature, might one become especially Jewish by reading (and writing) literature cross-culturally? I mean to suggest that in the translations of these three novels, Jewishness appears the very emblem of the derivation of identity through texts. And the *switch* to Jewishness, then, is an emblematic sign of cross-cultural identification through other people's texts, an affirmation of the way we read now. As such, in our contemporary moment, Jewishness has become something very, very good to write.

4

Karen Tei Yamashita's *Tropic of Orange* and the Transnational, Interethnic Imagination

A Hundred Shakuhachis

On a Los Angeles freeway overpass stands a white-haired old man with a raised baton, conducting the music of the traffic below. Depending on the time of day, traffic patterns, and the rhythm of peoples' lives, the music he guides into being can be "excruciatingly beautiful." "When it was really good," writes Karen Tei Yamashita, "it brought tears. He let them run down his face and onto the pavement, concentrating mightily on the delicate work at hand." Although "[t]hose in vehicles who hurried past under . . . [his] concrete podium most likely never noticed him" or felt "disconnected from a sooty, homeless man on an overpass," the old man's art has an unsuspected power: "[S]tanding there, he bore and raised each note, joined them, united families, created a community, a great society, an entire civilization of sound" (33–35).

This conductor of community is Manzanar Murakami, a character in Yamashita's 1997 novel *Tropic of Orange*. Once a surgeon and a family man, Manzanar walked away from all that and became a homeless freeway overpass conductor for reasons he cannot explain even to himself. His name records his history as "the first sansei born in captivity" (108), a Japanese American born at the Manzanar detention camp during World War II, and so we suspect that that archetypal Japanese American trauma may be at the root of his eventual unhinging, of his painfully acute sensitivity to the sounds of our civilization, his transformation of the traditional Asian practice of attentive silence into a fantastic art of inspired listening. This is to say that Asian American history and culture leave their traces in this ambitious novel, but that Yamashita extends these traces into "extravagant" designs, in

Sau-ling C. Wong's terms (see *Reading*), designs unanticipated in Asian American novelistic tradition.

Indeed, Yamashita's account of the cultural embarrassment caused by Manzanar's idiosyncratic practice reflects wryly on her own relations with the most conventional of Japanese American norms:

> The Japanese American community had apologized profusely for this blight on their image as the Model Minority. They had attempted time after time to remove him from his overpass, from his eccentric activities, to no avail. They had even tried to placate him with a small lacquer bridge in the Japanese gardens in Little Tokyo. But Manzanar was destined for greater vistas. He could not confine his musical talents to the silky flow of koi in a pond, the constant tap of bamboo on rock, or manicured bonsai. It was true that he had introduced the shakuhachi and koto to a number of his pieces, but he was the sort who imagined a hundred shakuhachis and a hundred kotos. (36–37)

There are ethnic artists whose eccentricity and largeness of vision strain the capacity of received forms and categories. One such is Karen Tei Yamashita, wildly imaginative and politically engaged, brilliant and humane, Asian, American, and Latin American, a writer who seems to view our collective life, like her alter ego Manzanar, from a position of unusually expansive vistas. A Japanese American born in California, Yamashita lived for a decade in Brazil, married a Brazilian, and in the first three of her novels spans the Americas by means of startlingly unconventional narrative strategies.[1] Writing in English for American audiences, Yamashita reformulates migrant stories and subjectivities, raising both dread and laughter while evoking the perils of the ethnically and nationally bounded imagination. Her work expands and complicates Asian American fictional interethnicity on a transnational scale.

Like her earlier books, Yamashita's third novel, *Tropic of Orange*, defies conventional literary categorization, exceeding the boundaries of most genres or subgenres to which we might at first glance assign it: postmodern satire, magic realism, Los Angeles disaster fiction, Asian American fiction, ethnic American fiction, Mexican fiction. Perhaps the most nearly adequate generic term would be "border novel," for in its formal elements and its plots, its landscape and its characterization, *Tropic of Orange* is deeply informed by the effort to render what José David Saldívar has called "the discursive spaces and the physical places" of the U.S.-Mexico border, and thus participates in "an *emerging* U.S.-Mexico *frontera* imaginary" in literature and culture (*Border* ix, xii). But if this is a text about the borderlands, then, as Claudia Sadowski-Smith puts it (in a somewhat different context), "readers of Yamashita's work may be asking themselves: What's Asian American about this?" (101). Yamashita's entire oeuvre has challenged standard notions of "what's Asian American," taking the Asian American novel to new places and welcoming into it new kinds of characters, broadening and complicating the geographical, historical, cultural, and generic contexts of representation in that body of literature.[2] And in *Tropic of Orange*, we might say that she has done the same for the literature of the border—identified heretofore almost exclusively with Chicano/a cultural production—by opening it up to Asian American and other populations and influences usually outside the borders of the border text.

Clearly, it would be insufficient to read such a novel exclusively within the parameters of Asian American literature. And yet, argues Rachel Lee, writing on Yamashita's first novel *Through the Arc of the Rain Forest*, it is important to consider Yamashita's work within that context because its "very oddities" can help us interrogate the "key hermeneutical options in Asian American literary and cultural studies" (Americas 107). For if the 1990s witnessed a "paradigm shift" in Asian American studies, from a national focus to the framework of a transnational Asian diaspora (Wong, "Denationalization" 2), Yamashita's fiction swells even this wider scope, connecting the diasporic Asian subject and the geopolitical, economic, and cultural dynamics of the Pacific Rim to the transnational space of the Americas, and the lives that transgress that most fortified border between North and South.[3] Thus, when Manzanar looks oceanward from his lofty perch, his view of the Pacific begins at "the southernmost tip of Chile" and then ascends in a sweeping arc "to the Galapagos, skirting the tiny waist of land at Panama, up Baja to Big Sur to Vancouver... to the Bering Strait," and then descends "from Vladivostok around the Japan Isles and the Korean Peninsula, to Shanghai... Ho Chi Minh City, through a thousand islands of the Philippines, Malaysia, Indonesia," and southward (171). But in another moment, when Manzanar turns to face his own city, he sees in Los Angeles an equal complexity. Like cultural critics who work with both transnational and U.S. paradigms, Manzanar perceives his home not only in a vast regional context, but also in its own dense and multifaceted local character, in a vertical layering that begins with "the very geology of the land, the artesian rivers running beneath the surface," and ascends through the "web of faults" and "the man-made grid of civil utilities"—gas, water, and power, to "the great overlays of transport—sidewalks, bicycle paths, roads, freeways," to "patterns and connections by every conceivable definition from the distribution of wealth to race, from patterns of climate to the curious blueprint of the skies" (57).

"*There are maps and there are maps and there are maps*," writes Yamashita. "The uncanny thing was that he could see all of them at once..." (56). Creating fictional worlds that juggle myriad conceptual maps, Yamashita manages simultaneously a global reach and a rich local specificity, interweaving large-scale visions of natural and human grandeur and disaster with small-scale illuminations of private yearnings and tragedies. As her work "highlights the global constitution of local identities" (R. Lee, *Americas* 111), families are formed, parted, and reunited by forces of world change; people from the most heterogeneous walks of life are all made personally subject to the same natural and political upheavals. To compare Yamashita's interethnic vision to the visions of Chang-rae Lee, Gish Jen, and the other Asian American authors considered in this study is thus to note the dynamic effects of her transnational paradigm, which situates local Asian American, other ethnic, and interethnic events and relationships in the convergence of far broader forces. What appears in Lee as a cacophonous New York City street scene of heterogeneous immigrant vendors, or in Jen as a glance at the pre-American lives that explain the behavior of the heroine's Chinese American parents, becomes in Yamashita sustained attention to human passages and interactions across seas and borders, and to the global economic and political changes to which they are intimately tied. Beginning with brief accounts of Yamashita's first two novels, both set in Brazil, this chapter will go on to argue that *Tropic of Orange* exemplifies the combined impact of the new transnational and interethnic paradigms on works of Asian American literature, becoming an allegory of imaginative "paradigm shift" itself.

Passage to Brazil

Yamashita's plots always begin with someone on the move, someone whose footsteps begin to set global changes in motion. In her most straightforward narrative, *Brazil-Maru* (1992), a realist historical fiction, Yamashita recovers a little-known chapter of Asian history in the Americas, the experiment in rural communal living on the part of idealistic Japanese immigrants to Brazil in the early twentieth century. *Brazil-Maru* portrays the attempts of this transplanted group to overcome the limits of national identity and build a civilization neither Japanese nor Brazilian but something new between the two; ultimately, however, it traces the idiosyncratic personalities and moral failings that undermine these utopian hopes.

Similarly bold in their crossing of borders but far from the tonalities of *Brazil-Maru* are the riotous worlds of Yamashita's first and third novels, in which bizarre and magical narrative strategies dramatize for American audiences the interdependent world in which we must come to see that we live. *Through the Arc of the Rain Forest* (1990) is an ebullient and chaotic fable about the world's encroachment upon the people and the rain forest of Brazil. As the agents of global capitalism converge on the tropics, nature undergoes bizarre transformations, while human invention thrives like the great rain forest itself, concocting comically hyper-organized global networks of commerce, communications, science, and religion. All the while, a mysterious, hard, gleaming substance called the Matacao surfaces in each acre of cleared forest. As intriguing as the Matacao, however, is the novel's narrator, a small black ball that rotates on its axis before the head of the hero Kazumasa Ishimaru, a Japanese immigrant to Brazil. Much could be said about this truly original narrative device, the ball (and I have done so at length elsewhere),[4] but suffice it here to say that, besides being a feminist, ethnic parody of narratorial omniscience—an absurdly visible, spherical attendant to the head of the hero that transforms the conventionally invisible and solipsistic Narrator into a being who values relationships—the ball seems to embody a desire for a global voice, a voice that could transcend the perceived limitations of an ethnic perspective and, as a credibly global historical witness, persuade readers to follow it across numerous old divides, to conceive a universal ecological imperative.

In Yamashita's most astonishing turn, late in the novel both the narrating ball and the marvelous Matacao are revealed to be eruptions of first-world waste plastic. Thus Yamashita's speaker places itself, its own powers of knowing, in the material realm of the global ecology. And even as it reminds us that we, too, are living lives inextricably bound up with waste plastic, it urges upon us our own awakening from matter to spirit, to the kind of global ecological consciousness needed to save the planet.

Tropic of Orange

Like its author, Yamashita's 1997 *Tropic of Orange* leaves behind the Brazil of her first two novels to settle in L.A., and yet this novel's vision is her most transnational to date. Instead of the spin of a ball, the movement at the heart of this text is a slow northward creep, the magical migration of the Tropic of Cancer across the U.S.-Mexico border to Los Angeles, trailing in its wake the illegal immigration of the entire culture and history of the Southern Hemisphere. *Tropic of Orange* explodes that furiously defended frontier and cultivates a multicultural sublime, assembling a cast of thousands in a postmodern, transnational, electronically wired L.A. In the region of the world she clears of national borders and unites under the sign of the Orange, Yamashita yokes South to North; illegal migrants to the safe; the homeless to the luxuried; and an ethnic spectrum of Mexican, Chicano, Japanese American, Singapore Chinese American, and African American characters together on an intricately plotted grid.

Whereas *Through the Arc of the Rain Forest* presents Brazil with tenderness and pathos, as the epic landscape for the gradually converging stories of diverse folkloric characters, the L.A. of *Tropic of Orange* is a divided, ungenerous home where people are separated by freeways, lifestyles, languages; race, ethnicity, and class; and relative access to housing, safety, transportation, the airwaves, and the Internet. But Yamashita's literary imagination in every way resists artificial division; when geography itself starts moving across national borders, *Tropic of Orange* becomes an allegory of the transnationalization of the U.S. novel. For what happens when a writer from California opens the southern borders of her literary imagination? To begin, the magic realism of the South arrives in realist L.A., causing more havoc than an earthquake: distorting time and space, bending the city southward, making streets and neighborhoods expand and contract, and forcing people to "MERGE, MERGE, MERGE" more profoundly than they ever have in freeway traffic (207).

Yamashita has remarked that, although she "used the metaphor of the land moving . . . it's actually the humans who have created this transition. . . . [T]hat has changed the landscape entirely, because they've taken their culture and their landscape with them" ("An Interview"). Newly entering the transnationalized U.S. text along with magic come the lives of the peoples of Mexico and Latin America, and the history and aspirations they carry with them on their passage to the North. The U.S.-Mexico border has become, Saldívar notes, "a paradigm of crossing, resistance, and circulation" (xiii). As *Tropic of Orange* renders this phenomenon—in lines of poetry that erupt from within the novel's prose—across the border comes a huge migrating throng:

> *[T]he kids selling Kleenex and Chiclets,*
> *the women pressing rubber soles into tennis shoes,*
> *the men welding fenders to station wagons and*
> *all the people who do the work of machines* (201)

They bear with them an astonishing load, beginning with

> *[T]he corn and the bananas*
> *the coffee and the sugar cane*
> *. . . the music and its rhythms,*

and including "*the halls of Moctezuma and all 40,000 Aztecs slain . . .* ," the Basilica of the Virgin of Guadalupe (on wheels), and the spirits of martyred revolutionaries, "*conquistadors, generals, and murderers, / African slaves, freedom fighters, anthropologists*"; in short, the whole South, with all of its "*cultural conflicts, political disruption, romantic language, with its one hundred years of solitude and its tropical sadness*" (201, 184, 171).

To be sure, this migration causes mighty shock waves when it reaches L.A. Rocking the realist world of a U.S. multicultural novel, the South brings to Los Angeles the heights and depths, the "excessive reality" of magic realism, which has come to be read as a revisionary postcolonial narrative mode, challenging "the binarisms, rationalisms, and reductive materialisms of Western modernity" (Zamora 498), especially the realist barriers that would defend the present from history, and the nationalist, even imperialist paradigm identified with traditions of the realist novel (see Faris 180). In contrast to the imperial real, magic realism here becomes the formal embodiment of boundary-crossing: of the unstoppable flow of people and of the literary imagination across the borders of nations.

And yet, this allegory of all-things-South-go-North does not portray the two regions as entirely separate entities now forcibly converging. Instead, Yamashita makes quite a different point with her central conceit, a magical orange (a seeming cousin, in the globe family, of the ball in *Through the Arc of the Rain Forest*). The Tropic of Cancer becomes visible as a "line—finer than the thread of a spiderweb—pulled with delicate tautness" and running through one particular orange, which falls from a tree at the exact moment of the summer solstice and is carried northward, the golden, spherical avatar of the migrating South (12). But, Yamashita informs us, the tree from which this navel orange fell was actually brought to its Mexican garden spot from Riverside, California, to be planted in the yard of a third-generation Chicano's nostalgic vacation home. And further, that tree may be a "descendent of the original trees first brought to California from Brazil in 1873 and planted by L.C. Tibbetts" (11). Thus the orange of the title does not merely embody the South, but rather, in its hybrid history, it illustrates the long-standing intricate relations of South and North. The migrating spherical fruit becomes this novel's marvelous emblem, a sign that readers must suspend not only our disbelief in the magical but also our expectations for an American novel, to grasp the different stories tellable within Yamashita's global vision.

In keeping with the novel's "border" energies of crossing and circulation, when the South reaches the North in this novel, what it finds is by no means a static, monolithic place, but a congregation of those who have crossed and continue to cross many other kinds of borders. The novel's point of beginning is the story of Rafaela Cortes and her young son Sol, who join the crowd flowing north as they return from her native Mexico to the husband and father they left in Los Angeles, the Singapore Chinese American Bobby Ngu. Bobby, who gained entrance into the United States by pretending to be a Vietnamese boat person, through prodigious labor and adaptability has become rich in name-brand appliances, and in his eclectic style of Americanness is described as "Chinese from Singapore with a Vietnam name speaking like a Mexican living in Koreatown" (15). Rafaela's marriage to Bobby, this is to say, is one of the key points in the novel where transnationalization fuses with the energy of American interethnicity, and ethnic subjectivity is enmeshed in a global and dialogic context. This complex vision of L.A. derives from Yamashita's own experience; having grown up in L.A. and spent ten years in Brazil, when she returned with her young family:

> I found a city that was very different, filled with people from all over the globe. I found living here very exciting. I reveled in being here again. I started to look at the literature of Los Angeles, but no one was talking yet about that change. I wrote the book to bring in those who have been invisible in the literature of Los Angeles. . . . also . . . I found my family part of this great movement of immigrants to the city, and I certainly identify with that movement. A friend of mine read the book and commented that there are no white characters in it. Well, somebody else gets to tell the story for a change. ("Karen Tei Yamashita" 340–41)

At first glance, the reader may expect *Tropic of Orange* to exemplify a far simpler scheme of U.S.-style pluralist egalitarianism, the kind that casts the multicultural crime-fighting teams in the movies or the friendly neighborhood on Sesame Street. Yamashita gives to each of seven main ethnic characters' stories seven discrete chapters, in first- or limited third-person narration, marked by the character's particular idiolect. A cleverly designed "HyperContexts" chart (which Yamashita has explained as a trace of the novel's genesis)[5] supplements the table of contents and helpfully organizes things, listing characters' names vertically and ranging their chapters across the horizontal axis of the seven consecutive days of the novel's span. But instead of containing each of the characters in an ethnic narrative enclosure, the chapters actually send them all busily into each others' lives and into the multicultural mix. Yamashita's ethnics thus emerge not as representatives of their ethnic groups—indeed there are only the barest suggestions of their connection to ethnic families—but as participants in a heteroglossic metropolis and region, who, through their discourse, their relationships, their work, and as the novel progresses, through the increasing interlacing of their stories, exceed ethnic and national definitions.

Bobby Ngu's chapters, for example, present a rich and rapid street argot that blends ethnic and commercial dialects, portraying even a lunch break as a polyglot experience:

> Got to get something to eat. Down the corner, there's a sign: Chinese burritos. Fish tacos. Ensopada. Camaron chow mein. Hoy Especial: $2.99. Comida to go. Por qué no?
>
> Bobby's got the takeout, the medicinal herbs, the *Miraculous Stop Smoking*. . . . Gets the water boiling, the tea steeping, the takeout nuked. . . . Tea don't go with

> the takeout. Chinese burritos. Chinamex. Who they trying to kid? But it's not bad. . . . (101)

Along with cuisines, languages intermix here with little trace of the immigrant linguistic agon we see in the world of Chang-rae Lee's *Native Speaker*. Perhaps Bobby's release into linguistic (and culinary) bricolage comes from having gone to school in L.A., rather than in suburban New York, largely among Latinos living in a vibrant, migrant Spanish despite their public education in English, or perhaps it comes from the sheer multiplicity of language possibilities around him and in his history; he has remade himself in too many cultural modes to be tormented by a binary language antagonism like the one that, for other reasons, obsesses Lee's Henry Park. For Bobby as well as for the novel's speakers of Spanish, black English, and other mother tongues, Yamashita's sense of an historically charged, ever-diversifying, and mobile linguascape (to coin a term on the model of Arjun Appadurai), makes possible a playfully ironic take on language differences, even for struggling immigrants who bring a different sound to American speech.

For two characters who are the third- and fourth-generation descendants of immigrants, ethnic identification is mediated by their immersion in the discourses of mass media and popular culture. Gabriel Balboa, a crusading Chicano newspaper reporter, narrates in the thrall of film noir; he thrives on investigating the gritty, unglamorous underside of L.A. life, "getting into the grimy crevices of the street and pulling out the real stories" (39). His attempt to build, furnish, and landscape the perfect getaway home in his ancestral Mexico is satirized as hopeless ethnic nostalgia, and is thwarted by cultural differences and natural forces alike. Gabriel's love interest is Emi, a Japanese American TV news producer so steeped in the corporate media culture, and in her brashness and irreverence so "distant from the Asian female stereotype" that "it was questionable if she even had an identity" (19). The figure closest to the author, one must note, in ethnic and gender terms, Emi mocks identity politics, actually saying to her own mother, "Maybe I'm not Japanese American. Maybe I got switched in the hospital" (21). I read this Emi as an outrageous rewriting of a pure-hearted, insipid character by that name from John Okada's *No-No Boy*, the best-known Japanese American novel.[6] Unlike Okada's Emi, this Emi really, really does want to talk about sex, and in every way she is anti-conventional among Asian American female characters: loud, opinionated, selfish, materialistic, technologically savvy, wickedly funny, a smasher of liberal pieties. Trying to embarrass her Chicano boyfriend in a sushi bar, she says loudly, "Gee, Gabe . . . Here we all are, your multicultural mosaic. There's you and me and the gays at the end of the bar and the guy with the turban. . . . There's even white people here" (127). "Cultural diversity is bullshit," she announces, half a page later, and turning to the sushi chef, asks him, "Don't you hate being multicultural? Her diva-esque moment comes when she challenges a patronizing white woman at the sushi bar—who offers shallow multiculturalist appreciations while wearing chopsticks in her hair—to wear two forks, instead, " 'Or would you consider that,' Emi paused, 'unsanitary'?" (129). In Emi, Yamashita offers an expressively contradictory American voice; she revels in the crass commercialism of her work in network TV ("It's not about good honest people like you . . . or whether we should make the world safe for democracy. It's about selling things: Reebok, Pepsi, Chevrolet, AllState, Pampers...") (126), but she objects in scathing terms to the commodification of her own ethnic culture, even while resisting any ethnic identification for herself.

Living another politics entirely, but similarly trouncing our expectations for ethnic characterization, is the grassroots activist Buzzworm, a "[b]ig black seven-foot dude, Vietnam vet" (described in the Asian/African interchapter) (27). Carrying a business card that reads, "*Angel of Mercy/ Central & South Central/...24 hrs/ 7 days,*" Buzzworm "walk[s] the hood every day, walkin' and talkin', making contact" (26), dispensing social service information and general encouragement, taking his eloquent black English into multiple cross-cultural street relationships, and scanning his Walkman to tune in to every conceivable musical style and radio language:

> *La equis la equis noventa y siete punto nueve!* Everybody was listening to the Mexican station.... Buzzworm.... was listenin' up too. Keeping up on the news.... Keeping up so's to be ready with the dialogue. Some wanted to pit black against brown, but... somebody had to be there to get the sides to see eye to eye. Order to see eye to eye, had to get with the program. Far as Buzzworm was concerned, program was the Mexican station.... Had to get behind another man's perspectives. Hear life in another sound zone. Walk to some other rhythms. (102–3)

As it complicates all of these ethnic identities, the novel consistently puts its characters in contact with the mass media, connecting them with what is most current in a wider collective sphere. In Buzzworm's instinct to "[keep] up on the news," in Gabriel and Emi's fixations with newspapers and TV newscasts, and in the up-to-the-minute texture of the talk, *Tropic of Orange* is a novel tuned in to the media that are attuned to change, to a present reality ever imminently becoming something else. And the kind of change the novel observes most closely is the changing impact of human movements across borders, the way that new patterns of migration and commerce are transforming the life of U.S. cities by making the migrant experience circular, global, diasporic (Lowe, "On Contemporary" 47; Hune, "Rethinking" 34). As noted in chapter 1, Appadurai explains that the United States now

> finds itself awash in... global diasporas, no longer a closed space for the melting pot to work its magic but yet another diasporic switching point to which people come to seek their fortunes though no longer content to leave their homelands behind. ("Heart of Whiteness" 803)

In passages on Bobby's beginnings in Singapore and Rafaela and Gabriel's travels back and forth between Mexico and L.A., on the masses who cross the border with the orange and the labor they do in the United States, on the multiplicity of radio stations to which Buzzworm tunes in and the L.A. populations—less immigrant groups than new, "delocalized" "*transnation*[s]"—that they serve (804), the novel portrays the new reality replacing the old, linear model of immigration to the United States.

This does not mean that Yamashita is any less sentimental, even reverential about contemporary immigration than writers whose fictions of Americanization have rested on the "melting pot" or "mosaic" ideologies that now seem limited by American exceptionalism. Indeed, as hard-nosed and cynical as her L.A. chapters can be, the chapters on the northward migration of the South recall the Brazil of *Through the Arc of the Rain Forest* in their unabashed emotionalism and heroic coloring. In part, as the italicized prose poetry, the magic realism, and the intermittent Spanish of these chapters suggest, Yamashita means to convey a distinctly Southern reality. But more important, the mass aspiration for a better life remains for her the most stirring phenomenon, with a transformative potential even for the North. In a moment of symbolic historical reckoning, Rafaela undergoes full-blown mythic translation into "a muscular serpent," embodying Latin America's people locked in "a horrific dance with death," and emerges hideously battered but triumphant over the forces of tyranny (221–22).[7] More marvelously still, carrying the orange from South to North is the fantastic figure of Arcangel, an ancient peasant/prophet/performance artist who displays superhuman strength, whose wit is undimmed, and whose 500-year memory retains all of the struggle, the labor, and the dreams of the peoples of Latin America.[8] This fabulous trickster erupts into lines of oratory to express the full scope of his capacious memory and his mission as sardonic prophet of cultural change:

The end of the world as we know it is coming!
It will come in 2012,
exactly ten cycles of fifty-two years
from the time Christopher Columbus
discovered San Salvador, Cuba, Haiti,
and the Dominican Republic in 1492! . . .
The great discovery!
The great curse!
And this because of a lousy bunch of spices
to hide the putrefaction of meat! (49)

These questing migrants bring to the novel, along with bilingualism and an expansive kind of memory, an infusion of authenticity and spirit, so that their arrival in the United States reveals the North as a place in need of more genuine forms of human meeting. When Arcangel gives his name at the border as "Cristobal Colón" and he and Rafaela lead the undocumented masses across the U.S. border on "*the gliding wings of a dream*" (199, 202), Yamashita has brought to the American novel not only a broader understanding of global migration but also a prophetic vision from the point of view of the uprooted, a migratory ethics. These ethics are put to the test in the novel's astonishing and comedic climax, a fantastic wrestling match between Arcangel in the role of the superhero "*El Gran Mojado*" (The Big Wetback) and a fearsome U.S. fighter "in a titanium suit with a head of raging fire" called SUPERNAFTA (258), attended by competing throngs who cheer for the interests of U.S. corporations or the Mexican poor.

By the time that the text's attention to the lives of individuals north and south of the border opens out to this freakish contest of titans, Yamashita has accustomed her readers to a novelistic project that, dramatizing the impact of transnational changes, oscillates between cameos and wide screen images, between the intimate and the historic, fusing individual plots of quest with mass-scale developments of enormous consequence. A telling difference, indeed, between Yamashita's interethnic vision and that of Chang-rae Lee is a tendency to treat masses not as a sublime spectacle for the individual's contemplation, but as characters in a much larger plot. In *Tropic of Orange*, as in *Through the Arc of the Rain Forest*, crowd scenes are Yamashita's best scenes.[9] In fact, in both novels, tragicomic scenes of the convergence of *several* fervent crowds, each following its own obsession, create climaxes on a gargantuan scale. And to be sure, there is something Rabelaisian about Yamashita's imagination, a strain inherited, it seems, by way of Latin American fiction, involving everything from a love of long lists—of the accretion that generates the sublime—to a proclivity for grotesque bodies, earthy comedy, and scenes of mass violence, illness, and death. These energies massive, sublime, and grotesque overcome the realist conventions of Asian American and multicultural U.S. fiction, opening the way for more global and more visionary narrative possibilities.

At the same time, Yamashita revises a literary genre already characterized by excess and sublimity: Los Angeles disaster fiction. *Tropic of Orange* brings to this venerable tradition Yamashita's transnational, interethnic vision and her progressive politics. In Mike Davis's account, the enormous body of disaster fiction and film that has destroyed Los Angeles an amazing three times a year on average since 1909, has been "rooted in racial anxiety," first about invading "alien" hordes from the East and South and later about the city's increasingly non-Anglo majority (290, 276, 282). *Tropic of Orange* turns the tables on such plots, firmly on the side of the "invaders" and those sympathetic to the city's ethnically changing character. Yamashita's own spectacular crisis plays out simultaneously in the magical migration of the Tropic and the resulting confusion of time and space in L.A.; in the U.S.-Mexico superhero prizefight; in a nefarious scheme of the cross-border smuggling of infant body parts and cocaine-infused oranges; and, under the deadly influence of those oranges, in the biggest L.A. freeway disaster of all history. When the rich are forced to abandon their luxury vehicles, these are immediately colonized by the homeless, who swiftly create a vast, self-sufficient village on the stalled freeway, and, while they await the inevitable raid by the LAPD, receive continuous live TV coverage, becoming the stars of wildly popular grassroots news and entertainment programming.

Before the frenzied backdrop of this plot, *Tropic of Orange* maintains its highly ordered, multicultural chapter structure, giving each major ethnic character the equal respect and attention due a traditional novelistic hero; it's just that each is swept up in or nearly destroyed by world changes of a colossal order. The happy multicultural insight that we are all connected and all equal cohabits frighteningly in Yamashita's oeuvre with the suspicion that we may all be leading one another headlong toward doom. And yet, a certain giddy enjoyment of the sheer piling up of life in Yamashita's work, a certain readerly (and, I would hazard, writerly) pleasure in making all these crossings—from South to North, from one ethnic story to the next, from the magical to the realist, from order to chaos—rescues her basically comic mode from tragedy. For even as the disasters accrue, we cannot help but read the unleashing of this marvelously connecting imagination, in the hemisphere and in the American novel, as a sign of hope. An intelligence hovers among us, we feel, that identifies and celebrates life's burgeoning energies even as it lets loose unbridled chaos.

A Vision of Nature

The boundary-crossing energies in Yamashita's work ultimately serve what seems to me a profoundly ecological vision, that is, a vision of human imbrication within the natural world. Not only in the overtly green politics of *Through the Arc of the Rain Forest*, but also in *Tropic of Orange*, Yamashita unfolds a postmodern vision that is at once ethical and centered on the power of nature, on the unpredictable, irrepressible natural energies that overcome artificiality, divisions, tyranny and oppression, and death itself. This is the ultimate context, I think, in which we must read Yamashita's experimentation with the interethnic, the transnational, and the sublime: an ethical politics derived from a vision of human subsumption in a wider ecology. Truer than a national border is the Tropic of Cancer, "a border made plain by the sun itself" (71). A more powerful reality than that of our cherished ethnic or national differences is our shared or contiguous inhabitation of a natural geography, as Manzanar knows, upon his elevated podium. This vision of human embeddedness in the natural finds its counterpart in the organic metaphors that continually animate the novel's man-made world: the freeway is "a great root system" and "a great writhing concrete dinosaur" (37), while the enormous trucks that jackknife and burn across five lanes are "the slain semis," "the great land-roving semis," "gawked" at by "the smaller vehicles of the automotive kingdom" (120). Human behavior, too, tends to be explained in the terms of natural processes. When the wealthy leave their vehicles, and the homeless, burned out of their hovels on public land, pour onto the freeway to take up residence, "[i]n a matter of minutes, life filled a vacuum, reorganizing itself in predictable and unpredictable ways" (120). Similarly, the mass-scale migration of the South is said to be "filling a northern vacuum" (171), an account that explains a vast human and geopolitical saga in the frank, reductive terms of natural science. Masses of people do what they do for the most intimate and eccentric reasons, but these reasons derive ultimately from natural processes of which people are but tiny elements.

This nature-centered vision sustains Yamashita's transnational political and environmentalist critique, in which nature's astonishing resilience renders absurd even as it registers the impact of human crimes against the Earth and its inhabitants. A brilliant such moment is the extended set piece in *Through the Arc of the Rain Forest* on the discovery of a "rain forest parking lot" deep in the Brazilian jungle, a huge field of crumbling and rusting "aircraft and vehicles of every sort of description," most likely the ruins of a clandestine 1950s or '60s U.S. military base. Without mentioning the violent human policies to which the "parking lot" likely bears witness, Yamashita lets nature comment by describing its ingenious adaptation to the perverse site, quoting scientific studies of the find: "The entomologists were shocked to discover that their rare butterfly only nested in the vinyl seats of Fords and Chevrolets and that their exquisite reddish coloring was actually due to a steady diet of hydrated ferric oxide, or rusty water." Another surprising find is "a new species of mouse, with prehensile tails, that burrowed in the exhaust pipes of all the vehicles," and featured "suction cups on their feet that allowed them to crawl up the slippery sides and bottoms of the aircraft and cars" and "impressive" colorings: "the females sported a splotchy green-and-brown coat, while the males wore shiny coats of chartreuse, silver, and taxi yellow" (99–100). And:

> One of the more exciting studies being undertaken was the documentation of the social behavior of a tribe of monkeys that had established territory in the carcasses of the bomber planes and their relation to a second tribe whose territory was decidedly the fossil remains of former gas-guzzling automotive monsters. A number of monkeys' skulls were found riddled with machine-gun bullets. . . . (101)

This jungle hybrid of human warfare technology and nature's irresistible will to transform stands as a marvelous model of the way the world works in Yamashita's oeuvre. Things and peoples meet and mix; here love blossoms; there invention and evil grow their consequences, as in the quirky serendipity of natural evolution. An ironic gaze observes it all.

It would seem inevitable for an ethnic novelist who holds such a vision to be drawn to the interethnic imaginative axis—in Yamashita not so much the axis of Werner Sollors's American "consent" (contractual as opposed to hereditary "descent" relations [*Beyond* 5–6]), but the axis of chance encounter—where life picks people up and puts them down changed, along unexpected paths. Ultimately Yamashita's work suggests that the "natural" convergence of peoples—individuals, groups, cultures, histories—creates a collective imagination that is itself a kind of organism, one in which we all participate, for good or ill. In remarks on the book, Yamashita has recalled the effect created in Los Angeles by the bizarre real-life/media meta-event of the 1994 O.J. Simpson freeway chase, which hovers in the background of *Tropic of Orange* (especially in extended riffs on the public appetite for oranges and orange juice, and in one gruesomely comic "football" catch):

> [W]hen O.J. was riding in that Ford Bronco, everyone knew that it was happening. There were people on freeways who came out to see if the Ford Bronco would pass. . . . They held signs out, waving at O.J. Or when the L.A. riots happened, people were going to sites they knew were near fires. So there was this conversation between the media (what was happening on television) and this physical event. There was an uncanny sense that the City had a "brain," or collective understanding. I think that it's similar to what's going on here [in *Tropic of Orange*]. . . . ("An Interview")

This novel thus attempts to replicate the phenomenon of a heterogeneous population that acts like a meta-being with a mind of its own, a creature uncontrollable by any of its parts, though made up of many people's individual choices. Yamashita's prefatory address reads in part:

> Gentle reader, what follows may not be about the future, but is perhaps about the recent past; a past that, even as you imagine it, happens. . . . No single imagination is wild or crass or cheesy enough to compete with the collective mindlessness that propels our fascination forward. We were all there; we all saw it on TV, screen, and monitor, larger than life.

O.J. is not the only media-induced public hallucination one thinks of here, of course; the phenomenon is now pervasive and chronic. Yamashita's apologia, for lack of a better term, implicitly contrasts the authorial imagination—which in various moments does attain to the wild and crass and cheesy—with a public, media-mediated mind against which "[n]o single imagination" could possibly compete. Her conception of the propulsive collective mind echoes Appadurai's notion that in the influence of the globalized mass media, "the imagination has become a collective social fact," even "an organized field of social practices" that constitutes "the key component of the new global order" (*Modernity* 5, 31).[10] Yamashita's address to readers casts the grotesque/sublime mass-media-age popular imagination as the book's model, its rain forest, if you will, the burgeoning natural phenomenon with which it cannot "compete." This is novelistic ambition on a Joycean scale, to be sure, but ambition matched by Yamashita's enormous affection for the collective mind (-lessness), which sets her tracing the features of its every hyped-up obsession with acuity and humor, even as she prepares the sublime catastrophe she sees it bringing on.

The lives of her selected ethnic individuals gradually coalesce toward the book's ending into one colossal Los Angeleno. Under the influence of "undulating patterns and the changing geography corrupting the sun's shadows, confusing time," "every sports event, concert, and whatnot was happening at the same time" (207, 205). While football, hockey, baseball, basketball, and boxing events are all taking place in public arenas,

> Placido Domingo belted Rossini at the Dorothy Chandler. . . . [t]he helicopter landed for the 944th time on the set of *Miss Saigon* at the Ahmanson, and Beauty smacked the Beast at the Shubert. Chinese housewives went for the big stakes in pai gow in the Asian room at the Bicycle Club. . . . Thousands of fans melted away with Julio Iglesias at the Universal Amphitheater. . . . King Tut had returned to LACMA; Andy Warhol to MOCA. The AIDS walk 5/10K run was moving through West Hollywood. . . . Chicanos marched from the Plaza de la Raza down Whittier to César Chávez in solidarity. . . . The middle class clamored in malls for summer sales; the poor clamored at swap meets. . . .
>
> The most horrific aspect of it was that it would all end at the same time. . . . (205–6)

Narrating the collective activities of "all seven million residents of Greater L.A. out on the town," Yamashita gradually transforms them into traffic—the physical embodiment of L.A.'s fevered "brain"—and prepares for the conductor Manzanar "the greatest jam session the world had ever known":

> In the next moment, they would all cram their bodies through exits, down escalators, through arcades . . . head toward their cars, their buses, their motorcycles and limousines . . . all slam their doors, all buckle their belts, all gun their motors . . . and CLICK, one two, SLIDE, three four, FLOMP, one two, BLAM. . . . REAR VIEW CHECK IT OUT . . . and a three and a four, CREEP ON OUT and a five and a six, and MERGE, MERGE, MERGE. They all converged everywhere all at once. (207)

Following this final, quintessentially Yamashitan sentence, the hyped-up pages that build the novel's climax present not only a freeway nightmare, but also multiple other convergences: the "approaching parade" of migration from the South; a sudden and confusing swap of languages across L.A.'s diverse TV and radio stations; the appearance "on overpasses and street corners . . . balconies and park benches" of Manzanar clones ("people [who] held branches and pencils, toothbrushes and carrot sticks, and conducted" [240, 233, 239]) and the swelling, celestial song of a spontaneous City of Angels choir.

When the apocalyptic blow comes, however, it is not some spontaneous combustion caused by mass fusion, but an airborne military attack on the homeless of the freeway, a predictable, politically realist event. A cold authorial eye observes life creating now convergence and cross-fertilization, now destruction and disaster. But these things work cyclically in Yamashita, here as in the end of *Through the Arc*, when after ecological apocalypse, the rain forest begins to return. Once death has had its hour in Los Angeles, Yamashita's requiem, completing the automotive motif, produces a comic but stunning moment, witnessed "bird's-eye" by Manzanar as he is evacuated by helicopter:

> the inflation of thousands upon thousands of automotive airbags, bursting simultaneously everywhere from their pouches in steering wheels and glove compartments like white poppies in sudden bloom. All the airbags in L.A. ruptured forth, unfurled their white powdered wings against the barrage of bullets, and stunned the war to a dead stop. (257–58)

What writer other than Yamashita could have imagined a city of automotive airbags into this sublimity? And though beauty descends into bathos in her next, typically sardonic turn, when postmodern commodification begins and "TV stations showed it over and over in slow motion" to the accompaniment of Pachelbel (265), the spontaneous, heterogeneous hugging that subsequently spreads all over the city marks the author's resiliently "cheesy" but affectionate human vision. Human aspiration as witnessed on a mass scale from a lofty perch, by the authorial composer/conductor of this book, is mindless, greedy, crass, violent, destructive, but never entirely disconnected from the beauty of nature's unfolding, as of "white poppies in sudden bloom."

The Buzz Plot

In a novel of this encompassing reach, little remains of the family-centered realist plot so important in the history of Asian American fiction, though Yamashita makes contact with that tradition in one plot of intergenerational separation and reunion; one character discovers late in the book that another is her long-lost grandfather. But the Asian family reunion never quite happens; this plot is overwhelmed by the powerful forces making the city spin. What takes its place, emerging in the very moment when the possibility of this reunion fails, is a key plot Yamashita's work shares with that of other contemporary Asian American novelists: the affiliation with African Americans and black culture, a plot of surprising resonance for the novels discussed at length in my chapters. Just as, in Lee's *Native Speaker,* the affiliation with blackness goes to the heart of the ambivalent portrayal of the possibilities of life in the multicultural American city, and as, in Jen's *Mona in the Promised Land*, it is key to the ruminations on the boundaries of family, community, and home, in *Tropic of Orange*, the black plot deepens the meditation on human imbrication in nature.

Given the prominence of nature in Yamashita's work, it would seem important that some of her characters are in tune with nature and others are not. That those carrying the orange across the border from the South are so seems as predictable as their comfort with magical happenings. But in L.A., most of the characters have no thought for the natural world, save two eccentrics: Manzanar, the crazy conductor whose awareness of a vast natural landscape seems one with his ability to hear the symphony of city traffic, and more surprisingly, Buzzworm, the African American Vietnam vet who works as a freelance "Angel of Mercy" in South Central. An inhabitant of a landscape mostly characterized by "[b]ushes, dried-up lawns, weeds, asphalt, and concrete" (31), Buzzworm cathects nature in the form of his neighborhood palm trees:

> [H]e really knew his palm trees. Family Palmaceae. Four thousand species. Tall ones called Washingtonia Robusta or Mexican Fan Palm.... Buzzworm was always talking about them like he was their personal gardener. You caught him staring at palm trees, seemed like he was talking to them.
>
> Sometimes he made people come out of their houses and appreciate what was on their own front lawn. They came out past their screen doors to take a look up at two spiky trunks topped with what, for all they cared, were giant mops.... But Buzzworm said, "These here are Phoenix Canariensis."
>
> "Phoenix Canary what? Buzzworm, what's this got to do with social services?"
>
> "You understand the species of trees in the neighborhood, you understand the nature of my work." (30–31)

Buzzworm has a holistic plan: "Restore the neighborhood. Clean up the streets. Take care of the people. Trim and water the palm trees" (83). He seems to believe that his neighbors in the home of L.A.'s notorious 1992 riots will not be truly well until they become attuned to and claim stewardship of their natural and their built landscape.

In placing Buzzworm and his rootedness in his South Central neighborhood at the heart of the book's ethical vision, Yamashita might be said to critique the racist exclusions historically conventional in L.A. fiction,[11] even as she firmly inscribes the memory of those awful days of 1992 in her novel. The riots stand along with the O.J. Simpson chase as the major public events haunting this novel's vision of the collective life of Los Angeles; in both, the actions of a criminalized black man or men on the move created spectacles of suspense and horror for a mass-media audience.[12] It is notable that in the character of Buzzworm, Yamashita offers a very different figure. Not only is her big, black, male, urban, Vietnam vet empathic, drug-free, smart, imaginative, and a devoted public citizen, and not only does he possess the attribute—atypical in representations of black men—of ecological mindfulness, but he is also a black man who moves about the streets of L.A. every day so as to make them more livable, to do good. The character most rooted, most at home in L.A., Buzzworm is the only person in the book who even speaks of a "neighborhood" that is his, and he loves his palms in part because, with their great height, they can be seen even by those who speed past his neighborhood on freeways, marking out "the place where he lived," becoming "symbols of the landscape, a beauty that could only be appreciated from afar" (33). Buzzworm's appreciation of the trees, even as it serves to reclaim African American belonging in L.A., also seems related to his tolerance of human difference. For his ecological view, the big picture he can see also makes him aware of the deep truth of human connectedness, as evident in the range of his outreach to the city's people, or in his habit of listening to the widest spectrum of L.A. radio stations, from which he tries to learn to speak new languages.

Generally Buzzworm seems to work among African Americans and Latinos, but in a significant design, Yamashita positions this compassionate, rooted, black multiculturalist as the person holding the gravely wounded Emi at the violent end. She is well out of her element when she must produce her TV news show live from the homeless freeway encampment and is slow to grasp the actual danger of it all. The reader is likely to be as shocked as she is that such a savvy and sardonic professional as herself could be shot when the military launches a helicopter gunship assault against those who have appropriated the cars of the wealthy. While the homeless run for cover, Buzzworm carries Emi underneath the palm trees and tries to save her life. The scene recalls (in reverse race terms) the moment in America's multiethnic human rights struggle when Japanese American activist Yuri Kochiyama held Malcolm X as he lay dying of a gunshot wound,[13] but Yamashita's black man and Japanese woman are a parodic, bathetic echo of that heroic pairing. Buzzworm and Emi are utterly mismatched—he mistrusts her values as much as she mistrusts his. Still, in the end, as Emi bleeds to death in his arms and yet manages to deliver her best line, the remarkable fact that it is a ventriloquized black line suggests, beyond the satire, a wistful iteration of the novel's interethnic hopes.

Echoing the memorable question of Rodney King—the police beating victim in solidarity with whom the 1992 riots erupted—Emi "look[s] deeply into his eyes" and says, "If *we* can jus' get along, maybe all our problems will go away." But Buzzworm replies, "Gonna take more than holdin' hands to start that revolution." "'Oh well,' Emi blew it off" (253). Though she is dying, her L.A. demeanor returns and she concentrates on staging for herself a truly cool death scene.[14] But her momentary "blackface" performance has interestingly multiple implications, as cross-race imitations often do.[15] It continues her mockery of "multiculti" politics and jokingly treats the famously videotaped victim's idealistic public entreaty as parrotable media camp, but beneath the laughter we also have to hear the adoption of a black voice so as to express a genuine desire for intergroup solidarity, a desire that has grown even in Emi, as the novel's interethnic plot thickened.

Neither her moment of cross-race vision nor the novel's arrival at a black-Asian embrace can save Emi, however, from her encounter with L.A.'s violent power relations.[16] Buzzworm does open her heart to us more fully than ever before, but if this is a predictably sentimental role for a black character, Yamashita does not enclose him in it;[17] it is Emi, not he, who dies dramatically under the freeway palms. Buzzworm goes home to the hood, to rest and start all over again his ministering rounds.

If Emi cannot be saved by the intersection of her plot with that of this rooted black L.A. citizen (or with the history of cross-race solidarity), neither can she be saved by what would seem a supremely redeeming connection—to an ethnic ancestor who is also the book's endearing authorial figure. For she reveals to Buzzworm, shortly before being shot, that she has caught sight—via helicopter news cam shot to her TV editing screen—of her long-lost grandfather, Manzanar Murakami, furiously conducting the music of the traffic disaster from his overpass. The plot drops its greatest surprise when Emi the anti-identitarian, postmodern creature of the web and the airwaves turns out to be made of Manzanar, of the history he so madly and compassionately embodies, sort of in the same way that the narrating ball of *Through the Arc* turns out to be made of the Matacao. But such substantive links, revealed by Yamashita, do not determine essentialist endings. Manzanar and Emi are not brought together until after she is dead; the plot of ethnic transgenerational reunion, perhaps too nostalgic for the hard edges of this book, is sacrificed in the shift to the interethnic and transnational paradigms.[18] What we get instead is a mourning for that very plot, as the bereaved Manzanar, accompanying Emi's body, scans the chaotic city while dangling from a helicopter gurney, watching the white poppies bloom.

Mixed Outcomes

Many stories need closing at the end of this crowded novel, however, and instead of either of these symbolically charged plots (the Asian familial or the Asian American/African American), Yamashita notably privileges a different romance in ending, the one that spans North and South, East and West. Bobby and Rafaela's Asian American/Latin American marriage frames the novel's deep structure of separation and conjunction, for we begin in Mexico with Rafaela and their son, Sol, the marriage temporarily abandoned; then on the trek north a threat to Sol's life provides one of the novel's suspenseful subplots; and Yamashita ends with this one family's magically real reunion amidst the frenzied Mexico-U.S. prizefight crowd at the Pacific Rim Auditorium. Much as in a similar plot in *Through the Arc* of the Japanese hero, his Brazilian love, and her two children, Yamashita reaches closure by restoring endangered children from the hands of mysterious bad guys to their rightful, interethnic families. The irrepressible life-urge—apparent in Sol, the sun's child—overcomes evil, differences, and borders, and in these multifaceted novels the precious and vulnerable transnational family unit is the highest value Yamashita's endings preserve.

These self-consciously melodramatic endings—an old-fashioned novelistic device with a postmodern touch—connect Yamashita's work once again to the novels of Lee and Jen. It seems fitting to reach closure by considering these exemplary texts' most significant common gesture toward futurity: their mixed children, the subject of the epilogue that follows. The notion of a transnational family perfectly encapsulates Yamashita's vision of resilient nature, triumphant over the national—and ethnic—borders that rise and fall in human history. In her oeuvre, borders seem not only artificial and unjust but also limiting, deadening, dull, compared to all that the unbounded, mobile imagination can bring to life. Traced through Yamashita's novels, the interethnic literary impulse of Asian American and U.S. fiction becomes part of a much larger post-national imperative: the imperative of imagined community, of human integration in an imagined ecology, on a global scale.

Epilogue

Mixed Races, Mixed Children, Mixed Outcomes

The Mixed Millennium

A striking but unremarked literary historical fact is that the fictional house of Asian America has rarely, until recently, contained a child of the third generation. A review of the best-known Asian American novels before the 1990s will find them well-occupied by struggling immigrants, their American-born children, and the dramatic tensions between the two, but—with a few exceptions—stopping short of imagining the next generation to be born. This phenomenon is certainly related to the "missing" marriage plot in Asian American narratives, in Patricia P. Chu's terms: Asian American fiction's strategic omission of the conventional marriage plot to suit the different demands of Asian American subject formation, where "marriage would signify . . . a full assimilation that has not yet occurred either in fact or in the symbolic realm of mainstream culture" (18–19).

The resonance of this analysis for the troubled marriage of the hero in Lee's *Native Speaker* and the comically deferred and displaced marriage of the heroine in Jen's *Mona in the Promised Land* is apparent. Yamashita uses marriage somewhat differently, to dramatize larger social processes of division and reintegration, as in the border-split marriage of Bobby and Rafaela, miraculously restored at the center of all convergence in the end of *Tropic of Orange*. But these three 1990s novels, despite their wide disparities in tone and sensibility, converge to center upon cross-ethnic marriages each of which produces an ethnically mixed child—fictional threesomes looking, as Lee's Henry Park fondly puts it, "like a family accident" (345).

While these marriages mark the growing prevalence of intermarriage in Asian and other U.S. ethnic communities as well as the era's multiculturalist ethos, they also point to a revision of the legacy of the "immigrant romance" of earlier Asian American fiction—which, Chu writes, "recounts the protagonist's search for a white partner to Americanize him or her" (19)—on the part of Asian American characters more easily reconciling themselves to a social order now grown more ethnically diverse and more inclusive. And most notably, the fact that the first substantial cohort of fictional third-generational Asian Americans is made up largely of mixed-race children presents us with an imaginative remaking of that order, indeed, with protagonists parenting a new order that is, as yet, not fully knowable. The interethnic child's fate or treatment in these novels—especially in the endings, each of which places the child as the horizon of the book's interethnic vision, the locus of its hopes, and the embodiment of a future that cannot yet articulate its nature—signals what is imagined as the realm of the possible, for the generation of part-Asian children now growing up amongst us, and for interethnicity as a literary project and a way of life.

Mixed-race characters have long had a special place in literature. Their very existence bespeaking a backstory that is at the least anti-conventional, and often redolent of intrigue and taboo, they seem to embody what is most compellingly narratable and readable in a literary plot. A venerable American literary tradition treats characters of mixed European and African American ancestry as inescapably symbolic figures, as scholars have extensively detailed. An historical study of mixed-race literature by Werner Sollors has contributed the most thorough account of the "tragic mulatto" genre, in which the "warring blood" of a light-skinned, "passing" hero or heroine melodramatically skews his or her romantic choices and public actions (Sollors, *Neither Black* 243).

In the U.S. social imaginary, the notion that being born of mixed parentage is an essentially aberrant (and thus tragic) fate long held sway, and an extensive, elaborate history of anti-miscegenation laws attempted to erect a bulwark against such births. But in the massive shift both in law and in cultural attitudes toward interracial mixing over the course of the twentieth century, propelled by the mid-century movement for African American civil rights, and by the subsequent era of ethnic identity politics, the meaning of racial in-betweenness has been profoundly re-thought. Substantial change is measured in the very fact that "mixed identity has become a matter of public discourse" (Prasad 8) at all. In the twenty-first century, we now commonly find affirmation of the social legitimacy of multiple-race identities in the policies of the U.S. government and of educational and social institutions, in print media and on the screens of popular culture.[1] Multiracial identity became an officially recognized status on the U.S. census in 2000, the result of what one observer calls "a grass-roots insurrection against simplistic racial constructs" (Ma 177).[2]

Scholars and theorists have contributed to this sea change as well, prominent among them Gloria Anzaldúa, whose visionary *Borderlands/La Frontera: The New Mestiza*, offers mixed-race identity as a paradigm for a prophetic consciousness that transcends binary racial thinking. Rather than a social pariah, the individual born of the encounter of two peoples, two histories, two collective stories, has come to be treated as the emblematic individual of our age, "physical proof of an increasingly global society . . . [and] a solder between various communities" (Prasad 8). Musing on the "heavyweight symbolic status" that accrues to people of mixed ancestry, author Rebecca Walker writes: "[W]e're the poster children for globalism, hybridization, humanism, and a dozen other cultural products predicated on transcending boundaries. . . . It's more than cool to be mixed, it's downright relevant" ("Introduction" 14). And Danzy Senna, author of the novel of mixed-race experience *Caucasia* (1999) writes in an extended parody titled "The Mulatto Millennium":

> Strange to wake up and realize you're in style. . . . It was the first day of the new millennium and I woke to find that mulattos had taken over. They were everywhere. Playing golf, running the airwaves, opening their own restaurants, modeling clothes. . . . According to the racial zodiac, 2000 is the official Year of the Mulatto. Pure breeds (at least the black ones) are out and hybridity is in. America loves us in all of our half-caste glory. The president announced on Friday that beige is to be the official color of the millennium. Major news magazines announce our arrival as if we were proof of extraterrestrial life. They claim we're going to bring about the end of race as we know it. (12)

Senna's essay takes on more ominous tones in an extended fantasy of "[t]he political strong arm of the multiracial movement, affectionately known as the Mulatto Nation (just 'the M.N. ' for those in the know)," which "decreed just yesterday that those who refuse to comply with orders to embrace their many heritages will be sent on the first plane to Rio de Janeiro, Brazil, where, the M.N.'s minister of defense said, 'they might learn the true meaning of mestizo power'" (15).

The warning is well taken, for a consensus "celebration of mixture" represents small advance from a consensus denigration of miscegenation, if it distracts us from persistent racism and class division, if it obfuscates power (Senna 20). But while it may smack of trendiness and downplay injustice, at the same time, the celebration of the "mulatto millennium" enacts a powerful symbolic change: the installation of new kinds of representative figures for the nation, figures of an America newly honest about its mixed nature and its connections to the larger world, figures for non-isolation, for the nation as the locus of the global. Barack Obama comes to mind, here, precisely; his exceptional qualities seem to instantiate a kind of American exceptionalism in which we could all believe: an honoring of our surpassingly mixed character.

"America is becoming a mestizo nation," declares Rubén Martínez (262). The son of a Mexican father and Salvadoran mother who grew up in Los Angeles, Martínez writes that both his youthful attempts at whiteness and his later adoption of a Latino identity were "fantasies, beautiful lies, Hollywood constructs":

> The truth was that I was always both, that dreaded ambiguity—and how Hollywood hates ambiguity! For to say that I am both is not a simple thing. What is American in me, what is Latino? Let's try the American: my Jewishness, my black-ness, my Asian-ness, my Scandinavian-ness, my immigrant-ness. And how about the Latino: Indian-ness, Iberian-ness, creole-ness, African-ness. . . . As if Chicano would be Chicano (or white, white, or Asian, Asian) in America without the cultural rock at the center of it all: the black. (257–58)

Here we return to Ralph Ellison—who knew that Americans are all part black, and who in this study's epigraph imagines a great figure of our mixedness coming slowly to birth. People of mixed race are "downright relevant," in Walker's terms, both because their growing numbers make them an important sector of the population, but also because the symbolic work that mixed-race Americans cannot help performing, even as they retain the legacies of the prejudicial racialization of their various forebears, is to body forth visibly what is true but often invisible about Americans all: that we come, culturally, from a profoundly mixed background.

Mixed Asian Characters

It is little wonder, amidst the rise of a mestizo U.S. cultural consciousness and an interethnic literary turn, that publications on the mixing of races now proliferate. Prominent among these are works in the genres of memoir and historical narrative, most often concerning the union of black and white—still the definitive binary in the national imaginary. The most widely read mixed-race memoirs have been Barack Obama's *Dreams from My Father* (1995), James McBride's *The Color of Water: A Black Man's Tribute to His White Mother* (1996), and Rebecca Walker's *Black, White, and Jewish* (2001); notably, however, in the persistence of the American "one-drop rule," the first two of these authors are generally identified not as "mixed" but as "black." Other important subgenres of late have been the family passing memoir, which recalls black family members who disappeared into a white life; recovered histories of the black and white branches of Southern families descended from slave plantations (ranging from little-known clans to the Jeffersons and Hemingses); and anthologies of essays or stories by writers of two racial or ethnic heritages.[3] While the body of U.S. fiction about mixed black-white characters is extensive, spanning the nineteenth and early twentieth centuries and including texts by, among many others, Charles Chesnutt, Mark Twain, William Faulkner, and Nella Larsen, fiction that takes up this familiar problematic has been uncommon since the rise of black cultural nationalism in the '60s, with notable exceptions among novels that hearken back to the slavery era.[4] As suggested earlier, the list of Native American writers who have pursued a poetics and problematics of "mixed blood" in stories that cross either tribal or Native European lines nearly matches the roster of best-known authors in the Native American literary canon.[5]

In Asian American literature the history of mixed-race figures is also long, and such characters have tended to be, like mixed black-white characters, at once "representative and exceptional figure(s)" within Asian American literature (Sheffer 132). The most noteworthy early mixed-race Asian American authors were the famous Eaton sisters, Winnifred and Edith, of Chinese and British parentage, who wrote under the pen names Onoto Watanna and Sui Sin Far. The two are often described as having taken up "diametrically opposed strategies" in their literary careers (Ma 166), Edith identifying with and sympathetically portraying working-class Chinese Americans, and Winnifred adopting the then-more glamorous identity of a Japanese rather than a Chinese author, repeatedly creating mixed-race heroines whose status as half-castes condemned them to plots of exoticized and often tragic romance.

Sheng-mei Ma locates in Watanna's work the prototype for a long-dominant Orientalist and essentialist form of cross-race romance in Asian American fiction that he designates by the ironic term "lomansu":

> Orientalist stereotypes are so spontaneously marshaled that romance becomes, as racist pidgin has it, "lomansu," with the proverbial confusion of "r" and "l" and with the hard-sounding suffix in place of the consonant "s." The pidgin spelling brings forth mixed race writers' collusion with the representation of the minority practiced by the hegemony, despite the intention of such romances to undermine cultural and racial stereotypes. (170)

A representative text is Chinese Belgian writer Han Suyin's *A Many-Splendored Thing* (1952), forerunner of the movie, TV series, and pop song "Love Is a Many-Splendored Thing," all dependent on a cold war/colonialist, Orientalist narrative of wartime romance between a Eurasian woman and Western man (170–71). Such schematic dramatizations of a mixed-race Asian condition have not entirely disappeared, even in our era of radical redefinitions of race and ethnicity (169–76), Ma contends.[6] Despite the path-breaking work of social scientists and cultural theorists on mixed-race identity, he claims, "The development of the Asian American mixed-race discourse is still in its initial stages." Rather than "discernible mixed-race characters and consciousness," we find characters who "[disappear] into one or the other race," or make just "cameo appearances" (186, 166).

My reading of recent Asian American literature accords only in part with Ma's argument. Though it must be said that Asian American literature since the massive cultural transformations of the mid-twentieth century shows a vigorous, revisionary engagement with the matter of intergroup encounter and romance, the meaning and import of ethnoracial mixing in that literature has often been an unsettled, deeply troubling question. For example, in the era of identity politics, mixed-race identity makes a "cameo appearance" in a secondary character who is a political enigma in Frank Chin's play *The Chickencoop Chinaman* (1972) (discussed in the Asian/African interchapter). The female character Lee, identified as "possible Eurasian or Chinese American passing for white" who "has borne several kids in several racial combinations" (3), functions as an indeterminate, unknowable element of the drama. If, in this intensely political, racially conflicted play, Lee were marked as definitely Asian, white, or black, like the other characters, we would have no trouble understanding her position—or rather, insofar as she is a sexualized female character whose role is emphatically subordinate to that of the primary male characters—what it means for the men to associate with her. But as "possibly Eurasian," Lee is mired in a symbolic uncertainty allied with the danger posed by her sexuality; her hypersexualization seems, in a typical formulation, a correlate of her mixed/indeterminate race. She cannot embody a political meaning, in a context where little else matters.

Even as cultural nationalist aesthetics shaded into the multiculturalist visions that have come to characterize ethnic American letters in the decades since Chin's agonistic drama, Asian American literature cannot be said to have produced a great many characters born of ethnoracial mixture, or to sustain anything we could call an affirmation of mixed-race consciousness. As with other areas of ethnic cultural production, Asian American nonfiction and popular discourse have engaged more energetically with mixed-race identity than has fiction; recent anthologies titled *Mixed*, *Mixing It Up*, and *Half and Half* include essay after essay in which East and South Asian Americans (among others) offer extended, searching reflections on their own experiences as mixed-race people (see note 4). The Internet yields an abundance of talk that articulates a positive, creative, even liberating conception of mixed-race identity in an ever-expanding vocabulary. A website called "mixedasians," for example, defines itself as "A community relating to the eurasian, biracial, multiracial, amerasian, mixed asian, blasian, hafu, half asian, and hapa," and cites its purpose as "to show the diversity found in mixed people and show that the idea of social race is starting to blur." Neither this evident pleasure in elaborating multiple new self-definitions nor this upbeat view on the blurring of social race is generally to be found in Asian American fiction, which seems largely haunted by a generic tradition in which mixedness is stigmatized and mixed-race people's stories are inherently sad ones. Rather than pleasure, Asian American mixed-race fiction has tended to produce what we probably should call, following Anne Anlin Cheng, the melancholy of mixed race.

One particularly dismaying genre is Asian American young adult fiction, which, according to an essay by Melinda L. de Jesús, tends toward a schematic presentation reminiscent of Ma's "lomansu." De Jesús reports a body of work replete with young heroines whom racial mixture has rendered torn and anxious, less on the positive model of "cultural fusion" than on that of melodrama and tragedy. Longing to assimilate into white social circles, and often caught in "a heterosexual love triangle" that favors her choice of "the white boy" over the Asian American (314–15), the typical heroine causes the critic to lament "yet another mixed race Asian American girl raised in a white household who denies and/or is denied her racial identity" (326).

A subgenre that witnesses even more dire stigmatization of the racially mixed is Asian American (adult) fiction about children of marriage or romance between U.S. soldiers and Asian women. In such texts, a mixed heritage brings racial and geopolitical conflict into the heart of the protagonists' existence, leaving them tragically bound by the enigma of their identity. The part-Filipino, part-Anglo brothers of Brian Ascalon Roley's *American Son* (2001) are locked in a tragic understanding of their inheritance, which instances a history of geopolitical and racial domination; embracing the legacy of their white father is not a viable option for their sense of honor and self-respect, which they seem able to uphold only by imitating the brutally violent protocols of L.A. Latino gangs. Heinz Insu Fenkl's *Memories of My Ghost Brother* (1996) recalls a Korean childhood haunted by violence, shame, and loss among the mixed-race children of Korean mothers and U.S. G.I. fathers in the Vietnam War era. Growing up in Pupyong among prostitutes and beggars, the young Heinz longs for intimacy with the powerful, blond father (of German American origin) who periodically lives with him and his mother, at the same time fearing this alien presence, whom he knows belongs to "the clan that kills people whose skin is the color of mine" (133). His world and the father's U.S. army world are irreparably separate; hearing his father sing with an army buddy, the boy knows that his own voice could never "merge" and "[join]" in this way with his father's, for he "would forever be tainted by . . . Koreanness" (253). The familial knot of love and power is more hideously twisted when Heinz discovers that his father earlier forced his mother to make a terrible sacrifice—giving up an older son by another man—before he would grant her the status of his legal wife and Heinz that of his son, and give them both the promise of a future in America.

One figure born of the coupling of an American soldier and an Asian woman who transcends that plot to embody a nascent mixed-race consciousness is perhaps the best-known mixed-race character in Asian American fiction, the poignantly rendered Joey Sands, son of a Filipino prostitute and an unknown African American serviceman in Jessica Hagedorn's *Dogeaters* (1990) (discussed in chapter 1). The most compelling character in the novel, and the second of two personified narrators, Joey possesses black mestizo looks that make him the exotic object of many Manila tourists' and servicemen's desires. But Joey's character arcs with the transformation of Hagedorn's complex, multifaceted plot, as he grows from a self-anesthetizing junkie and prostitute of the Manila slums to a figure increasingly alive to the larger world and—after witnessing a major political assassination—engaged with his country's political future, ending as a revolutionary guerilla. Other characters in the novel are Spanish or American Filipino mestiza/os—a form of mixedness that seems to bring them, simply, worse cases of the obsession Hagedorn's characters share for all trends and commodities American and/or European. But although Joey does not deeply investigate blackness or race mixture, or articulate their possible meanings for him, his socially aberrant Filipino-black identity makes him a kind of visionary outsider, positioned to see past conventional pieties to the violent falsehoods that his people must uncover and overcome.

The Melancholia of Visible Mixture

Insofar as Joey shares the melancholia of other mixed-race Asian American characters, he is plagued by a racial self-consciousness that operates within a specifically visual economy. Mixedness gives many Asian American literary characters a special kind of visual racial status: the status of a visual puzzle, of a visuality up for public interrogation, in which every evaluating gazer feels in need of and entitled to an accounting of the ethnic strains that produced that face and that coloration. As Chinese Euro-American writer Paisley Rekdal puts it:

> Appearance is the deciding factor of one's ethnicity, I understand; how I look to the majority of people determines how I should behave and what I should accept to be my primary culture.... Any struggle to assert myself as more than what I seem to be is exhausting. A choice, I realized, either could be made by me or asserted for me. (15)

The social imperative to respond appropriately to the question, "What are you?" haunts the consciousness of several of Don Lee's characters, including his (non-mixed) Korean American character Danny, in the story "Yellow" (discussed in chapter 1) and two characters in his 2004 novel *Country of Origin*. Lee has remarked that he came to write mixed-race characters in this novel because most of his students nowadays are mixed and "they think in different ways about culture"; also his friendship with mixed-race novelist Danzy Senna was "incredibly influential" during the time of the writing (Personal interview). But Lee apparently was not moved by these living models, in composing a novel that takes on mixed-race experience more centrally than any other treated in this study, to write a celebratory treatment of the subject. *Country of Origin* presents us, rather, with mixed-race melancholics who are lifelong prisoners of the panoptical gaze of racialization, as obsessed with others' reading of their looks as any sufferer of DuBoisian double consciousness. The two of Lee's three protagonists who are of mixed heritage both experience that background and its stigmatizing social visibility as a profound emotional lack and the cause of a persistent, existential unhappiness.

The male American protagonist, Tom Hurley, resembles Danny of "Yellow" in his self-consciousness about his exotically different looks:

> [H]e had those mixed-blood *hapa haole* features that women liked: thick, wavy black hair, a straight nose, angular cheekbones and jaw, long, girlish eyelashes. He was half-white and half-Korean, but when asked about his ethnicity, he always said Hawaiian, a declaration of racial neutrality that, more often than not, let him avoid further inquest. (12)

For Tom, like Danny, the looks that make him at once vain and, "[w]hen people asked what he was" (115), prone to automatic lies, also make him emotionally shallow, incapable of deep interpersonal contact. This condition is compounded, for Tom, by an American childhood with a white U.S. military father and a Korean mother, in which "At each new post or town or city, he had just tried to blend in . . . but it had never quite worked," for "[h]is mother, his Asianness, always seemed to single him out as different, as other" (125). This sort of self-consciousness characterizes Tom throughout much of the novel, but the plot that takes him past a dead-end affair with a married, blonde American woman into a surprisingly happy ending strongly suggests that reconciling himself to his mixed-race condition and rejecting the panopticon economy that long shaped his self-regard are essential to his well-being. We last see Tom happily married to a "Filipina-Portuguese-Korean-Scottish" woman (308), raising three kids in Hawaii, which had always been "the one place he'd ever visited where he hadn't had to explain himself, where it had seemed possible to be both Asian and American at the same time" (115), and tellingly—for one who early on "worked hard to keep fit and trim and tan" (12)—having become, "no getting around it—fat"; "He had let himself go" (306). This is Lee's portrait of a mixed person's release into the serenity of looking unexceptional.

But Lee's much less fortunate female protagonist dies early in the book, and so sad is the slow unraveling of flashbacks that retell her life up to the moment of that death, while Tom and others try to discover what befell her, that it would be hard to think of the drifting career of Lisa Countryman as anything but that of a contemporary, globally migratory, tragic mulatta. In her American youth, Lisa suffered from constant public derision of her mixed Japanese African features, which inspired a range of tributes:

> [S]he had heard it all, from whites and blacks alike, neither of whom cared for her peculiar mulatto mix: gook monkey, bamboo coon, chigga jigaboo, dim-sum

> casco yellowbone chinkamo slopehead nine-iron UFO ping-pang yangmo bucket-head. (19)

It was oddly more difficult for Lisa, though, when after puberty her features changed and her skin lightened, so that "[p]eople now mistook her for Italian, Israeli, Hawaiian, French, Native American, Russian, Lebanese—*some*thing, some sort of exotic dark mixture, but not really dark, not a real darkie, not—God forbid—black" (19). This intense visual scrutiny has left Lisa feeling, depending on her company,

> [N]ever black enough, or Oriental enough, or white enough, and everyone always felt deceived if she didn't announce her ethnic taxonomy immediately upon meeting them . . . as if she were trying to pass. But just as often, when she did claim racial solidarity with a group, people didn't believe her, suspecting she was merely trying to appropriate the radical-chic color of the month. (67)

Visually indeterminate race has thus left Lisa feeling, from earliest childhood, "that she was bad, that she was worthless, that she was unlovable" (210): "People hate me. . . . I should look ethnic. . . . I've been a freak all my life" (210). The stigma of mixed parentage causes her to experience her very selfhood as a lack, the "self-as-loss" that Cheng identifies as racial melancholia (127).

Lee eventually reveals that Lisa was born to a Korean mother and African American G.I. father in Japan, but abandoned shortly after birth to an orphanage there, and later adopted by an African American couple who raised her in the United States. Her tragic life makes a full circle, then, when Lisa returns in her early twenties to search for her birth mother in Japan, the primary setting of Lee's novel. For Lee's Japan is a place depicted as obsessed with racial purity, systematically and cruelly excluding the racially other, a hell for mulattoes. A Japanese character spent several years of his childhood in the United States:

> From personal experience, Kenzo knew about the state of racial equality in America. It was sound in theory, but not in practice. It was a glorious dream, but just a dream. It would never work. It had never worked—not anywhere, not anytime in history—and the US was the only country foolish and hypocritical enough to try.
>
> Like the rest of the world, Japan prized its homogeneity. It was all very orderly and predictable, unambiguous, and very reassuring, the dictates of the group, the importance of tradition, the building of *seron*—consensus. Without *seron*, there was anarchy, the disintegration of society, such as what was happening in America today. . . . (130–31)

Late in the book we learn that Lisa's birth mother was *zainichi* Korean, descended from those brought to Japan during the WWII occupation of their country, a woman of such low rank in Japan that she must repress her origins in order to have a singing career. Lisa's mother's shameful status, combined with the African American identity of her G.I. father, made Lisa as a baby ineligible for a normal birth certificate, and had she grown up in Japan, would have made her a non-citizen of her birth country, "illegitimate and stateless," not "eligible for schooling, health care, any kind of public assistance," or even a passport to leave the country that rejected her. At the orphanage where she lived till age four, "the children taunted her without mercy" (235–37). Her adoption and removal to the States, then, took her to a place where, though freakish, she was at least legally enfranchised.

Some twenty years later, alone in the world after the accidental death of her adoptive parents, Lisa travels to Japan only to be cruelly rejected by her still-fearful birth mother. By the end of the novel, we understand why in an earlier scene, Lisa is depressed enough to overdose on drink and drugs. In that early scene, we last see her amazed to find herself choking, unable to breathe, consciously approaching death "terrified, and very, very alone," aware that "no one would really miss her" (25).

So it is a real surprise, when the detective plot closes and all loose ends are tied up, to find ourselves, in Lee's stunning final scene, within a consciousness we had thought extinguished, Lisa's. In her very last moment "just before [her heart] stopped beating," Lisa dreams of herself at four years old, but "the girl, with fate and fortune, she might have been"—perfectly reunited with her Japanese mother and African American father, and migrating to America with them by ship: "[T]hey were finally here, the California coast before them" on "a brilliant morning" (314–15). The last lines deliver a vision of America shining with promise:

> As they passed under the Golden Gate Bridge, Lisa imagined what her mother must have been feeling right then, seeing the United States for the very first time. A land where all was possible, where truth prevailed, goodness was rewarded, and beauty could be found in the meeting of outcasts. Oh, what a sight, Lisa marveled.
>
> We are orphans, all of us, she thought. And this is our home. (315)

The golden, immigrant dream evoked in these lines is simultaneously negated because it arises in the last thoughts of a woman who does not know that this is her dying dream, and who never, even in America, lived out such a promise. Lee's extraordinary ending is an elegy for the America that was supposed to have been, registering through the complexity of its layers both a wistful longing and a tragic indictment. *Country of Origin* depicts an America that did not become a haven for the differently and the multiply raced. While the final words, "this is our home," summon our deepest hopes for the United States—the novel's own country of origin—for this tragic heroine, the phrase that designates the nation can, in a terribly ironic equation, mean only her death.

The In-Betweenese

Contrasted to Lee's Lisa, the figure of Catalina in Patricia Chao's *Mambo Peligroso* (2005) (discussed in chapter 1) seems to inhabit a different symbolic cosmos. She does carry deep loss within her: the loss of Cuba, Cubanness, and her Cuban father, who killed himself during the revolution, losses of a kind she shares with thousands of other Cuban Americans. But because the "country of origin" in Chao's novel is one that affirms and even encourages race mixture, rather than despises it, Catalina's mixed Cuban and Japanese-ness never makes her a freak or unlovable alien, in Cuba or in the United States. Being the daughter of a Japanese Cuban mother does not place her in a separate category, gives her no special form of melancholia beyond that of the expatriate community as a whole. People do notice and sometimes fetishize her visible difference—a lover calls her "chinita" (145), vaguely naming her Asianness—but her race mixture does not plague her or limit her vistas. Rather, it seems to contribute to Catalina's interest, narratability, her possibilities as a character, part of what makes readers wonder what she will eventually come to be. And though that coming-to-be is characterized by struggle, danger, and tragedy, as well as exhilaration, it is shaped by her own realizations and choices, not by the way she is framed by (male) others, as in the case of Frank Chin's Lee, or by any spectator of her racial makeup, as in the case of Don Lee's Lisa. Most important, the novel's tragic death is not hers. The fact that her heritage does not include the more stigmatizing African strain surely enhances Catalina's plot possibilities, but regardless, it is a notable moment in Asian American literary history when Chao imagines an ethnically mixed Asian American female character who is the self-sufficient, non-tragic heroine of her own novel of quest, and whose mixed ancestry does not limit or doom her, but rather, gives her a challenge to puzzle out. At the same time, as rapturously caught up as she is in matters Cuban—above all, in mambo dancing—Catalina seems to arrive very belatedly (on the second-to-last page) at any interest in the Japanese element of her identity, so perhaps she is one of Ma's characters who "[disappear] into one or the other race," a lapse for which Senna's "Mulatto Nation" would surely reprimand her.

Among all the recent Asian American novels to feature mixed characters, I have found only one full-out paean of praise to the future forecastable from widespread, increasing genetic mixing. In Jiro Adachi's *The Island of Bicycle Dancers*, the Korean Japanese New York immigrant Yurika has an admirer in the novel's most prominent white character, redundantly called Whitey, who provides such an expression of delight, in a vision not untainted by a sexualizing appetite for the mixed body:

> He saw the fastest-growing ethnic groups in the country forming an Asian-Latin empire where Yurika's dimples, her lips, her sloping back, her two-tone hair, became a beauty ideal from coast to coast, from Nuevo Saigon to San Singapore. He wrote about a future where the streets were full of tasty ethnic cocktails like Yurika, people not fully part of one culture or another but smack in the middle of two or three. Their growing numbers were shrinking the world at an exponential rate, so that this middle, this in between, mushroomed into regions populated by people like Yurika of yellowish brown flesh and lovely eyes the shape of mango pits, the lands of the In-Betweenese. (33)

It is somewhat easier to excuse Whitey's fetishizing regard when we read that he welcomes "the shrinking of the Anglo race . . . [and] prided himself on being a living embodiment of his own race's cosmic downward mobility":

> Whitey had come to believe that his acne . . . was a gross allergic reaction to the Anglo trappings that surrounded him. . . . Whitey was much happier now that he was

> surrounded by Latinos, blacks, and other downwardly mobile whites—mostly artists and junkies of the East Village and Lower East Side. His skin had improved considerably, though scars remained. Still, though, on days when he had too many deliveries to corporate banks in the Wall Street area or law offices around Rockefeller Center, small whiteheads appeared around his chin and on his earlobes. In this way . . . he considered himself Betweenese—a Virginian-Anglo-white boy who never fit in with his own people—not at the prep school he had attended, not in any of the summer jobs at country clubs or banks. . . . As a child, he had always rooted for Indians when he watched old John Ford Westerns with his family. He was drawn to food-oriented cultures. . . . (34)

The spontaneous reaction of Whitey's skin, through which Adachi figures white skin as marred, nonideal, might also be read as a refusal of the invisible privilege of whiteness, which Whitey explicitly rejects to claim the name of a Betweenese, even if there is a patronizing tone to his gastronomic interest in the rest of the population. More troubling in a novel that seeks to transcend racist stigmas is that Yurika's romantic choice of the dark-skinned Bone over Whitey seems to come down to his physicality; she describes him as being "like an animal," and calls him "[h]er animal man" (73). Bone's attractions are all sexual, where pimply Whitey's are his mind and heart. Despite its venture into the land of the In-Betweenese, Adachi's novel does not disprove Ma's argument that, while we wait for treatments of race mixture that fully problematize racial categories and affirm a mixed, fluid, or syncretic postethnic consciousness, we still find reiterations of some of the old racist dividing lines, and not much beyond "cameo appearances" of the truly mixed at heart.

Mixed Kids

But we should not discount "cameo appearances" when they are made by children. Children are potent signifiers in literature, sites of potential and unfolding meaning, of a consciousness at the limit of what the text can articulate. In fictional worlds that do not admit many children, such as those of Jane Austen, for example, when they do appear—as in a novel of self-absorbed adult society like *Emma*— "[I]nfants and children will figure as living emblems of a world beyond the self" (Castle xvii). I want to argue that the representation in contemporary Asian American fiction of mixed-race babies, particularly as the plot-culminating product of fictional interethnic romances, should be understood as a significant gesture toward the multiracial consciousness whose absence in this literature Ma laments. In narratives about mixed children, Susan Gubar writes in *Racechanges*, "[T]he hybridity of the child signals . . . a distinct rupture from the past into an unprecedented, strange, post-racist future," "hold[ing] out the promise of a redemptive transracial consciousness" (232, 207). In the Asian American novels considered here, what each child promises is not precisely the same transracial consciousness, but a projection of the fiction's distinctive interethnic imagination into the future. If rather flat as a character and scarcely speaking in the text, each fictional child is a powerfully symbolic presence.[7] Each seems a hypothesis, a proposed form of existence beyond melancholia or fetish, a natural, untainted, new consciousness with an integrity of its own. It would be hard to overstate the importance of the death of Mitt, the ethnically mixed son of the hero of *Native Speaker*, for that book's interethnic vision. Mitt had been a "wondrous" phenomenon (285), beloved for a uniqueness inseparable from his embodiment of ethnic fusion. Henry recalls "his boy's form . . . so beautifully jumbled and subversive and historic," and adds, "No one, I thought, had ever looked like that" (103). Henry's lingering grief for his child throughout the novel profoundly chastens interethnic hope, and the evocation of the absent Mitt amidst the hubbub of a classroom of multiethnic immigrant kids makes the novel's ending bittersweet. Finishing (and publishing) his book, Chang-rae Lee does not send out into the world a "child" whose message is purely promise, but rather, as when Lelia writes each exiting student's "lovely" and "difficult" name on a sticker pressed to his or her chest, in *Native Speaker* he sends out a substitute, a child for whom our hope is tempered by the knowledge of grief.

Io, the ethnically mixed child of Mona Chang and Seth Mandel, appears only in the last few pages of Gish Jen's *Mona in the Promised Land*, but as I suggested in chapter 3, she is key to the comic ending, both as evidence of the fruition of hybridity and as another alternative form of achieved relationship (besides that of the crucial mother-daughter reunion) to the ironized marriage plot; in Io, Mona produces a fully hybrid girl. The strange choice of her name seems to signify above all that in Mona and Seth's marriage neither the Chinese nor the Jewish prevails—but rather the yuppie postmodern and its affectation of Greek (what meaning can be derived from the classical Io's alter identity as a cow, however, remains a mystery). The sunny but not idealizing portrait of her—falling and almost crying, but righting herself to clap at the happy ending—is of a piece with the novel's own lack of pretension, its way of mocking its earnest investment in a multicultural ideal. What is "redemptive" about Io, to use Gubar's term, is that she simply embodies our interethnic future—or is that our present?—a moment when Mona's risky 1970s extra-ethnic quest is resolved by the "millennial" fact of the birth of many, many such interethnic children.

Yamashita's Sol, as suggested in chapter 4, is a mixed child so obviously right with nature that the inability of his parents or anyone around him to get over ethnic, racial, or national differences seems plainly wrong. His northward progress amidst the migrating throng helps make that transnational quest seem utterly natural, too. And by closing with the restoration of his safe future, Yamashita makes her novel's interethnic project seem in the process of spreading, irresistibly as rain forest growth, beyond the book's covers.

These children of the interethnic impulse might also be read as emblems of their novels' resistance to another kind of subject: the consolidated ethnic identity that, in Anne Anlin Cheng's words, has typically served to close "the ethnically representative novel and its *Bildung*" (137). For Yamashita most obviously, any such consolidation of identity is utterly overthrown by the interplay of multiple subjectivities, ethnic and racial differences, mixed and migratory families. In Jen's *Mona*, much more the individualist bildungsroman, the exuberant plot of the heroine's identity "switch" culminates in a heterosexual marriage ending that mocks and resists itself, and the spectacle of an intermarrying bride endlessly deferring the matter of her name. And in Lee's *Native Speaker*, the plot of an ethnic outsider's angst, too, ends in ongoing deferral of identity, with the hero masked, and his stance in the scene provisional, melancholic, apart—recalling the dark epigraph from Whitman, and recalling as well the figure of Ellison's invisible man, who in Cheng's reading resistantly holds to nonidentity in the end (137). But building on the vision of the invisible man, Lee's Henry Park points attention, in his ending, to someone outside himself; his gaze is turned to the classroom of multicultural kids who become representative "of who we are," in a larger sense. Lee's ending can help us see that in an important way, all three of these novels ultimately turn things over to the hybrid child, who takes the place of an ethnically reified subject. These new interethnic fictions thus can be seen to work beyond the arrival at an achieved ethnic identity and toward the open possibilities of hybrid subjectivities.[8]

In the transnational family reunions of Yamashita's endings, the restoration of the mixed child to the parents, the interethnic lovers to one another, despite massive upheavals around them, starts the world over again anew. In her novel and in the others studied here, new beginnings take place in a transformed local landscape, a new "ethnoscape," a reimagined homescape, if you will. These examples confirm that the Asian American novel, still engaged in a historically resonant quest to "claim America" as a home for Asian Americans, has also become a place that invites others in—other kinds of characters and literary forebears and other readers, too—in the hope of reinventing home together. The most potent sign of the promise of such a home is the unanimity of their closing visions, in which—the forces of greed, division, and animosity momentarily in check—the future of the mixed child looks bright. Whatever uncertainties attend the rapidly changing ethnic character of our communities, nations, relationships, and lives, we may well expect that the mixed children who mark the close of these and other contemporary ethnic American novels carry the promise of a thriving and increasingly open-ended ethnic literature.

NOTES

Preface

1. These children also evidence the widespread race mixing in contemporary fiction, a subject addressed in this study's epilogue, on mixed-race characters in Asian American fiction. On race mixture and interracial people, see Werner Sollors's work, especially *Neither Black Nor White Yet Both* and his edited volume *Interracialism*; see also Susan Koshy, *Sexual Naturalization*; as well as Gubar, Hollinger, and Perlmann.

2. On the failure of multiculturalism to bring social and economic justice, see James Kyung-Jin Lee, xiv.

3. See, for example, Robin Truth Goodman's highly critical materialist reading of Keri Hulme's *The Bone People* and other winners of Mobil Oil's Pegasus Prize for Literature, and their relationship to the values of corporate globalization (95–117).

4. On this point, see Daniel Y. Kim (*Writing* xvi–xviii); see also Marable.

5. For a defense of extended close reading in ethnic literary scholarship, see Daniel Y. Kim (*Writing* 246–49). See also the volume *Literary Gestures: The Aesthetic in Asian American Writing* by Rocío G. Davis and Sue-Im Lee, especially the introduction by Sue-Im Lee.

Chapter 1

1. A *New York Times* article on the winner of the 2008 Nobel Prize in Literature underscores this point. Praising the later work of Jean Marie Gustave Le Clézio, Professor Antoine Compagnon remarks, "It has an openness to others, to other cultures, to the South, to minorities. This is a very current sensibility" (Lyall).

2. I refer to the common assumption of recent literary criticism expressed, for example, in a remark of Werner Sollors, reading ethnic texts as "not mere reflections of existing

differences but also . . . productive forces in nation-building enterprises" (*Invention* xv). My point is that contemporary ethnic texts are also productive forces in building something that transcends the nation.

3. Friedman also cites Clifford in this regard.

4. See, for example, two influential volumes: *Cultures of United States Imperialism* (1993), edited by Amy Kaplan and Donald E. Pease, and *The Futures of American Studies* (2002), edited by Donald E. Pease and Robyn Wiegman.

5. Edna Acosta-Belén notes, in an essay on hemispheric Latino/a studies:

> Emerging from the transnational sociocultural system that characterizes the Americas are significant cultural and linguistic transformations and exciting hybrid configurations, multicultural crossovers that are forcing scholars to rethink, redefine, and transgress the conventional boundaries of what we do in our respective academic disciplines . . . .The traditional disciplines are opening their borders to paradigms that favor more connected or integrated approaches to the social realities, to paradigms that view societies as complex conglomerates of hybrid cultures, contested identities, and conflicting and uneven power relations. (244–45)

6. For a related theoretical contribution, see Lenz.

7. On the growing self-consciousness and public activism of people of mixed-race heritage, see Hollinger; Perlmann. See also the epilogue, "Mixed Races, Mixed Children, Mixed Outcomes."

8. For a useful revision of Sollors, see Brogan, especially pp. 13–15. For criticisms of the ethnicity school, see Sau-ling C. Wong, *Reading*, p. 4; Wald.

9. I refer to the title of Thomas J. Ferraro's important study, *Ethnic Passages: Literary Immigrants in Twentieth-Century America*.

10. See Clifford, *Routes*; and Gilroy, *The Black Atlantic*.

11. For an excellent, brief discussion of these terms and their contested applications, see Marable.

12. I would thus count myself among those A. Robert Lee, in *Multicultural American Literature*, describes as follows:

> [O]ther liberal-leftists back a multicultural ethos to the hilt as the very ground-condition of all future American politics, as important to the shaping of the nation's power arrangements as class, gender, or region. In this sense, ethnicity is to be understood as live human dynamic, busy in contradiction, contestatory as need be, anything but inert category. (3)

13. See Sollors's *Neither Black Nor White Yet Both: Thematic Explorations of Interracial Literature*; *Interracialism: Black-White Intermarriage in American History, Literature, and Law*; and *An Anthology of Interracial Literature: Black-White Contacts in the Old World and New*.

14. Consideration of the texts of Latino/a literature is, regrettably, largely absent from my discussions in this study, though cultural critique in this tradition is key to my analyses, here and in chapter 4, on the work of Karen Tei Yamashita.

15. For this energetic term I am indebted to Erika Meitner.

16. Among the numerous Native American authors whose work features mixed-blood characters (on which matter see the epilogue, note 5), Louise Erdrich has written many, among them the memorably fierce would-be saint Pauline Puyat of *Tracks* (1988), who, unloved and unlovable among her tribe, turns to self-mortification in a Catholic convent. Erdrich has also written central white characters, such as those in *The Beet Queen* (1986) and *The Master Butchers Singing Club* (2003). But her 2004 novel, *Four Souls*, signals a new

moment when its plot turns, remarkably, upon cross-race Indian-white sexual and romantic relationships. The formidable Fleur Pillager, she of mysterious powers who avenges the theft of her family's land at the end of *Tracks*, manages to become in *Four Souls* the healer, the wife, and the deliberate ruin of John James Mauser, the wealthy white man who built his mansion upon her loss and from her trees. Another plot climaxes in Mauser's sister-in-law's joyful emergence from the rigid social restrictions of her caste, into an embrace of cross-race love with his manservant, Fantan.

17. I refer to the stereotype of the tragic mulatto, interestingly dissected by Sollors in *Neither Black Nor White Yet Both*. For a discussion of recent novels that reclaim and reinflect mixed-race identity, see the epilogue, "Mixed Races, Mixed Children, Mixed Outcomes."

18. The movement here beyond the "color line" and into a multiracial consciousness is echoed in the appearance, in late twentieth-century African American letters, of numerous personal memoirs and historical accounts that search into cross-race family histories, meditating on the ordinary, near-invisible, familial interraciality of our culture (on such texts see the epilogue, especially note 3). We might locate a similar interest in novels with interracial dynamics like Morrison's *Paradise* (1998) and *A Mercy* (2008) and, earlier, Octavia Butler's science fiction slavery novel *Kindred* (1979), as well as the eccentric *Oreo* (1974), by Fran Ross, which riffs with comic brilliance on the parallelism and possibilities of black-Jewish fusion.

19. One might start with early-century Jewish American stories that position immigrant children in tense tests of loyalty between their Old World parents and figures of white normativity encountered in American schools. See for example Mary Antin, "The Lie" (1913) and Anzia Yezierska, "Children of Loneliness" (1923); this opposition is comically updated in Grace Paley's tale of stardom in a public school Christmas pageant, "The Loudest Voice" (1959). The trend continues through alternately terrifying and exhilarating visions of the multiethnic New York City streets, such as Henry Roth's 1934 *Call It Sleep*, Michael Gold's *Jews Without Money* (1930), and Kate Simon's *Bronx Primitive* (1982). Jewish American literature of the mid-century offers numerous explorations of, on the one hand, the anxieties of suburbanization, assimilation into whiteness, and intermarriage, such as Bruce Jay Friedman's *Stern* (1962), and much of the early and even the recent Philip Roth, and, on the other hand, the plight of and the possibilities of engagement with African Americans. A sympathetic impulse toward African Americans is observable as early as the lynch poems of the immigrant Yiddish poets Yehoash in the teens and Berish Vaynshteyn in the '30s, and becomes widespread from the 1960s on, notable in the complex fictional studies of Grace Paley, Stanley Elkin, and Norma Rosen, and in particularly intense, vexed, and dialogic form in the fiction of Bernard Malamud.

20. On contemporary avant-garde Jewish culture, see the interchapter "Cross-ethnic Jewishness in Asian American and Other Contemporary Fiction," note 8.

21. The trend is notably strong in Jewish women's texts; in an essay on the relationship of Jews to multiculturalism, Cheryl Greenberg has made the suggestive claim that Jewish American women tend to align themselves more fully with multiculturalism than do Jewish men (60).

22. In my first book, I constructed a chain of the interlinked cross-ethnic book blurbs (by the ethnic women writers whose books were on my shelf) to illustrate the point that African American and Caribbean women writers should be understood to participate in the "horizontality" of contemporary literary influence (Rody, *The Daughter's Return* 13–15). On "the global writing of books" and their circulation through transnational "literary systems," see Walkowitz (528).

23. Hollinger develops this term, which he derives from Mitchell Cohen and Bruce Ackerman.

24. Ellison lists Hemingway, Eliot, Malraux, Dostoevsky, and Faulkner.

25. For a discussion of the history and implications of the term "Asian American," see Sau-ling C. Wong, *Reading*; see also Koshy, "The Fiction"; Chuh.

26. On the evolution of Asian American literary and cultural critique, see Cheung, "Re-Viewing"; Wong, "Denationalization" and *Reading*; Lowe, *Immigrant*; R. Lee, *Americas* (5–11); Li (17); Lim and Ling; Kim, Preface; Hagedorn, "Introduction; Bow.

27. Yen Le Espiritu's 1992 book *Asian American Panethnicity* explores the history of and possibilities for social and political affinity and alliance among Asian Americans across national and ethnic differences. King-kok Cheung's edited collection *An Interethnic Companion to Asian American Literature* first used the term "interethnic" in Asian American scholarship. Her book presents essays in each of which a scholar introduces and surveys a distinct, ethnically defined body of Asian American literature; in the second part, scholars' essays discuss trends and theoretical problems germane to all. While Cheung's text is "interethnic" in the sense that it "seeks to fulfill the dual purpose of introducing the distinctive literary histories of constituent Asian American groups and of bringing out issues that connect them" ("Re-Viewing" 20), I use the term differently, to name a dynamic that actively shapes Asian American literary texts, a pattern of imaginative affiliation and exchange with other peoples, texts, and cultures, sometimes within but largely outside of Asian America.

28. For example, Sau-ling Cynthia Wong cites this notion, deriving it from Maxine Hong Kingston's *China Men*; Wong also uses the term in a discussion of the need to resist "mainstream American" cultural norms (Wong, *Reading* 14). Describing changes in Asian Americanist critical practice in 1997, King-Kok Cheung writes, "The shift has been from seeking to 'claim America' to forging a connection between Asia and America . . ." ("Re-Viewing" 1).

29. In the wake of the entrance of over twenty million new immigrants to the United States since 1965 (Mendoza and Shankar xvii), critics have come to speak, once again, of an "immigrant" literature—in contrast to the "ethnic" literature of the mid-twentieth century, a category that came to be so named after the severe legal restrictions of the 1920s ended the heyday of early-century immigration and of "immigrant literature" as well (Mendoza and Shankar xx–xxi).

30. See the Asian/African interchapter on the term's invention.

31. I'll note with regret that the novels treated at length in the chapters to come are all by East Asian Americans, so that texts by South Asian American authors have unfortunately been excluded from extensive consideration. But the overview that closes this chapter discusses several South Asian American texts and authors.

32. Wong is citing the title of a study by James W. Loewen, *The Mississippi Chinese: Between Black and White* (1971).

33. On the controversy over *Blu's Hanging*, see for example Chiang, Seo, and Takahama.

34. On interracial literature, including cross-race romance plots and plots of the "tragic mulatto," see Sollors, *Neither Black Nor White Yet Both*.

35. But this anger interestingly sends him in his teens into a boxing plot, a throwback to days of more visceral struggle for immigrant Asian Americans, the thirties of the Filipino men in Peter Bacho's stories, the forties of the Chinese American boy in Gus Lee's *China Boy*, or the black boxer worship of the Asian American men in Frank Chin's *Chickencoop Chinaman* (all discussed in the first interchapter). Boxing is understood by most around Lee's Danny to be inappropriate for this child of the middle class 1980s, destined to be a college-educated professional; says his mother, "Boxing's only for poor people. I thought you're not so dumb" (214). But boxing is also for angry outsiders who feel they have to fight their way in, as Bacho

explains in a story discussed in the Asian/African interchapter (see Bacho, "A Manong's Heart"). It is noteworthy that Lee creates a well-off 1980s character who harbors alienation and rage akin to that of earlier, poorer immigrant Asians.

36. Chu also recalls the history of marriage as "a site where American legislators and cultural discourses have sought to inscribe the rejection of Asian immigrants as potential citizens": the exclusion from immigration of Asian women, the prohibition of interracial marriages (19).

37. Also see the epilogue, note 7, on Lahiri's novel *The Namesake* (2003).

38. For example, each man appreciates the other's different masculine style. Jerry receives the gentle, long-haired Paul's "usual lovechild hug, wiry and sneaky strong" (74), and notes his "combination of bardic and new age male sensitivity" as well as his inability to drink much because of a "genetically challenged liver" (94, 96). Paul praises Jerry's "beautiful machine expertise": "You're the sort of fellow who's totally reliable, in the mechanical arts"; "[I]f there's anybody I'd trust, Jerry [to fly a private plane], it would be you" (94–95).

39. The death of Jerry's pregnant daughter, Theresa, though it doesn't prevent the birth of her and Paul's child, is unfortunately suggestive about marriageability in Lee's novels; it ends what would have been the first marriage of two Asian Americans in his oeuvre to date.

Interchapter

1. See for example the violent repression of 1930s Filipino migrant workers in Bulosan. By one report, Japanese Americans in internment camps were treated by white officials as if they were black: "At the Poston internment camp, a staff person complained that many of the facility's officials knew little about Japanese Americans but 'almost automatically transferred attitudes held about Negroes to the evacuees'" (Lipsitz 201, citing Daniels, 36).

2. Important contributions to this emerging area include Prashad's 2001 study of "the peoples who claim the heritage of the continents of Asia and Africa," *Everybody Was Kung Fu Fighting*, which attempts to recount "how these two cultural worlds are imbricated in complex and varied ways through five centuries and around the globe," from the time of the slave trade to the emergence of "polycultural kung fu" in the period of U.S. black revolutionary activism (x, 146); George Lipsitz's chapter on Asia in the mind of black nationalists in *The Possessive Investment in Whiteness*; Gary Y. Okihiro's essay "Is Yellow Black or White?" which traces the shared history of "a kindred people, African and Asian Americans" (34); Daniel Y. Kim's literary examination of the interracialism of "black and yellow men" in *Writing Manhood in Black and Yellow: Ralph Ellison, Frank Chin, and the Literary Politics of Identity* (2005); and jazz musician Fred Ho's and scholar Bill V. Mullen's *Afro Asia: Revolutionary Political and Cultural Connections between African-Americans and Asian-Americans* (2008). Other suggestive explorations in the Asian-African American vein include James Kim's "The Legend of the White-and-Yellow Black Man," on racial triangulation in the Hollywood martial arts film *Romeo Must Die*; LeiLani Nishime's piece on the black-Asian buddy cop movie *Rush Hour*; Jelena Šesnić's essay on male homosocial identification in *China Boy* and *Native Speaker*; Yung-Hsing Wu's essay on Ralph Ellison and Chang-rae Lee (on which literary connection, see chapter 2); and, in the *AfroAsian Encounters* volume on "the mutual influence of and relationships between members of the African and Asian diasporas in the Americas" (1), numerous essays on literary, popular film, and musical imbrications. For a further list, see Raphael-Hernandez and Steen (13–14 note 1).

3. According to Prashad,

> Scholars who began to research AfroAsian interaction . . . demanded that ethnic studies shift its epistemological horizon from pluralist inclusion within a culture of hierarchy to solidarity based on scrupulous attention to the interests of different pan-ethnic formations in the rat race of bureaucratic multiculturalism. . . . ("Foreword" xx)

Contributions to the field grew particularly, he notes, in the years following the Black-Korean riots of the early 1990s (xiv–xv, xx).

4. Lipsitz is citing Yasuko II Takezawa, *Breaking the Silence: Redress and Japanese American Ethnicity* (Ithaca, NY: Cornell UP, 1995).

5. Present-day dimes bear the visage of Franklin D. Roosevelt, of course, but in Bulosan's 1930s, they bore a figure of Lady Liberty.

6. I thank Susan Fraiman for this point.

7. On "emasculation" see among others Eng; J. Ling; and Cheung, "The Woman Warrior Versus the Chinaman Pacific."

8. James Kim's essay "The Legend of the White-and-Yellow Black Man," a reading of white-black-Asian male violence in the Hollywood martial arts film *Romeo Must Die*, offers a suggestive theory of "triangulated racial desire," an "ambivalent desire for a racial other circulated through a system of three terms" (165). Kim's "triangulation" integrates Eve Sedgwick's theory of the triangulated homoerotic desire that places a woman's body between two desiring men, and Eric Lott's theory of white male "love" and "theft" of black men and their culture (165). On this subject, see also chapter 2.

9. Indeed, discussing the *Aiiieeeee!* anthologies, Daniel Y. Kim claims that "the polemics of Chin and his colleagues are driven by an impulse to project a literary image of what might be termed Yellow Power" (125).

10. See Samir Dayal on racial triangulation surrounding "black-and-brown interactions," including romances, in recent films (88).

11. A parallel encounter is the meeting on Alcatraz Island, during the 1969 Native American protest, of the Chinese American hero of Shawn Wong's *Homebase* with a Native American man who resembles his grandfather. The old man tells the hero that his ancestors came from China thirty thousand years ago and, moreover, that his own grandfather was a Chinese immigrant. Underscoring their multilayered solidarity, the man also informs the hero of a history he does not know: that of the imprisoned Chinese on the island next to Alcatraz, Angel Island.

12. On the politics of Asian American hip-hop and its reception, see Wang.

Chapter 2

1. Lee may have had little to do with his book's paperback cover art, of course. My assertion about the covers of African Americans' books rests on an unscientific survey of the book covers on my shelf, which reveal a distinct and not-so-subtle pattern to the color coding of ethnic novels. To cite just a few examples, a text by an African American, Gloria Naylor's *The Women of Brewster Place*, shows a preponderance of black, with white accents; a text about a mixed-race person, Danzy Senna's *Caucasia*, advertises its subject in a self-conscious balance of black and white shapes and spaces; and well-known texts by Asian Americans such as Maxine Hong Kingston's *The Woman Warrior* and Amy Tan's *The Joy-Luck Club* wear the Orient all over them, in dramatic reds or flamboyant yellow dragons.

2. Daniel Y. Kim has recently written, in a similar vein, that "*Native Speaker* seems a text tailor-made for an emergent paradigm in American and Ethnic Studies" called "intercultural" or "interracial" ("Do I" 233–34).

3. Lee has remarked that his character Henry struggles "to become a 'native speaker' . . . of his self" (Monaghan)

4. Elaine Kim writes, "Those of us who chafe at being asked whether we are Chinese or Japanese as if there were no other possibilities . . . are sensitive to an invisibility that seems particular to us" ("Home" 272). Her essay on the Korean American experience of the Los Angeles riots also discusses the general American ignorance of the "centuries of extreme suffering" of the Korean people, which shapes the "rich and haunted lode of Korean national consciousness" carried as a legacy by Korean Americans (271, 284).

5. Janice's character suggests another strategic ethnic omission: the odd near-absence of Jews from this novel of New York politics and ethnic life. The presence of Jews is mentioned briefly among the ranks of Kwang's campaign workers and the neighbors in Henry's suburban childhood, but no individual characters emerge; and Jews are not engaged in the novel in substantial ways. I could not help but read the feisty Polish-American character Janice Pawlowsky, with her commitment to Kwang's progressive politics, her Berkeley law degree, her plump sexiness, and her verbal sass, as an omitted Jew—perhaps omitted for reasons not unlike those I hypothesize in relation to Lee's omission of important black characters: the avoidance of unwanted conflict or complication.

6. Verbal and syntactic repetition interestingly links this passage to and contrasts it with a passage on compulsory assimilation to whiteness in Frank Chin's *Chickencoop Chinamen* discussed in the Asian/African interchapter. Chin's hero recalls parental advice: "Don't be seen with no blacks, get good grades, lay low, an apple for the teacher, be good, suck up, talk proper, and be civilized" (26).

7. Morrison writes, "It is no accident and no mistake that immigrant populations (and much immigrant literature) understood their 'Americanness' as an opposition to the resident black population" (*Playing* 47). Among studies of white ethnics' performance of non-blackness, see the following vividly titled books: Michael Rogin, *Blackface, White Noise: Jewish Immigrants in the Hollywood Melting Pot*; Karen Brodkin, *How Jews Became White Folks, and What That Says about Race in America*; Noel Ignatiev, *How the Irish Became White*.

8. The year 1991, one year before, also saw violence and protest boycotts of Korean-owned stores in both Los Angeles and New York City.

9. On race and the L.A. riots see Robert Gooding-Williams, *Reading Rodney King/Reading Urban Uprising*. On Koreans and blacks in particular, see Elaine Kim and Sumi Cho in that volume. For a sociological and psychological analysis of Korean-black relations, see Dae Young Kim and L. Janelle Dance; and for a general treatment of urban black-Korean-Jewish relations, see Jennifer Lee. McFerson's 2006 volume, *Blacks and Asians*, takes on many aspects of relations between the two groups in the United States and elsewhere.

10. On all of these terms, see Clarence Major's *From Juba to Jive: A Dictionary of African-American Slang*.

11. In this he resembles the "perverse variation" on Eng's racial castration described by James Kim, discussing the Chinese American character Han, who in the Hollywood martial arts film *Romeo Must Die* fluidly takes on many identities in "a kind of erasure": "emptied of his ethnicity, Han effectively becomes a blank slate on which other identities can be written" and is thus "emasculated through a process of *deracination* systematically stripping him of his yellowness" (J. Kim 162). Henry's plight also accords strikingly with a problematic in the work of playwright and novelist Frank Chin, which Daniel Y. Kim reads as "hunger for the kinds of racialized masculinity that men of other races embody without effort" (*Writing* 203). Chin has written explicitly of "the chameleon Chinaman," who is "[h]ungry, all the time hungry . . . looking for color, trying on tongues and clothes

and hairdos, taking everyone elses [sic], with none of our own, and no habitat, our manhood just never came home" (qtd. in D. Kim 36).

12. But see Park and Wald for a different view on the representation of the Korean housekeeper, Ahjuma.

13. See also a mention of Kwang pursuing Henry (144) and courting behavior between the two (178).

14. What happens to the colonialist plot, for example, in the toast Henry makes to his wife Lelia?: "To Lee. . . . The person who taught me how to curse out loud. And mean it" (198). Here the hero casts himself as Caliban who, taught language by the colonizer, uses it to curse him back. Yet several differences are suggestive: unlike Prospero, Lelia actually teaches the savage his curses, and teaches him loudness too; Henry does not use these against her, but against others. While not a Korean value, loudness suggests resistance to the silence enforced by a colonizing language and culture. Intimacy modifies the anticolonial scenario also in that Henry actually makes the toast to "Lee," using English to recast his wife's name in his own language, in a shortened form that must be—to hero and author alike—much more familiar and congenial than "Lelia," a name Henry might well have added to his list of English words ("*Frivolous. Barbarian.*"), which, in their abundance of *l*'s and *r*'s, "someone must have invented . . . to torture" Korean speakers. "English," Lee memorably writes, "is a scabrous mouthful" (233–34).

15. Or, as Daniel Y. Kim has gone so far as to put it, "The urban masses . . . comprise the central collective protagonist of *Native Speaker*" ("Do I" 233). Kim's reading of Lee's engagement with African American literary and cultural paradigms, especially his "attempt to conjure a novel form of interracial political identification," accords with my interethnic emphasis (235).

16. But then again it recalls the voracious imagination of Wittman Ah Sing, Maxine Hong Kingston's refiguration of Frank Chin in the hipster protagonist of her novel *Tripmaster Monkey: His Fake Book*. Liam Corley writes that in *Native Speaker*, Lee "performs an equivalent claim to universality that depends, as Whitman's did, upon a narcissistic focus on the embodied self as the representative figure of humanity," and thus "revises Whitman's heritage of representative Americanness to include the immigrant experience as central" (67).

17. In these lines from Whitman's "The Sleepers," darkness is the nullity of death. But as the speaker travels amidst vistas of the world's many peoples, all mixed and equal in their sleep, among many others he comes upon sleeping Africans and slaves. See Corley for an interesting reading of the intertextual node of the shipwreck motif: "The spectacle from which Whitman here turns is a shipwreck," he writes, and thus "[t]he starting point for any explication of the poem's meaning within *Native Speaker* is . . . the wreck of the *Golden Venture*" (67), an incident alluded to in the novel. The illegal immigrant Chinese of this doomed ship were forced to swim to shore in New York harbor, resulting in many deaths.

18. Similarly, Daniel Y. Kim writes: "Lee's narrative ultimately constructs the aesthetic realm, in neo-Romantic terms, as a domain of abundant recompense. The City that Kwang fails to remake politically, Henry as narrator is able to remake through the figurative power of language" ("Do I" 251).

19. And, as Rachel Lee puts it, Kwang in this way also "construes the undocumented worker (the 'illegal immigrant') as the . . . quintessential American" ("Reading" 349).

20. Kwang is also shown being abusive to his wife, carrying on an extramarital affair, and, while driving drunk, causing serious injury to a young Korean sex worker, facts that seriously undercut his public rhetoric about "family." I thank an anonymous reader for these points.

21. In this sense, Mitt's death is another form of symbolic castration, for it ends Henry's power to generate that dreamed-of larger self.

22. On Mitt and the implications of the ending of *Native Speaker*, see also the epilogue.

23. In my experience, some readers view with suspicion the politics of multicultural community in this class scene, in particular the role of the white woman's voice, which, unlike Henry's muted voice, is vested with the power to grant legitimacy by saying everyone else's "difficult" name, and even to extend these immigrant children "citizenship" ("Everybody, she says, has been a good citizen" [349]). Certainly Lelia acts from a position of considerable race and class privilege here, but, as others have argued, surely we can read her as attempting to stretch herself beyond that privilege: when pronouncing the children's "dozen lovely and native languages" doing "the best she can" to get them right; acting silly and undignified to bring her students confidence; and in conferring classroom "citizenship," imaginatively countering the status of many of these children's illegal-alien families (in a plot that has seen the deportation of many such families). By endorsing this defense of Lelia, of course, I not-so-opaquely defend the position of the white English teacher in the multicultural classroom, a position I often inhabit. But Lee, it seems to me, is fully aware of the contradictions and inequalities of a situation he renders with humor and grace.

Chapter 3

1. "In high school," Jen has said in an interview, "these writers were like gods to me"; "I continue to greatly esteem these writers, and to admire what Roth has called 'red-faced literature,' a literature that is out there emotionally, not quite so restrained . . . " ("So").

2. It may be useful to emphasize that my operative term here is "Jewishness" rather than "Judaism," to indicate culture rather than religious practice (though the two are not entirely separable), and more, to indicate an ethnic condition and signifier, as understood either from within or from without. Exactly what constitutes "Jewishness" in all these senses is, of course, a complex and changing matter, given enormous variations in the lives of Jews in many times and places. But I speak here primarily of Jewishness in America, about which historian Jenna Weissman Joselit writes, "What was once a comprehensively ordered, fully integrated system of beliefs and behaviors had come undone, its constituent parts disaggregated and reassembled. In the alchemy of America, a new form of Jewish identity emerged—Jewishness—whose expression had as much, and perhaps more, to do with feeling 'Jewish at heart' than with formal ritual" (293–94).

3. I thank Swan Kim for an early comment to me about the distinctiveness of tone in *Mona,* and for her paper on the ideology of "compulsory American happiness" in the novel.

4. An exception might be Gus Lee's *China Boy* (1991), for which point I heartily thank an anonymous reader.

5. A couple of possible exceptions that come to mind are Grace Paley's late 1950s story, "The Loudest Voice," and Galina Vromen's 2002 story "The Secret Diary of a Bat Mitzvah Girl," in both of which—coincidentally?—young Jewish American girls fearlessly and vocally drag resistant families into the arena of American cultural hybridization.

6. In this regard, see Jen's epigraphs, all of which celebrate "flux and motion" and the joining of new groups, the first two in the specific terms of cross-ethnic identification:

> I'm becoming Chinese, I know it. – Richard Rodriguez
> And having grown up next door to Skokie, Illinois—the land of perpetual spring, a Rosenbloom on every corner—I knew more Yiddish than Japanese. – David Mura

7. On her own speaking voice, Jen has related the following story:

> My mother told me that once they had made up their minds that America was going to be their home, they also decided they wanted their kids to speak English so well

no one would be able to tell their parents were Chinese. And what was the result? One of my boyfriends in college once made everyone in the room close their eyes, listen to me talk, and tell him what they heard. And, of course, they all said, "New York Jew!" ("Culturally Speaking" 1, 3)

8. This is the title of a collection of essays, edited by Seltzer and Cohen, cited here.

9. Prominent examples might be the novels and stories of Abraham Cahan or Anzia Yezierska. See also the extensive selections in *Jewish American Literature: A Norton Anthology* (ed. Chametzky et al.).

10. My thanks to Dean Franco for pointing to a tradition of nineteenth- and early twentieth-century American Jewish writers who asserted the equivalence of Jewish and American values, including Rabbi Isaac Mayer Wise, Emma Lazarus, Horace Kallen, and Mary Antin.

11. On white ethnics' option to choose to remain ethnic, see Mary Waters.

12. Jen has spoken of the genesis of the second novel in a chance encounter with someone she had known in her Scarsdale high school; the meeting, she says, "jogged my memories," inspiring her to produce the first chapter of the book ("So").

13. The narrative retrospect also creates sociological anachronisms. Mona's adoption of Jewishness in the early 1970s might be said to apply a 1990s multicultural sensibility prematurely; she thinks of ethnicity as a mentality, a way of life, a choice, some years before most American Jews shifted from conceiving Jewishness as a religious, national, or ethnic identity to a cultural identity (Waxman 7–8, Farber and Waxman, "Cohesion and Conflict" 91), from "a community of belief based on a system of shared prescriptive values" to "a community of shared individual feelings," a change deriving in large part from "the primacy of personal choice in America" and "the individualized perception of modern religious belief" (Farber and Waxman, "Constructing" 193–94). I thank my student Lauren Akselrod for her sociological insights.

14. Jen has discussed her own cross-ethnic acculturation:

I'm not Jewish, but I thought about it a lot as a teenager, and reexamined a lot of those thoughts while writing the book. . . . who I am is a person who assimilated a great deal of the Jewish culture I grew up in, as I think everybody who lives in the New York area has. The fact is that you can't grow up in New York without learning some Yiddish, without the culture leaving its mark on you. In the parts of this book that were consciously controlled, I did want to honor that. One of my friends from childhood described the novel as "a love letter to Scarsdale." ("So")

15. Thank you, Sarah Stein.

16. The name "Gish Jen," one might note, is a kind of postmodern simulacrum of Asianness on the part of an American daughter. As Jen recounts it, some friends in high school gave her the nickname "Gish" to replace her actual name, "Lillian" (which she disliked), after the silent screen star Lillian Gish. Jen later adopted "Gish" as a pen name on a whim and has kept it ever since ("Gish Jen"). In my experience, readers often make the ironic mistake of taking "Gish" for an "exotic," Chinese name.

17. Jen has named Austen as a "really big influence on me" in her youth ("MELUS Interview" 113).

18. This era saw the development of new Jewish American spiritual practices and institutions like the chavurah movement (grassroots, experimental, egalitarian prayer and study communities) and later the movement called Jewish Renewal (which draws upon Jewish mystical traditions; feminist, environmentalist, and pacifist politics; and even non-Western spiritual traditions to reinvigorate Jewish practice).

19. In "Why America Has Not Seemed Like Exile," Stephen J. Whitfield writes:

> America has done more than to provide a relatively open society in which anti-Semitism has been minimal, a state that has been uncoupled from an official religion, an economy relatively free of barriers to entry, a relatively democratic culture. America has also put Jewish history out of its misery, and has given Jews an opportunity to pursue happiness and to discredit the "lachrymose" conception of their Old World origins. This promise has constituted something new in the experience of the Diaspora. (257)

20. On the idea of home in Asian American texts, in our era of migration, see Francia.

21. But in the strange and unresolved plot of the attacker's sexual assault on Mona and its aftermath, Jen sketches out, to my view, an area in which subjectification still reigns in the plot of her female Asian American subject: sex and gender relations. Though Seth arrives and stops the attack, in the ensuing weeks, the attacker blends into Seth, amidst role-playing games intended to help Mona's recovery that blur suspiciously into sexual seduction; the reader cannot ever forget Seth's association with the attacker. Mona's victimization, or at least her objectification by aggressive male manipulators of her plot, is then underscored when the farcical ending reveals that Sherman-on-the-phone all those years was an act performed by a trio of young men, of whom the last is Seth. Comically tricked back into a relationship with Seth by a male conspiracy, Mona must suppress feelings of rage and humiliation, and must rationalize the rightness of her return to the relationship. In terms of sexuality, then, she is shown to be more "subjectless" than she is in racial terms. She develops no "switching" mechanism that can restore her agency in this regard (though there's a mention near the end of a hope to one day "open a door and discover—to her utter stupefaction and relief—Sherman turned into a woman"!) (298).

22. Of course, the two protagonists' choices are very different in one important sense: that Coleman Silk completely disavows his black roots, attempts to erase them entirely, pretending always to have been a Jew; whereas Mona, born a crucial few decades later in the moment when "civil rights [is] on TV" (6), and into the less completely confining racialized identity of Chinese American, believes she can be two things at once, and by virtue of conversion, indeed can. Hers is the multiethnic American dream; Coleman Silk's the racial nightmare.

23. Viet Thanh Nguyen has argued that "Asian American intellectuals . . . prefer to see . . . the objects of their critical inquiry as bad subjects," who "reject dominant ideology"; "the discourse of the bad subject's primary role is to prevent" the "suture" of "the racialized individual back into dominant American culture," instead "demonstrating the fractures and ruptures of American culture in regard to racial and other inequalities" (144).

24. See Lin on the way that Mona's phone relationships, in particular, "[undermine] a notion of personal identity as fixed in a stable, racially unitary body," to suggest that racial identity is performative (50).

25. To add to the density of literary allusion, the ensuing episode also tips a hat to a comedic episode in the cross-race relations of *Huckleberry Finn.*

26. I am indebted to Dean Franco for this critique, and also for underscoring, for me, the ways that Camp Gugelstein is allowed and controlled by the contingencies of white privilege, as well as being a satiric rendition of Jewish attempts to partner with 1960s and '70s black activists.

27. It seems important, however, that readers of both books may be led to suspect black characters for some time before the Latinos are formally accused; African Americans are in this way not untainted by blame. I thank Deborah McDowell for this insight.

28. My thanks to Caroline Tran.

29. On this subject see Wendy Ho, *In Her Mother's House*.

30. Io was a muse whom Zeus romanced, and whom he turned into a cow, to protect her from Hera's rage.

31. Along these lines, Jen has notably remarked, in response to readings of the novel:

> I want to question why it's funnier for an Asian-American woman to consider switching identities like that than it would be for, [for] example, an Irish-American. There's some racist component to that formulation. . . . how is it that people who don't even know us very well feel free to tell us about our identity and how we're living up to it? . . . Asian-Americans are held up to a different standard in that regard than Caucasian Americans, and there's an assumed power differential there that I want to question. . . .
>
> It's not as much of a joke for a white person to try Buddhism as it is for a Chinese person to try Judaism. People have found the book hilarious . . . but there are also serious issues there that I hope they'll consider as well. ("So")

32. In a fine cross-ethnic reading, Jonathan Freedman observes the influence of Jewish American writer Grace Paley on Jen's "Birthmates," which he sees as a revision of Paley's parable of Jewish-African American cohabitation in "The Long Distance Runner" from the vantage point of Asian Americans, who "have not yet come to terms with the equivocal racial position they occupy" (300–302). I would add that this irresolution is underscored, in Jen's version, by the fact that the Asian American protagonist is less optimistically tuned into "what in the world is coming next" than is Paley's Faith in her ending (258), as emblematized in Jen's final image of a malformed, aborted child.

And to expand the Jen-Paley intertextual linkage, I would suggest that the title story in Jen's collection, "Who's Irish?" also strongly recalls Paley. The voice of its bossy Chinese American grandmother astonished by her granddaughter's park behavior, and her dawning affection for "the voice of Bess," her Irish American counterpart (16), resonate with the powerful, comically rendered, maternal talkers populating New York City parks, apartments, and windows in Paley's oeuvre, and with the profound respect of her narrating alter ego, Faith Darwin, for the voices of many sorts of others.

Interchapter

1. An excellent study is Neil R. Davison's *James Joyce, Ulysses, and the Construction of Jewish Identity: Culture, Biography, and "the Jew" in Modernist Europe*, which discusses the history of scholarship on this subject. Among studies of the literary representation of Jews, see Nochlin and Garb, *The Jew in the Text: Modernity and the Construction of Identity*.

2. Further, Freedman's chapter "Transgressions of a Model Minority" traces a nineteenth- and twentieth-century history of the social and imaginative entwinement of Jewish and Asian Americans in American discourse, including parallel stereotypes of both Orientalizing and "model minority" varieties.

3. The grotesque Jewish father, Morton Sass, plays a vivid role in Sterling Lung's "racial castration," most notably in a farcical men's room scene during the Lung-Sass wedding, when Sterling misunderstands his father-in-law's challenge to demonstrate his best punch as a demand that he show his penis for inspection, and when the father actually places the wedding ring on Sterling's finger (161–63). For comparison, see David Eng's reading of the "hysterical impotence" he finds rampant among the male characters in Louie's earlier short story collection *Pangs of Love* (Eng 193–203).

4. Similarly, Sterling's friend, the butcher Fuchs, who "has muttonchop sideburns and a nose with hairs like alfalfa sprouts," can suddenly appear to Sterling like "a man from an

earlier time in human history, someone who could effortlessly tilt back the chin of a lamb and slash its throat" (5, 7).

5. A slighter but more disturbing engagement with Jewishness appears in a subplot to *American Son*, Brian Ascalon Roley's 2001 novel about the terrifying vulnerability of a teenaged, half-Filipino American protagonist to the relentless racism and violence in his Los Angeles world. Written at a far greater distance from Jews than the novels of Jen or Louie, this novel shows the economic disparity and racial self-hatred that afflict Louie's Sterling Lung becoming a total barrier to interethnic relationships, and sufficient cause, even, for violent hostility. Several references to wealthy L.A. Jews portray them as utterly unsympathetic to those less fortunate and more racialized, but even the reader who adjusts to this consistently hostile portrait of Jews may be shocked when Roley's working-class Asian American coming-of-age story articulates a new limit to interethnic American solidarity, reaching its abrupt climax in a scene of violent vengeance on a young Jewish boy, a victim who is plainly innocent but seems to earn his victimization by obliviousness to his unjust access to unequal power, transnational mobility, and American assimilation. The beating of the younger, weaker Jewish boy is what finally allows the Filipino American youth to feel "strong," in the book's last line.

To be sure, Roley's subtle characterization makes Gabriel's rise to this strength a deeply ambivalent outcome, causes us to root for this young man's better qualities so that the ending, announcing his entrance into a violent adulthood, is sharply disappointing. But it is inescapable that "Jewish" here has ceased to mean "parallel group capable of solidarity with Asian immigrants," as in the works of Bulosan, Okada, Gus Lee, or Gish Jen, and means instead something more like "rich and powerful white people, incapable of empathy for us, enemies." Roley's portrayal of seemingly insurmountable class barriers in this local context and of a startling degree of anti-Jewish feeling render impossible the mutuality of Jen's 1960s and '70s, New York suburban world, or any desire to be like or be with or befriend Jews.

6. On Eliot's modernist appropriations, see Harish Trivedi, "'Ganga Was Sunken': T. S. Eliot's Use of India"; on the ethics of global pop cultural appropriation, see Neil Lazarus, "'Unsystematic Fingers at the Conditions of the Times': Afropop and the Paradoxes of Imperialism."

7. And Smith blurs distinctions further with her black Jewish characters.

8. The late twentieth-, early twenty-first-century crop of New Jew cool manifestations include, besides the remarkable, ever-morphing, globalizing klezmer revival, phenomena arising from a downtown, avant-garde New York Jewish scene such as the campy *Heeb* magazine, the short fiction anthology *Lost Tribe: Jewish Fiction from the Edge* (ed. Zakrzewsky), and the wealth of Jewish-hybrid musical manifestations (rap, reggae, Latin) chronicled in Jonathan Schorsch's article "Making Judaism *Cool*." Schorsch finds in these "grooves" of "post-baby boomers, alive to ethnicity and the rise of religiosity since the 1980s," many of whom are *ba'alei teshuvah* (returnees to religion), cause for both hope and suspicion; as a whole, "Jewish cool signifies a kind of amusing and perverse but much needed *tikkun* or repair, for Judaism and our culture at large," but is sometimes guilty of "mere posture" (33–36). Calling this movement Radical Jewish Culture, after a John Zorn project, Jonathan Freedman argues that it "expands the notion of Jewish otherness into a cultural politics of alterity that contests . . . the assimilationist, acculturated notion of Jewish identity . . . in the name of something older": "the heterogeneity, the multiplicity, the hybridity" of Jewish culture throughout history (with echoes of Lisa Lowe's Asian Americanist paradigm) (20, 21–22). For an engaging reading of Tony Kushner, contemporary avant-garde Yiddish culture, and gay klezmer, see Dean Franco (143–52).

Vincent J. Cheng examines suspicious, non-Jewish versions of "Jewish chic," practiced by people other than Jews; citing Emmanuel Levinas, he speaks of "imperialist nostalgia," when Poles in Cracow and Warsaw hold revivals of Yiddish culture, fifty years after its decimation in their region (108–9).

Chapter 4

1. On the subject matter appropriate to a novel Yamashita has said, "For me, it has to be big"; a novel must be ambitious in its scope (Personal interview). Yamashita is also the author of plays, short stories, and poetry. Her fourth novel, *Circle K Cycles*, combines fiction, essays, and collage to examine the lives of Japanese Brazilians who have migrated to Japan. For a bibliography and discussion of her work, see Sugano.

2. Two 1990s novels by Japanese American women share some of the concerns and the innovative features of Yamashita's *Tropic of Orange*: Cynthia Kadohata's futuristic L.A. disaster novel *In the Heart of the Valley of Love* (1992), and Ruth Ozeki's *My Year of Meats* (1998), which straddles the United States and Japan in its concern with global commercial and ecological issues.

3. On this subject see R. Lee (*Americas* 106–13). Also on Yamashita's transnational attention see Sadowski-Smith (100–108).

4. See Rody, "Impossible Voices: Ethnic Postmodern Narration in Morrison's *Jazz* and Yamashita's *Through the Arc of the Rain Forest*."

5. Speaking to my class at the University of Virginia in March of 2009, Yamashita gave a stunning account of the origins of *Tropic of Orange* in a Lotus software program she was playing with while at a dull secretarial job. Intrigued by the potential of the columns she could create, she began writing a novel in chart form. When the book was in publication, she insisted to her editor that this matrix of the novel be preserved in the "HyperContexts" chart (Yamashita, Lecture).

6. When asked, however, Yamashita replied that she was thinking only of a cousin of hers by that name (Personal interview). Okada's Emi is a beautiful, modest, patriotic Japanese American woman waiting for the husband who refuses (for reasons of family shame) to return to her from World War II Europe. There is more than a little (racialized) male fantasy in her characterization, especially in her "legs . . . like a white woman's" (83), and in the fact that she is secretly starving for someone like the hero, Ichiro, to come along. The morning after a friend sends Ichiro silently to her bed, she tells him not to speak of their lovemaking: "Talking will make it sound bad and unclean and it was not so" (93).

7. Sadowski-Smith notes that, given Rafaela's surname, Cortes, her former address on "Calle Malinche," and her assailant's name, Hernando, their combat recasts the conquest of Mexico by Hernán Cortés, to give victory to the indigenous woman. Rafaela's defeat of Hernando while in the shape of a snake also "rewrites the myth of Aztlán, which is symbolized by the image of an eagle devouring a snake" (101–2).

8. Yamashita has said that she based Arcangel's character on performance artist Guillermo Gómez-Peña ("An Interview"). Sadowski-Smith argues that through Arcangel Yamashita reconfigures "precolonial mythologies and Mexican national traditions" as "signs of cross-cultural and trans-national activism." For more on Arcangel, including the connection of "*El Gran Mojado*" to "a Mexican tradition of masked superheroes" ranging from Zorro to Subcomandante Marcos, see Sadowski-Smith (106).

9. One of Yamashita's favorite movies, she has remarked laughingly, is *Spartacus*; she loves the fact that, instead of some high-tech simulation, "you have a cast of thousands—literally thousands!" (Personal interview).

10. Appadurai's *Modernity at Large* also accords with Yamashita's vision in his focus on "media and migration" as key forces in the "rupture" of modernity: "This mobile and unforeseeable relationship between mass-mediated events and migratory audiences defines the core of the link between globalization and the modern" (3–4).

11. Yamashita recalls that she grew up in L.A. amidst "a black culture—now it's Latino but then it was black." The Asian American kids she knew, she recalls, all wanted to walk, talk, and act black (Personal interview).

12. On the L.A. riots, see chapter 2, notes 4, 8, and 9. Perhaps the absence of Korean American characters in Yamashita's multiculturalist novel can be understood in similar terms to the ones I use in discussing the diminished role of blacks (and of Jews) in Chang-rae Lee's *Native Speaker*.

13. I am grateful to the anonymous reader from Indiana University Press who pointed out this connection.

14. Yamashita has spoken humorously about wanting to give the self-dramatizing Emi a protracted death scene, one that went on and on and on (Lecture).

15. Eric Lott's influential book on blackface minstrelsy, *Love and Theft*, argues for the "contradictory racial impulses at work" in such cross-race imitations: "[S]ymbolic crossings of racial boundaries—through dialect, gesture, and so on—paradoxically engage and absorb the culture being mocked or mimicked" (4, 29).

16. But Yamashita ironizes even the notion of such an embrace: "Emi smiled. 'Who'd a thought you and I'd get this close?' She might have embraced him, but her limbs had ceased to feel" (253).

17. Similarly, Buzzworm's character reiterates certain tendencies of white American portrayals of African Americans; his strong sense of home gives him an aura of authenticity that is nearly a cliché among black characters created by non-black authors, as is the treatment of blackness as redemptive. Still Buzz transcends stereotype in being simply the most decent character in the book, its moral center, who spends his days trying to help people out of every kind of trouble.

18. But we might also read Emi as being both ironized and punished, in part, for her disloyalty to family. My thanks to Susan Fraiman for this insight.

Epilogue

1. Also culturally important has been the growth and public acceptance of mixed-race families created through adoption, often of international and especially Asian children; such a family is portrayed in Jen's *The Love Wife*.

2. On the history of and controversy over the representation of multiracial people in the U.S. census, see Perlmann; Hollinger.

3. Family passing memoirs include Shirlee Taylor Haizlip's *The Sweeter the Juice: A Family Memoir in Black and White* (1994), and Bliss Broyard's *One Drop: My Father's Hidden Life—a Story of Race and Family Secrets* (2007). Histories of black and white families descending from slave plantations include Edward Ball's *Slaves in the Family* (1998), Henry Wiencek's *The Hairstons: An American Family in Black and White* (2000), and Annette Gordon-Reed's *The Hemingses of Monticello: An American Family* (2008). Some anthologies are *Two Worlds Walking: Short Stories, Essays, and Poetry by Authors with Mixed Heritages*, edited by Diane Glancy and C. W. Truesdale (1994), *Half and Half: Writers on Growing Up Biracial and Bicultural*, edited by Claudine Chiawei O'Hearn (1998), *Mixing It Up: Multiracial Subjects*, edited by SanSan Kwan and Kenneth Spiers (2004), and *Mixed: An Anthology of Short Fiction on the Multiracial Experience*, edited by Chandra Prasad (2006).

4. These include Margaret Walker's *Jubilee* (1966), Alex Haley's *Roots* (1976), Gayl Jones's *Corregidora* (1975), Barbara Chase-Riboud's *Sally Hemings: A Novel* (1979), and Charles Johnson's *Oxherding Tale* (1982). Another vivid African American exception is the black-Jewish heroine of Fran Ross's *Oreo* (1974).

5. Important twentieth-century fiction writers who have written mixed-blood characters are D'Arcy McNickle, N. Scott Momaday, Leslie Marmon Silko, Louise Erdrich, Michael Dorris, Gerald Vizenor, and Sherman Alexie. On this subject see Owens, *Mixedblood Messages: Literature, Film, Family, Place*.

6. Ma argues that several ostensibly enlightened texts about racial mixture by mixed-race Asian American authors in the multicultural era have not actually emerged from the "lomansu" mold; his examples are plays by Velina Hasu Houston and Dmae Roberts and novels by Aimee E. Liu.

7. I thank my student Rebecca Marsh for her insights into mixed-race children in these fictions.

8. Ethnically or racially mixed children perform similar roles in several other recent Asian American fictional texts by Jen and others. In Jen's story "Who's Irish?" (1999), a Chinese-Irish American granddaughter who goes naked in the park and mocks discipline embodies baffling, multiethnic America to her Chinese grandmother: "I am not exaggerate. Millions of children in China, not one act like this" (12). And Bailey Wong, whose name reiterates the Euro-Chinese American marriage of parents Blondie Bailey and Carnegie Wong in Jen's *The Love Wife*, is repeatedly contemplated as the harbinger of a new, not yet knowable interethnic order. Comments a neighbor, "When I look at that boy, all I can think is, Is this the new face of America?" (157). Though Bailey's surprising blondness makes him a visually disturbing emblem of race mixture (his father calls him "the Wong heir, even with the wong hair" [161]), this toddler remains untroubled by the differences he visibly bridges, in the final scene allowing himself to be fed by two mother figures, one white and one Chinese (378). At the end of Chang-rae Lee's *A Gesture Life* (1999), a Korean-African American grandson (via an adopted daughter) whom the hero must save from drowning seems an avatar of the post-identitarian world overtaking the world of traumatic ethnic and national division that is the hero's past. See the interchapter "Cross-ethnic Jewishness" for discussions of the symbolic functions of the Chinese Jewish sons of the protagonist in David Wong Louie's *The Barbarians Are Coming*.

A novel that stops short of the mixed-child ending makes a notable comparison. Gogol Ganguli, the Bengali American hero of Jhumpa Lahiri's *The Namesake* (2003), ends still distinctly unmarriageable, after a failed relationship with a white woman and a divorce from another Bengali American, both clearly missteps in the resolution of his identity: neither a total flight from nor a total return to his upbringing will do. But the closing page leaves him beginning at last to read the stories of the Russian writer Nikolai Gogol, whose surname he has awkwardly carried all his life, in a cross-cultural naming that emblematizes the heterogeneous matrix of his identity, which he only now begins to confront in its fullness. It is instead Gogol's sister Sonia, a secondary and less troubled character, who is about to be married in the book's final pages, and she looks headed for a comic, interethnic resolution worthy of Gish Jen or Zadie Smith: her fiancé, Ben, is, remarkably enough, "half-Jewish, half-Chinese," and Gogol "can easily imagine her, a few years from now, with two children in the back seat" (270, 284). This double ending retains, then, a familiar Asian American fictional protagonist's anomie and irresolution, even while pointing toward the comic possibility of a mixed-child ending, drawing on what seems the emblematic American mixture of the moment, a fusion of weighty ancients made to incarnate lighthearted possibility.

REFERENCES

Acosta-Belén, Edna. "Reimagining Borders: A Hemispheric Approach to Latin American and U.S. Latino and Latina Studies." In Butler, ed. *Color-Line to Borderlands* 240–64.

Adachi, Jiro. *The Island of Bicycle Dancers*. New York: Picador-St. Martin's, 2004.

Anderson, Wanni W., and Robert G. Lee. "Asian American Displacements." In Anderson and Lee, eds, *Displacements and Diasporas: Asians in the Americas*, 3–22.

———, eds. *Displacements and Diasporas: Asians in the Americas*. New Brunswick: Rutgers UP, 2005.

Antin, Mary. "The Lie." 1913. In Chametzky et al., eds. 191–206.

Anzaldúa, Gloria. *Borderlands/La Frontera: The New Mestiza*. San Francisco: Spinsters-Aunt Lute, 1987.

Appadurai, Arjun. "The Heart of Whiteness." *Callaloo* 16.4 (1993): 796–807. Rptd. from *Public Culture* 5.3 (Spring 1993).

———. *Modernity at Large: Cultural Dimensions of Globalization*. Minneapolis: U Minnesota P, 1996.

"Austen, Jane." *The Free Dictionary by Farlex*. March 7, 2007. <http://encyclopedia.farlex.com/Austen%2ctJane>.

Bacho, Peter. "Rico," "The Second Room," "August 1968," "A Manong's Heart," "A Family Gathering." *Dark Blue Suit and Other Stories*. Seattle: U Washington P, 1997.

Bakhtin, M. M. *The Dialogic Imagination: Four Essays*. Ed. Michael Holquist. Trans. Caryl Emerson and Michael Holquist. Austin: U Texas P, 1981.

Ball, Edward. *Slaves in the Family*. New York: Farrar, Straus, and Giroux, 1998.

Bauer, Dale M., and Susan Jaret McKinstry, eds. *Feminism, Bakhtin, and the Dialogic*. Albany: State U of New York P, 1991.

Bhabha, Homi K. *The Location of Culture*. London: Routledge, 1994.

Biale, David, Michael Galchinsky, and Susanna Heschel, eds. *Insider/Outsider: American Jews and Multiculturalism*. Berkeley: U California P, 1998.

———. Introduction. Biale et al. 1–13.

Bow, Leslie. "'For Every Gesture of Loyalty, There Doesn't Have to Be a Betrayal'": Asian American Criticism and the Politics of Locality." *Who Can Speak? Authority and Critical Identity*. Ed. Judith Roof and Robyn Wiegman. Urbana: U of Illinois P, 1995. 30–55.

Brodkin, Karen. *How Jews Became White Folks and What That Says about Race in America*. Rutgers: Rutgers UP, 1998.

Brogan, Kathleen. *Cultural Haunting: Ghosts and Ethnicity in Recent American Literature*. Charlottesville: UP of Virginia, 1998.

Broyard, Bliss. *One Drop: My Father's Hidden Life—a Story of Race and Family Secrets*. New York: Little, Brown, 2007.

Bulosan, Carlos. *America Is in the Heart*. 1946. Seattle: U of Washington P, 1973.

Butler, Johnnella E., ed., *Color-Line to Borderlands: The Matrix of American Ethnic Studies*. Seattle: U Washington P, 2001.

Butler, Octavia. *Kindred*. New York: Doubleday, 1979.

Castle, Terry. Introduction. *Emma*. By Jane Austen. Ed. James Kinsley. Oxford: Oxford UP, 1995. vii–xxviii.

Chametzky, Jules, John Felstiner, Hilene Flanzbaum, and Kathryn Hellerstein, eds. *Jewish American Literature: A Norton Anthology*. New York: Norton, 2001.

Chan, Jeffery Paul, Frank Chin, Lawson Fusao Inada, and Shawn Wong. *Aiiieeeee! An Anthology of Asian American Writers*. Washington, DC: Howard UP, 1974.

———. *The Big Aiiieeeee! An Anthology of Chinese American and Japanese American Literature*. New York: Meridan, 1991.

Chao, Patricia, "Author Interview: Patricia Chao on *Mambo Peligroso*." <http://www.harpercollins.com/author/authorExtra.aspx?authorID=1667&isbn13=9780060734183&displayType=bookinterview>.

———. *Mambo Peligroso*. New York: HarperCollins, 2005.

Charles, John Christopher. "Talking Like White Folks: Freedom and the Rise of the Post World War II African American White-Life Novel. Diss. U of Virginia, 2007.

Chase-Riboud, Barbara. *Sally Hemings: A Novel*. New York: Ballantine, 1979.

Cheng, Anne Anlin. *The Melancholy of Race: Psychoanalysis, Assimilation, and Hidden Grief*. New York: Oxford UP, 2001.

Cheng, Vincent J. *Inauthentic: The Anxiety Over Culture and Identity*. New Brunswick: Rutgers UP, 2004.

Cheung, King-kok. *Articulate Silences: Hisaye Yamamoto, Maxine Hong Kingston, Joy Kogawa*. Ithaca: Cornell UP, 1993.

———. *An Interethnic Companion to Asian American Literature*. New York: Cambridge UP, 1997.

———. "Re-Viewing Asian American Literary Studies." In Cheung, ed. *An Inter-Ethnic Companion to Asian American Literature*. 1–36.

———. "The Woman Warrior versus the Chinaman Pacific: Must a Chinese American Critic Choose between Feminism and Heroism?" *Maxine Hong Kingston's The Woman Warrior: A Casebook*. Ed. Sau-ling Cynthia Wong. New York: Oxford UP, 1999: 113–33.

Chiang, Mark. "Aesthetics and the Crisis of Asian American Cultural Politics in the Controversy over Blu's Hanging." In Davis and Lee 17–34.

Chin, Frank. *The Chickencoop Chinaman*. 1972. *The Chickencoop Chinaman and The Year of the Dragon: Two Plays*. Seattle: University of Washington P, 1981.

Chin, Marilyn. "How I Got That Name." *The Norton Anthology of Modern and Contemporary Poetry*. Third Ed. Volume 2. Ed. Jahan Ramazani, Richard Ellmann, and Robert O'Clair. New York: Norton, 2003. 1013–16.

———. "We Are Americans Now, We Live in the Tundra." *A Fierce Brightness: Twenty-Five Years of Women's Poetry*. Ed. Margarita Donnelly, Beverly McFarland, and Micki Reaman. Corvallis, OR: Calyx, 2002. 37.

Cho, Sumi K. "Korean Americans vs. African Americans: Conflict and Construction." In Gooding-Williams, ed. *Reading Rodney King/Reading Urban Uprising*. 196–211.

Choi, Susan, *The Foreign Student*. New York: HarperCollins, 1998.

Chu, Louis. *Eat a Bowl of Tea*. New York: Lyle Stuart, 1961.

Chu, Patricia P. *Assimilating Asians: Gendered Strategies of Authorship in Asian America*. Durham: Duke UP, 2000.

Chuh, Kandice. *Imagine Otherwise: On Asian Americanist Critique*. Durham and London: Duke UP, 2003.

Clifford, James. *Routes: Travel and Translation in the Late Twentieth Century*. Cambridge: Harvard UP, 1997.

Corley, Liam. "Just Another Ethnic Pol: Literary Citizenship in Chang-rae Lee's *Native Speaker*." *Transnational Asian American Literature: Sites and Transits*. Ed. Shirley Geok-lin Lim, John Blair Gamber, Stephen Hong Sohn, and Gina Valentino. Philadelphia: Temple UP, 2006. 55–74.

Daniels, Roger. *Concentration Camps USA: Japanese Americans and World War II*. New York: Holt, Rinehart and Winston, 1971.

Davis, Mike. *Ecology of Fear: Los Angeles and the Imagination of Disaster*. New York: Metropolitan/Henry Holt, 1998.

Davis, Rocío G., and Sue-Im Lee. *Literary Gestures: The Aesthetic in Asian American Writing*. Philadelphia: Temple UP, 2006.

Davison, Neil R. *James Joyce, Ulysses, and the Construction of Jewish Identity: Culture, Biography, and "the Jew" in Modernist Europe*. Cambridge: Cambridge UP, 1996.

Dayal, Samir. "Black-and-Tan Fantasies: Interracial Contact Between Blacks and South Asians in Film." In Raphael-Hernandez and Steen, eds, *AfroAsian Encounters*. 86–100.

De Jesús, Melinda L. "'Two's Company, Three's a Crowd?': Reading Interracial Romance in Contemporary Asian American Young Adult Fiction." *LIT* 12 (2001): 313–34.

Di Filippo, Paul. "Taking Flight: The story of a regular guy trying to rise above his limitations." *Washington Post Book World*. March 21, 2004. T07.

Donovan, Josephine. "Style and Power." In Bauer and McKinstry, eds, *Feminism, Bakhtin, and the Dialogic*. 85–94.

Eisen, Arnold. *Galut: Modern Jewish Reflection on Homelessness and Homecoming*. Bloomington: Indiana UP, 1986.

Ellison, Ralph. *Invisible Man*. 1947. New York: Vintage, 1972.

———. "Twentieth-Century Fiction and the Black Mask of Humanity." 1946. "The World and the Jug." 1953. *Shadow and Act*. New York: Random House, 1964.

———. "What America Would Be Like Without Blacks." 1970. *Going to the Territory*. New York: Random House, 1986.

Eng, David L. *Racial Castration: Managing Masculinity in Asian America*. Durham: Duke UP, 2001.

Engles, Tim. "'Visions of me in the whitest raw light': Assimilation and Doxic Whiteness in Chang-rae Lee's *Native Speaker*." *Hitting Critical Mass* 4.2 (1997): 27–48.

Erdrich, Louise. *The Beet Queen*. New York: Holt, 1986.

———. *Four Souls*. New York: HarperCollins, 2004.

———. *The Master Butchers Singing Club*. New York: HarperCollins, 2003.

———. *Tracks*. New York: Harper & Row, 1988.

Espiritu, Yen Le. *Asian American Panethnicity: Bridging Institutions and Identities*. Philadelphia: Temple UP, 1992.

Farber, Roberta Rosenberg, and Chaim I. Waxman, "Cohesion and Conflict: Jews in American Society." In Farber and Waxman, eds, *Jews in America*. 89–94.

———. "Constructing a Modern Jewish Identity." In Farber and Waxman, eds, *Jews in America*. 191–95.

———. eds. *Jews in America: A Contemporary Reader*. Hanover and London: Brandeis UP, UP of New England, 1999.

Faris, Wendy B. "Scheherazade's Children: Magical Realism and Postmodern Fiction." In Zamora and Faris, eds, *Magical Realism*. 163–89.

Felski, Rita. "The Doxa of Difference." *Signs* 23.1 (Autumn 1997): 1–21.

———. "Modernist Studies and Cultural Studies: Reflections on Method." *Modernism/Modernity* 10.3 (2003): 501–17.

Fenkl, Heinz Insu. *Memories of My Ghost Brother: A Novel*. New York: Dutton, 1996.

Ferraro, Thomas J. *Ethnic Passages: Literary Immigrants in Twentieth-Century America*. Chicago: U of Chicago P, 1993.

Fischer, Michael M. J. "Ethnicity and the Post-Modern Arts of Memory." *Writing Culture: The Poetics and Politics of Ethnography*. Ed. James Clifford and George E. Marcus. Berkeley: U California P, 1986. 194–233.

Fishkin, Shelley Fisher. *Was Huck Black?: Mark Twain and African American Voices*. New York: Oxford UP, 1993.

Foer, Jonathan Safran. *Everything Is Illuminated*. New York: Houghton Mifflin, 2002.

———. *Extremely Loud and Incredibly Close*. New York: Houghton Mifflin, 2005.

Forrest, Leon. "Leon Forrest at the University of Kentucky: Two Interviews." *Leon Forrest: Introductions and Interpretations*. Ed. John G. Cawelti. Bowling Green: Bowling Green State U Popular P, 1997. 286–98.

Foucault, Michel. "Of Other Spaces." *The Visual Culture Reader*. Second Edition. Ed. Nicholas Mirzoeff. London and New York: Routledge, 2002. 229–36.

Francia, Luis H. "Inventing the Earth: The Notion of 'Home' in Asian American Literature." *Across the Pacific: Asian Americans and Globalization*. Ed. Evelyn Hu-DeHart. New York: Asia Society/ Philadelphia: Temple UP, 1999. 191–218.

Franco, Dean J. *Ethnic American Literature: Comparing Chicano, Jewish, and African American Writing*. Charlottesville: U Virginia P, 2006.

Freedman, Jonathan. *Klezmer America: Jewishness, Ethnicity, Modernity*. New York: Columbia UP, 2008.

Freud, Sigmund. *Group Psychology and the Analysis of the Ego*. Trans. and ed. James Strachey. New York: Norton, 1959.

Friedman, Bruce Jay. *Stern. New York: Simon and Schuster, 1962.*

Friedman, Susan Stanford. *Mappings: Feminism and the Cultural Geographies of Encounter*. Princeton: Princeton UP, 1998.

———. "Migrations, Diasporas, and Borders." *Introduction to Scholarship in Modern Languages and Literatures*. Third Edition. Ed. David G. Nicholls. New York: Modern Language Association, 2007.

Galchinsky, Michael. "Scattered Seeds: A Dialogue of Diasporas." In Biale et al., eds, *Insider/Outsider*. 185–211.

Gates, Henry Louis, Jr. "The Language of Slavery." The Slave's Narrative. Ed. Charles T. Davis and Henry Louis Gates, Jr., eds. New York: Oxford UP, 1985. xi–xxxiv.

Gilroy, Paul. *The Black Atlantic: Modernity and Double Consciousness*. Cambridge: Harvard UP, 1993.

Glancy, Diane, and C. W. Truesdale, ed. *Two Worlds Walking: Short Stories, Essays, and Poetry by Authors with Mixed Heritages*. Minneapolis: Two Rivers P, 1994.

Gold, Michael. *Jews Without Money*. New York: Liveright, [1938, c1930].

Gooding-Williams, Robert, ed. *Reading Rodney King/Reading Urban Uprising*. New York and London: Routledge, 1993.

Goodman, Robin Truth. *World, Class, Women: Global Literature, Education, and Feminism*. New York: RoutledgeFalmer, 2004.

Gordon-Reed, Annette. *The Hemingses of Monticello: An American Family*. New York: Norton, 2008.

Greenberg, Cheryl. "Pluralism and Its Discontents: The Case of Blacks and Jews." In Biale, et al., eds, *Insider/Outsider*. 55–87.

Gubar, Susan. *Racechanges: White Skin, Black Face in American Culture*. New York: Oxford UP, 1997.

Hagedorn, Jessica. *Dogeaters*. New York: Penguin, 1990.

———. Introduction. *Charlie Chan Is Dead: An Anthology of Asian American Fiction*. Ed. Hagedorn. New York: Penguin, 1993.

Haizlip, Shirlee Taylor. *The Sweeter the Juice: A Family Memoir in Black and White*. New York: Simon and Schuster, 1994.

Haley, Alex. *Roots*. New York: Doubleday, 1976.

Han, Suyin. *A Many-Splendored Thing*. New York: Little, Brown, 1952.

Hardt, Michael and Antonio Negri. *Empire*. Cambridge: Harvard UP, 2000.

Ho, Fred. "Kickin' the White Man's Ass: Black Power, Aesthetics, and the Asian Martial Arts." In Raphael-Hernandez and Steen, eds, *AfroAsian Encounters*. 295–312.

Ho, Fred and Bill V. Mullen, eds. *Afro Asia: Revolutionary Political and Cultural Connections between African-Americans and Asian-Americans*. Durham: Duke UP, 2008.

Ho, Wendy. *In Her Mother's House: The Politics of Asian American Mother-Daughter Writing*. Walnut Creek, CA: AltaMira P, 1999.

Hollinger, David A. *Postethnic America: Beyond Multiculturalism*. New York: HarperCollins, 1995.

Holston, James, and Arjun Appadurai. "Introduction: Cities and Citizenship." *Cities and Citizenship*. Ed. James Holston. Durham: Duke UP, 1999.

Hune, Shirley. "Asian American Studies and Asian Studies: Boundaries and Borderlands of Ethnic Studies and Area Studies." In Butler, ed., *Color-Line to Borderlands*. 227–39.

———. "Rethinking Race: Paradigms and Policy Formation." *Amerasia Journal* 21.1–2 (1995): 29–40.

Ignatiev, Noel. *How the Irish Became White*. New York; London: Routledge, 1995.

Jaggi, Maya. "Flight Checks." *The Guardian*. July 3, 2004. <http://www.guardian.co.uk/books/2004/jul/03/featuresreviews.guardianreview17>.

Jameson, Fredric. "Notes on Globalization as a Philosophical Issue." *The Cultures of Globalization*. Ed. Fredric Jameson and Masao Miyoshi. Durham: Duke UP, 1998. 54–77.

Jen, Gish. "About Gish Jen: A Profile by Don Lee." *Ploughshares* 26.2/3 (Fall, 2000): 217–22.

———. "Culturally Speaking: Gish Jen '77, B'87 on the American Experience." Interview with Lilli Leggio. *Radcliffe News* 15.1 (December 2001–January 2002). 1, 3.

———. "Gish Jen." *Home to Stay: Asian American Women's Fiction*. Ed. Sylvia Watanabe and Carol Bruchac. Greenfield Center, NY: Greenfield Review P, 1990. 52.

———. *The Love Wife*. New York: Vintage-Random House, 2004.

———. "MELUS Interview: Gish Jen." *MELUS: The Journal of the Society for the Study of the Multi-Ethnic Literature of the United States* 18.4 (Winter 1993): 111–21.

———. *Mona in the Promised Land*. 1996. New York: Vintage-Random House, 1997.

———. "So, aren't you going to ask if I'm Jewish?" Interview with Ron Hogan. *The Beatrice Interview*. March 2, 2007.<http://www.beatrice.com/interviews/jen/> 1996.

———. *Typical American*. 1991. New York: Plume-Penguin, 1992.

———. *Who's Irish? Stories*. New York: Knopf, 1999.

Johnson, Charles. *Oxherding Tale*. Bloomington: Indiana UP, 1982.

Jones, Gayl. *Corregidora*. 1975. Boston: Beacon, 1986.

Joselit, Jenna Weissman. *The Wonders of America: Reinventing Jewish Culture 1880–1950*. New York: Hill and Wang, 1994.

Kadohata, Cynthia. *In the Heart of the Valley of Love*. New York: Viking, 1992.

Kang, Younghill. *East Goes West: The Making of an Oriental Yankee*. New York: Scribner's, 1937.

Kaplan, Amy, and Donald E. Pease, eds. *Cultures of United States Imperialism*. Durham: Duke UP, 1993.

Kim, Dae Young, and L. Janelle Dance, "Korean-Black Relations: Contemporary Challenges, Scholarly Explanations, and Future Prospects." In McFerson, ed., *Blacks and Asians*. 153–70.

Kim, Daniel Y. "Do I, Too, Sing America? Vernacular Representations and Chang-rae Lee's Native Speaker." *Journal of Asian American Studies* 6.3 (October 2003): 231–60.

———. *Writing Manhood in Black and Yellow: Ralph Ellison, Frank Chin, and the Literary Politics of Identity*. Stanford: Stanford UP, 2005.

Kim, Elaine H. "Home Is Where the *Han* Is: A Korean American Perspective on the Los Angeles Upheavals." In Gooding-Williams, ed., *Reading Rodney King/Reading Urban Uprising*. 215–35.

———. Preface. *Charlie Chan Is Dead: An Anthology of Contemporary Asian American Fiction*. Ed. Jessica Hagedorn. New York: Penguin, 1993.

———. "'Such Opposite Creatures': Men and Women in Asian American Literature" *Michigan Quarterly Review* XXIX.1 (Winter 1990): 68–93.

Kim, James. "The Legend of the White-and-Yellow Black Man: Global Containment and Triangulated Racial Desire in *Romeo Must Die*." *Camera Obscura* 55, 19.1 (2004): 151–79.

Kim, Runyoung. *Clay Walls*. Sag Harbor, NY: Permanent, 1986.

Kingston, Maxine Hong. *China Men*. New York: Knopf, 1980.

———. *Tripmaster Monkey: His Fake Book*. New York: Knopf, 1989.

———. *The Woman Warrior: Memoirs of a Girlhood Among Ghosts*. New York: Vintage-Random House, 1976.

Knadler, Stephen. "Unacquiring Negrophobia: Younghill Kang and the Cosmopolitan Resistance to the Black and White Logic of Naturalization." *Jouvert: A Journal of Postcolonial Studies* 4.3 (Summer 2000). March 7, 2007. <http://social.chass.ncsu.edu/jouvert/v4i3/knad.html.>

Koshy, Susan. "The Fiction of Asian American Literature." *Yale Journal of Criticism* 9.2. Rptd in Wu and Song, eds, *Asian American Studies*. 467–95.

———. *Sexual Naturalization: Asian Americans and Miscegenation*. Stanford: Stanford UP, 2004.

Krishnan, Sanjay. *Reading the Global: Troubling Perspectives on Britain's Empire in Asia*. New York: Columbia UP, 2007.

Krupat, Arnold. *The Turn to the Native: Studies in Criticism and Culture*. Lincoln and London: Nebraska UP, 1996.

Kwan, SanSan and Kenneth Spiers, ed. *Mixing It Up: Multiracial Subjects*. Austin: U Texas P, 2004.

Lahiri, Jhumpa. *Interpreter of Maladies: Stories*. New York: Houghton Mifflin, 1999.

———. *The Namesake*. New York: Houghton Mifflin, 2003.

Lazarus, Neil. "'Unsystematic Fingers at the Conditions of the Times': Afropop and the Paradoxes of Imperialism." *Recasting the World: Writing after Colonialism*. Ed. Jonathan White. Baltimore: Johns Hopkins UP, 1993. 137–60.

Lee, A. Robert. *Multicultural American Literature: Comparative Black, Native, Latino/a and Asian American Fictions*. Edinburgh: Edinburgh UP, 2003.

Lee, Chang-Rae. *Aloft*. New York: Riverhead, 2004.

———. *A Gesture Life*. New York: Riverhead, 1999.

———. "An Interview with Chang-rae Lee." By Sarah Anne Johnson. *The Writer's Chronicle* 37.6. (May/Summer 2005): 3–11.

———. Interview with Chang-rae Lee. By Kenneth Quan. *Asia Pacific Arts*, UCLA Asia Institute. <http://www.asiaarts.ucla.edu/article.asp?parentid=11432>.

———. *Native Speaker*. New York: Riverhead, 1995.

Lee, Don. *Country of Origin*. New York: Norton, 2004.

———. Personal interview. Charlottesville, VA, March 20, 2008.

——— "Question and Answer with Don Lee." In Lee, *Yellow: Stories*.

———. "Yellow." In Lee, *Yellow: Stories*. 197–255.

———. *Yellow: Stories*. New York: Norton, 2001.

Lee, Gus. *China Boy*. New York: Penguin-Dutton, 1991.

Lee, James Kyung-Jin. *Urban Triage: Race and the Fictions of Multiculturalism*. Minneapolis: U Minnesota P, 2004.

Lee, Jennifer. *Civility in the City: Blacks, Jews, and Koreans in Urban America*. Cambridge: Harvard UP, 2002.

Lee, Rachel C. *The Americas of Asian American Literature: Gendered Fictions of Nation and Transnation*. Princeton: Princeton UP, 1999.

———. "Reading Contests and Contesting Reading: Chang-rae Lee's Native Speaker and Ethnic New York." *MELUS: The Journal of the Society for the Study of the Multi-Ethnic Literature of the United States*, 29:3–4 (2004 Fall-Winter): 341–52.

Lenz, Günter H. "Toward a Dialogics of International American Culture Studies: Transnationality, Border Discourses, and Public Culture(s)." In Pease and Wiegman, eds. *The Futures of American Studies*. 461–85.

Li, David Leiwei. *Imagining the Nation: Asian American Literature and Cultural Consent*. Stanford: Stanford UP, 1998.

Lim, Shirley Geok-lin, and Ling, Amy. Introduction. *Reading the Literatures of Asian America*. Ed. Lim and Ling. Philadelphia: Temple UP, 1992.

Lin, Erika. "Mona on the Phone: The Performative Body and Racial Identity in *Mona in the Promised Land*." *MELUS: The Journal of the Society for the Study of the Multi-Ethnic Literature of the United States* 28.2 (Summer 2003): 47–57.

Ling, Amy. "Cultural Cross-Dressing in *Mona in the Promised Land*." *Asian American Literature in the International Context: Readings on Fiction, Poetry, and Performance*. Ed. Rocío G. Davis and Sämi Ludwig. Hamburg: LIT, 2002. 227–36.

Ling, Jinqi. "Identity Crisis and Gender Politics: Reappropriating Asian American Masculinity." In Cheung, ed., *Inter-Ethnic Companion*. 312–37.

Lipsitz, George. *The Possessive Investment in Whiteness: How White People Profit from Identity Politics*. Revised and Expanded Edition. Philadelphia: Temple UP, 2006.

Loewen, James W. *The Mississippi Chinese: Between Black and White*. (1971). Second Edition. Prospect Heights, IL: Waveland, 1988.

Lott, Eric. *Love and Theft: Blackface Minstrelsy and the American Working Class*. New York: Oxford UP, 1993.

Louie, David Wong. *The Barbarians Are Coming*. New York: Berkley-Penguin, 2000.

———. *Pangs of Love: Stories*. New York: Knopf-Random House, 1991.

Lowe, Lisa. "On Contemporary Asian American Projects." *Amerasia Journal* 21:1–2 (1995): 41–52.

Lowe, Lisa. *Immigrant Acts: On Asian American Cultural Politics*. Durham: Duke UP, 1996.

———. "Multiculturalism." *The Oxford Companion to Women's Writing in the United States*. Ed. Cathy N. Davidson and Linda Wagner-Martin. New York: Oxford UP, 1995. 589–91.

Lyall, Sarah. "Restless Literary Explorer From France Wins a Nobel." *New York Times*. October 10, 2008. A10.

Ma, Sheng-mai. "The Necessity and Impossibility of Being Mixed-Race in Asian American Literature." *Reconstructing Hybridity: Post-Colonial Studies in Transition*. Ed. Joel Kuortti and Jopi Nyman. Amsterdam; New York: Rodopi, 2007.

Major, Clarence. *From Juba to Jive: A Dictionary of African-American Slang*. New York: Penguin, 1994.

Marable, Manning. "We Need New and Critical Study of Race and Ethnicity." *Chronicle of Higher Education*. February 25, 2000. B4.

Martínez, Rubén. "The Next Chapter: America's next great revolution in race relations is already under way." *New York Times Magazine*. July 16, 2000. 10–11.

McBride, James. *The Color of Water: A Black Man's Tribute to His White Mother*. New York: Riverhead, 1996.

McCunn, Ruthanne Lum. *Thousand Pieces of Gold: A Biographical Novel*. Boston: Beacon, 1981.

McFerson, Hazel M., ed. *Blacks and Asians: Crossings, Conflict, and Commonality*. Durham: Carolina Academic P, 2006.

Mendoza, Louis and S. Shankar, eds. *Crossing Into America: The New Literature of Immigration*. New York: New, 2003.

Michaels, Walter Benn. *Our America: Nativism, Modernism, and Pluralism*. Durham: Duke UP, 1995.

———. "'You who never was there': Slavery and the New Historicism, Deconstruction and the Holocaust." *Narrative* 4.1 (January 1996): 1–16.

mixedasians. 20 November, 2008. <http://www.mixedasians.com>.

Monaghan, Peter. "A Korean-American Novelist's Impressive Debut." *Chronicle of Higher Education* 41.30 (April 7, 1995): A7.

Morrison, Toni. *A Mercy*. New York: Knopf, 2008.

———. *Paradise*. New York: Knopf, 1998.

———. *Playing in the Dark: Whiteness and the Literary Imagination*. New York: Vintage, 1993.

———. "Unspeakable Things Unspoken: The Afro-American Presence in American Literature." Rptd. in Wonham, ed. 16–29.

Most, Andrea. *Making Americans: Jews and the Broadway Musical*. Cambridge and London: Harvard UP, 2004.

Mukherjee, Bharati. "Immigrant Writing: Give Us Your Maximalists." *The New York Times Book Review*. 28 August, 1988. 1.

———. *The Middleman and Other Stories*. New York: Ballantine, 1988.

Mullen, Bill V. "Persisting Solidarities: Tracing the AfroAsian Thread in U.S. Literature and Culture." Raphael-Hernandez and Steen. 245–59.

Mura, David. *The Colors of Desire: Poems*. New York: Anchor, 1995.

Murray, David. "Translation and Mediation." *The Cambridge Companion to Native American Literature*. Ed. Joy Porter and Kenneth M. Roemer. Cambridge: Cambridge UP, 2005. 69–83.

Nguyen, Viet Thanh. *Race and Resistance: Literature and Politics in Asian America*. New York: Oxford, 2002.

Nishime, LeiLani. "'I'm Blackanese': Buddy-Cop Films, *Rush Hour*, and Asian American and African American Cross-racial Identification." *Asian North American Identities: Beyond the Hyphen*. Ed. Eleanor Ty and Donald C. Goellnicht. Bloomington: Indiana UP, 2004. 43–60.

Nochlin, Linda, and Tamar Garb, eds. *The Jew in the Text: Modernity and the Construction of Identity*. New York: Thames and Hudson, 1996.

Obama, Barack. *Dreams from My Father: A Story of Race and Inheritance*. New York: Times Books-Random House, 1995.

O'Hearn, Claudine Chiawei, ed. *Half and Half: Writers on Growing Up Biracial and Bicultural*. New York: Pantheon, 1998.

Okada, John. *No-No Boy*. 1957. Seattle: U of Washington P, 1992.

Okihiro, Gary Y. "Is Yellow Black or White?" *Margins and Mainstreams: Asians in American History and Culture*. Seattle: University of Washington P, 1994. 31–63.

Oster, Judith. *Crossing Cultures: Creating Identity in Chinese and Jewish American Literature*. Columbia: U Missouri P, 2003.

Owens, Louis. *Mixedblood Messages: Literature, Film, Family, Place*. Norman: U Oklahoma P, 1998.

Ozeki, Ruth. *My Year of Meats*. New York: Viking, 1998.

Paley, Grace. *The Collected Stories*. New York: Farrar, Straus, & Giroux, 1994.

———. "The Long-Distance Runner." In Paley, *The Collected Stories*. 242–58.

———. "The Loudest Voice." In Paley, *The Collected Stories*. 34–40.

Palumbo-Liu, David. *Asian/American: Historical Crossings of a Racial Frontier*. Stanford: Stanford UP, 1999.

Park, You-me, and Gayle Wald. "Native Daughters in the Promised Land: Gender, Race, and the Question of Separate Spheres." *American Literature* 70.3 (September 1998): 607–33.

Pease, Donald. "American Studies: An Interview with Donald Pease." By John Eperjesi. *Minnesota Review* 65–66 (Fall/Spring 2006): 121–32.

Pease, Donald E., and Robyn Wiegman, eds. *The Futures of American Studies*. Durham: Duke UP, 2002.

Perlmann, Joel. "Reflecting the Changing Face of America: Multiracials, Racial Classification, and American Intermarriage." In Sollors, ed. *Interracialism*. 506–33.

Prasad, Chandra, ed. *Mixed: An Anthology of Short Fiction on the Multiracial Experience*. New York: Norton, 2006.

Prashad, Vijay. *Everybody Was Kung Fu Fighting: Afro-Asian Connections and the Myth of Cultural Purity*. Boston, MA: Beacon P, 2001.

———. "Foreword: 'Bandung is Done'—Passages in AfroAsian Epistemology." In Raphael-Hernandez and Steen xi–xxiii.

Radhakrishnan, R. "Postcoloniality and the Boundaries of Identity." *Callaloo* 16.4 (Fall 1993): 750–71. *JSTOR* University of Virginia Library, Charlottesville, VA. March 7, 2007. <http://links.jstor.org/sici?sici=0161-2492%28199323%2916%3A4%3C750%3APATBOI%3E2.0.CO%3B2-O>.

Ramazani, Jahan. *The Hybrid Muse: Postcolonial Poetry in English*. Chicago: U Chicago P, 2001.

Raphael-Hernandez, Heike, and Shannon Steen, eds. *AfroAsian Encounters: Culture, History, Politics*. New York: New York UP, 2006.

Reddi, Rishi. *Karma and Other Stories*. New York: HarperCollins, 2007.

Rekdal, Paisley. *The Night My Mother Met Bruce Lee: Observations on Not Fitting In*. New York: Pantheon, 2000.

Rody Caroline. *The Daughter's Return: African-American and Caribbean Women's Fictions of History*. New York: Oxford UP, 2001.

———. "Impossible Voices: Ethnic Postmodern Narration in Morrison's Jazz and Yamashita's *Through the Arc of the Rain Forest*." *Contemporary Literature* 41.4 (2000): 618–41.

Rogin, Michael. *Blackface, White Noise: Jewish Immigrants in the Hollywood Melting Pot*. Berkeley: U of California P, 1996.

Roley, Brian Ascalon. *American Son*. New York: Norton, 2001.

Ross, Fran. *Oreo*. [1974]. Boston: Northeastern UP, 2000.

Roth, Henry. *Call It Sleep*. 1934. New York: Picador, 2005.

Roth, Philip. *The Human Stain*. Boston; New York: Houghton Mifflin, 2000.

Ruppert, James. "Mediation and Multiple Narrative in Contemporary Native American Fiction." *Texas Studies in Language and Literature*. 28.3 (1986): 209–25.

Rushdie, Salman. "In Defence of the Novel, Yet Again." *Step Across This Line: Collected Non-Fiction 1992–2002*. London: Jonathan Cape, 2002.

Sadowski-Smith, Claudia. "The U.S.-Mexico Borderlands Writes Back: Cross-Cultural Transnationalism in Contemporary U.S. Women of Color Fiction." *Arizona Quarterly* 57.1 (Spring 2001): 91–111.

Saldívar, José David. *Border Matters: Remapping American Cultural Studies*. Berkeley: U of California P, 1997.

———. "The Limits of Cultural Studies." *American Literary History* 2.2 (1990): 251–66.

San Juan, Jr., E. "The Ordeal of Ethnic Studies in the Age of Globalization." In Anderson and Lee, eds, *Displacements and Diasporas*. 270–90.

Schorsch, Jonathan. "Making Judaism *Cool*." *Tikkun* 15.2 (March/April 2000): 33–36.

Schwartz, Lynne Sharon. "The Melting Pot." 1987. Solotaroff and Rapoport, eds. 284–317.

Segal, Lore. "The Reverse Bug." 1989. Solotaroff and Rapoport, eds. 318–32.

Seltzer, Robert M. "Introduction: The Ironies of American Jewish History." In Seltzer and Cohen, eds, *The Americanization of the Jews*. 1–16.

Seltzer, Robert M., and Norman J. Cohen, eds. *The Americanization of the Jews*. New York: New York UP, 1995.

Senna, Danzy. *Caucasia*. New York: Riverhead, 1999.

———. "The Mulatto Millennium." In O'Hearn, ed., *Half and Half*. 12–27.

Seo, Diane. "Authentic Characters or Racist Stereotypes? Some Asian Americans Describe Lois-Ann Yamanaka's Writing as Socially Irresponsible. Yet High-Profile Authors and Others Defend Her No-Holds-Barred Style." *Los Angeles Times*. July 23, 1998. E1.

Šesnić, Jelena. "'Histories That All of Us Should Know': Asian American Masculinities in Interethnic Perspective." *SRAZ* (*Studia Romanica et Anglica Zagrabiensia*) LII (2007): 87–107.

———. Unpublished essay. 2002.

Shange, Ntozake. *for colored girls who have considered suicide / when the rainbow is enuf: a choreopoem*. 1975. Reprint, New York: Collier-Macmillan, 1989.

Sheffer, Jolie Alexandra. *Imagining America: The Psychology of Race and Gender in Representations of the National Family, 1880–1920*. Diss. U of Virginia, 2006.

Shohat, Ella, and Robert Stam. *Unthinking Eurocentrism: Multiculturalism and the Media*. London and New York: Routledge, 1994.

Silko, Leslie Marmon. *Ceremony*. New York: Penguin, 1977.

Simon, Kate. *Bronx Primitive: Portraits in a Childhood*. New York: Viking, 1982.

Smith, Zadie. *The Autograph Man*. New York: Random House, 2002.

———. *White Teeth*. New York: Random House, 2000.

Solataroff, Ted, and Nessa Rapoport, eds. *Writing Our Way Home: Contemporary Stories by American Jewish Writers*. New York: Schocken, 1992.

Sollors, Werner. *An Anthology of Interracial Literature: Black-White Contacts in the Old World and New*. New York: New York UP, 2004.

———. *Beyond Ethnicity: Consent and Descent in American Culture*. New York: Oxford UP, 1986.

———, ed. *Interracialism: Black-White Intermarriage in American History, Literature, and Law*. New York: Oxford UP, 2000.

———, ed. *The Invention of Ethnicity*. New York: Oxford, 1989.

———. *Neither Black Nor White Yet Both: Thematic Explorations of Interracial Literature*. New York: Oxford UP, 1997.

Spivak, Gayatri Chakravorty. *Death of a Discipline*. New York: Columbia UP, 2003.

Sugano, Douglas. "Karen Tei Yamashita." *Asian American Novelists: A Bio-Bibliographical Critical Sourcebook*. Ed. Emmanuel S. Nelson. Westport, CT: Greenwood, 2000. 403–8.

Suh, Seung Hye, and Robert Ji-Song Ku. "The New Immigration and the Literature of Asian America." In Mendoza and Shankar, eds. 314–26.

Sundquist, Eric J. *To Wake the Nations: Race in the Making of American Literature*. Cambridge: Harvard UP, 1993.

Tajima-Peña, Renee. *My America, or, Honk If You Love Buddha*. Documentary. Prod. Quynh Thai. National Asian American Telecommunications Association and Independent Television Service, 1996.

Takahama, Valerie. "Controversial Adventures in 'Paradise': Bully Burgers and Pidgin." *The Orange County Register*. February 15, 1996. E01. <http://www.swarthmore.edu/Humanities/pschmid1/engl52a/engl52a.1999/yamanaka.html>

Tan, Amy. *The Joy-Luck Club*. New York: G.P. Putnam's Sons, 1989.

Trivedi, Harish. "'Ganga Was Sunken': T. S. Eliot's Use of India." *The Fire and the Rose: New Essays on T. S. Eliot*. Ed. Vinod Sena and Rajiva Verma. Delhi: Oxford UP, 1992. 44–62.

Vaynshteyn, Berish. "Lynching." In Chametzky et. al., eds., *Jewish American Literature*. 412–13.

Vromen, Galina. "The Secret Diary of a Bat Mitzvah Girl." *Best Jewish Writing 2002*. Ed. Michael Lerner. San Francisco: Jossey-Bass, 2002. 54–63.

Wald, Alan. "Theorizing Cultural Difference: A Critique of the 'Ethnicity School.'" *MELUS: The Journal of the Society for the Study of the Multi-Ethnic Literature of the United States* 14.2 (1987): 21–33.

Walker, Margaret. *Jubilee*. New York: Houghton Mifflin, 1966.

Walker, Rebecca. *Black, White, and Jewish: Autobiography of a Shifting Self*. New York: Riverhead, 2001.

———. Introduction. In Prasad, ed. 13–18.

Walkowitz, Rebecca L. "The Location of Literature: The Transnational Book and the Migrant Writer." *Immigrant Fictions: Contemporary Literature in an Age of Globalization. Contemporary Literature*. Ed. Walkowitz. 47.4 (Winter 2006): 527–45.

Wang, Oliver. "These Are the Breaks: Hip-Hop and AfroAsian Cultural (Dis)Connections." In Raphael-Hernandez and Steen, eds. 146–64.

Waters, Mary. *Ethnic Options: Choosing Identity in America*. Berkeley, London: U California P, 1990.

Waxman, Chaim I. "The Sociohistorical Background and Development of America's Jews." In Farber and Waxman, eds., *Jews in America*. 7–15.

Whitfield, Stephen J. "Why American Has Not Seemed Like Exile." *Jewish In America*. Eds. Sara Blair and Jonathan Freedman. Ann Arbor: U Michigan P, 2004. 239–64.

Whitman, Walt. "The Sleepers." *The Complete Poems*. Ed. Francis Murphy. Harmondsworth, Middlesex, England: Penguin, 1975. 440–49.

Wiegman, Robyn. *American Anatomies: Theorizing Race and Gender*. Durham: Duke UP, 1995.

Wiencek, Henry. *The Hairstons: An American Family in Black and White*. New York: St. Martin's, 2000.

Williams, Sherley Anne. *Dessa Rose*. New York: William Morrow, 1986.

Wisse, Ruth. "Jewish Writers on the New Diaspora." In Seltzer and Cohen, eds., *The Americanization of the Jews*. 60–78.

Wong, Sau-ling Cynthia. "Chinese/Asian American Men in the 1990s: Displacement, Impersonation, Paternity, and Extinction in David Wong Louie's *Pangs of Love*." *Privileging Positions: The Sites of Asian American Studies*. Ed. Gary K. Okihiro, Marilyn Alquizola, Dorothy Fujita Rony, and K. Scott Wong. Pullman, WA: Washington State UP, 1995. 181–91.

———. "Denationalization Reconsidered: Asian American Cultural Criticism at a Theoretical Crossroads." *Amerasia Journal* 21:1–2 (1995): 1–27.

———. *Reading Asian American Literature: From Necessity to Extravagance*. Princeton: Princeton UP, 1993.

Wong, Shawn. *Homebase*. New York: I. Reed Books, 1979.

Wonham, Henry B., ed. *Criticism and the Color Line: Desegregating American Literary Studies*. New Brunswick: Rutgers UP, 1996.

Wood, James. "Fundamentally Goyish." *London Review of Books* 24.19 (October 3, 2002). March 7, 2007. <http://www.lrb.co.uk/v24/n19/wood02.html>.

Wright, Richard. *Native Son*. 1940. New York: Perennial, 1987.

Wu, Frank H. Foreward. In McFerson, ed. xi–xvii.

Wu, Jean Yu-Wen Shen, and Min Song, eds. *Asian American Studies: A Reader*. New Brunswick: Rutgers UP, 2000.

Wu, Yung-Hsing. "Native Sons and Native Speakers: On the Eth(n)ics of Comparison." *PMLA* 121:5 (October 2006): 1460–74.

Yamanaka, Lois-Ann. *Blu's Hanging*. New York: HarperCollins, 1997.

Yamashita, Karen Tei. *Brazil-Maru*. Minneapolis: Coffee House, 1992.

———. *Circle K Cycles*. Minneapolis: Coffee House, 2001.

———. "An Interview with Karen Tei Yamashita." Jean Vengua Gier and Carla Alicia Tejeda. *Jouvert: A Journal of Postcolonial Studies* 2.2 (1998): 94 pars. March 7, 2007. <http:/social.chass.ncsu.edu/jouvert/v2i2/yamashi.htm.>.

———. "Karen Tei Yamashita." Interview by Michael S. Murashige. King-kok Cheung, ed., *Words Matter: Conversations with Asian American Writers*. Honolulu: U Hawai'i P; Los Angeles: UCLA Asian American Studies Center, c2000. 320–42.

———. Lecture. ENMC/AM 317, "Contemporary Interethnic Fiction." University of Virginia, Charlottesville. March 26, 2009.

———. Personal interview. Washington, D.C. December 30, 2000.

———. *Through the Arc of the Rain Forest*. Minneapolis: Coffee House, 1990.

———. *Tropic of Orange*. Minneapolis: Coffee House, 1997.

Yehoash. "Lynching." 1919. In Chametzky et al., eds., *Jewish American Literature*. 142.

Yezierska, Anzia. "Children of Loneliness." 1923. In Chametzky, et. al., eds., *Jewish American Literature*. 234–44.

Zakrzewsky, Paul. *Lost Tribe: Jewish Fiction from the Edge*. New York: Harpercollins, 2003.

Zamora, Lois Parkinson. "Magical Romance/Magical Realism: Ghosts in U.S. and Latin American Fiction." In Zamora and Faris, eds., *Magical Realism*. 498–550.

Zamora, Lois Parkinson, and Wendy B. Faris, eds. *Magical Realism: Theory, History, Community*. Durham: Duke UP, 1995.

INDEX